"One organization with a long record of success in helping people find jobs is The Five O'Clock Club."
FORTUNE

"The Five O'Clock Club's arrival in D.C. reflects the growing importance of . . . career development."
The Washington Post

"Many managers left to fend for themselves are turning to the camaraderie offered by [The Five O'Clock Club]. Members share tips and advice, and hear experts."
The Wall Street Journal

"If you have been out of work for some time . . . consider The Five O'Clock Club."
The New York Times

"Wendleton has reinvented the historic gentlemen's fraternal oasis and built it into a chain of strategy clubs for job seekers."
The Philadelphia Inquirer

"Organizations such as The Five O'Clock Club are building . . . an extended professional family."
Jessica Lipnack, author, *Professional Teams*

"[The Five O'Clock Club] will ask not what you do, but 'What do you want to do?' . . . [And] don't expect to get any great happy hour drink specials at this joint. The two-hour seminars are all business."
The Washington Times

"The Five O'Clock Club's proven philosophy is that job hunting is a learned skill like any other. The Five O'Clock Club becomes the engine that drives [your] search."
Black Enterprise

"Job hunting is a science at The Five O'Clock Club. [Members] find the discipline, direction and much-needed support that keeps a job search on track."
Modern Maturity

"Wendleton tells you how to beat the odds—even in an economy where pink slips are more common than perks. Her savvy and practical guide[s] are chockablock with sample résumés, cover letters, worksheets, negotiating tips, networking suggestions and inspirational quotes from such far-flung achievers as Abraham Lincoln, Malcolm Forbes and Lily Tomlin."
Working Woman

"On behalf of eight million New Yorkers, I commend and thank The Five O'Clock Club. Keep the faith and keep America working!"
David N. Dinkins, former Mayor,
The City of New York

"Kate Wendleton has written a sage and sensible book for the turbulent 90's."
Harvey Mackay, author of *Swim with the Sharks Without Being Eaten Alive*

"Everyone who has met Kate knows that she has a genius for caring about others."
David Rottman, vice president and manager, Career Services,
Chase Manhattan Bank, New York City

"During the time I was looking for a job I kept Kate's books by my bed. I read a little every night, a little every morning. Her common-sense advice, methodical approach, and hints for keeping the spirits up were extremely useful."
    Harold Levine, coordinator, Yale Alumni Career Resource Network

"Everyone talks about 'taking charge' of their lives; Kate Wendleton shows you how. One of the savviest and most effective career counselors that I know teaches that—even in the toughest of times—you can (and deserve to) find work that is right for you."
    Robert Mintz, director of Human Resources, Time, Inc., Magazines

"Today's job market is the toughest I've seen, and it requires the combination Kate has struck: shrewdness about the hiring process and the courage to face inner issues. Great work!"
    William Pilder, chairman, TransKey

"Kate Wendleton offers a wealth of pragmatic, uplifting advice for the job seeker. A person who follows Kate's formula would certainly get my attention, even if I'd already rejected his or her résumé."
    Carole F. St. Mark, president,
    Pitney Bowes Logistics Systems & Business Services

"Kate breaks the process into doable steps that are easy to understand."
    Albert Prendergast, senior vice president, Human Resources, Mastercard International

"A one-woman crusade against unemployment—Kate Wendleton and The Five O'Clock Club!"
    Roberta Mell,
    vice president, National Advertising, Home Box Office

"Kate is one of the most singularly creative and energetic persons I have ever met. She is completely dedicated to the 'proposition of possibilities' in peoples' lives, and that dedication comes shining through."
    Dan Ciporin, president,
    Dealtime.com

"The Five O'Clock Club books are 'what works now.' This indispensable, no-excuses guide to job-hunting and career building provides a step-by-step approach to organizing your search . . . targeting the job you want . . . getting in for the meetings . . . beating out the competition . . . and turning the interview into an offer."
    Jack Schlegel, New York Advertising & Communications Network

"Thank you, Kate, for all your help. I ended up with four offers and at least fifteen compliments in two months. Thanks!"
    president and CEO, large banking organization

"I have doubled my salary during the past five years by using The Five O'Clock Club techniques. Now I earn what I deserve. I think everyone needs The Five O'Clock Club."
    M. S., attorney, entertainment industry

"I'm an artistic person, and I don't think about business. Kate provided the disciplined business approach so I could practice my art. After adopting her system, I landed a role on Broadway in *Hamlet*."
    Bruce Faulk, actor,
    Manhattan (currently touring Europe in a play)

"Kate's books bring her enthusiastic, thought-provoking style to print. A must-read for every person who has a job, wants one, or may be contemplating changing it."
    Richard Schneyer, chair, Career Services Committee, Annual Convention,
    National Society of Fund Raising Executives

INTERVIEWING
and
SALARY NEGOTIATION

Kate Wendleton

http://www.FiveOClockClub.com

The
Five
O'Clock
Club®

Career Press / 1999

To order this title, please call toll-free 1-800-CAREER-1 (NJ and Canada: 201-848-0310) to order using VISA or Mastercard, or for informaiton on books from Career Press.

The Career Press, Inc., 3 Tice Road, PO Box 687, Franklin Lakes, NJ 07417

Library of Congress Cataloging-in-Publication Data

Wendleton, Kate.
   Interviewing and salary negotiation : For job hunters, career
   changers, consultants and freelancers / Kate Wendleton.
     p.   cm.
   Includes bibliographical references and index.
   ISBN 1-56414-434-8 (pbk.)
   1. Employment interviewing.   2. Job Hunting   I. Title
HF5549.5.I6W458   1999
    650.14--dc21   99-16467
                                         CIP

For information, address The Five O'Clock Club,
300 East 40th Street - Suite 6L - New York, New York 10016
http://www.FiveOClockClub.com

For Richard, Sara, Paul and Martin

*Perhaps the truth lies in what most of the world
outside the modern West has always believed,
namely that there are practices of life,
good in themselves, that are inherently fulfilling.*

*Perhaps work that is intrinsically rewarding
is better for human beings than work
that is only extrinsically rewarded.*

*Perhaps enduring commitment to those we love
and civic friendship toward our fellow citizens
are preferable to restless competition
and anxious self-defense.*

*Perhaps common worship,
in which we express our gratitude and wonder
in the face of the mystery of being itself,
is the most important thing of all.*

*If so, we will have to change our lives
and begin to remember
what we have been happier to forget.*

Robert N. Bellah, Richard Madsen, William Sullivan,
Ann Swindler, and Steven Tipton, *Habits of the Heart*

Preface

Dear Member or Prospective Member of The Five O'Clock Club:

I am very happy to bring you this book.

When I started The Five O'Clock Club in Philadelphia in 1978, professionals and managers who were job hunting came to my apartment every Thursday evening. Career consultants from corporations and consulting firms taught us their job-hunting techniques. I will be forever grateful to those experts who helped us get started. We were able to compare their approaches. We experimented. We tried various job-hunting techniques and reported our results back to the group.

At The Five O'Clock Club, it was not enough for us to learn about job hunting—we wanted to learn about the job *hiring* process. What happens when your résumé crosses the desk of a hiring manager? How effective are direct-mail campaigns? Why does one person find a job quickly, while someone else takes longer—even though both work hard and are equally well qualified?

This book series answers those questions. We found that there is no one job-hunting technique that works. Job-hunting formulas hold true in the aggregate, but may not for a specific situation. The techniques that work depend, to a large extent, on the industry in which you are interested, the kind of job you want to have within that industry, and on your own style and personality.

This book gives you guidelines, but also gives you flexibility in deciding which job-hunting approach is right for you. When you understand what is happening and why, you can be in a better position to plan your own job-hunting campaign, and not rely so much on chance or on what a specific expert tells you.

Job hunting can be thought of as a project—much like any project you might handle in your regular job. Most of the approaches in this book are businesslike rather than intensely psychological. Thinking of job hunting in a business-type way allows you to use the problem-solving skills you might use at work.

This book series is organized for busy people like you. Skip to the part you need. If you already know what you want in your next job, go directly to our book *Getting Interviews* to learn the most powerful, up-to-date techniques available today for getting interviews. If you have an interview coming up, *Interviewing and Salary Negotiation* will give you the latest ideas for getting what you want, including how to assess the interview and turn it into a job offer.

I feel duty-bound to address the issue of career planning. Most people are interested in job-hunting techniques but don't want to give much thought to what they should do with their *lives*. So read *Targeting the Job You Want* to make sure your job targets are correct. Most job hunters think it was the smartest thing they did in their searches. Make the wise decision to spend the time it takes to give your life some direction and a real sense of satisfaction.

These books are the result of years of research into how successful job hunters land the best jobs at the best pay. This series replaces the very successful and popular *Through the Brick Wall* series, and with the addition of new material, takes job search to an even higher level of sophistication. Together, these books provide the most detailed explanation of the search process :

- *Targeting the Job You Want* tells you *where* to look for a job. It is a relatively painless way to think about the career-planning process. In addition, it contains the most comprehensive job-search bibliography around.
- *Getting Interviews* tells you *how* to get job leads—part-time or full-time, freelance or consulting. In addition, it contains worksheets which you may copy for your own use.
- *Interviewing and Salary Negotiation* (this book) tells you The Five O'Clock Club way to interview, get the offer and negotiate.
- *Building a Great Résumé* is quite simply the best résumé book on the market. It uses the résumés of real people and tells you their stories. It refers to over 100 industries and professions.

In addition to interviewing, following up and negotiating, this book covers the overview of the job-search process. That way, you are not forced to refer to the other books when you are in the middle of this one.

Finally, in each book you will find a lot of inspirational writing. I have needed it myself often enough, as have the many unemployed and unhappy working people with whom I have worked. The techniques by themselves are worthless without the right frame of mind. I hope the quotations will inspire you as they have inspired me and my fellow job hunters.

Thank you for supporting The Five O'Clock Club through your purchase of this book. Because of people like you, we can keep the program going and spread to new cities so we'll be there when you need us. Our goal is, and always has been, to provide the best affordable career advice. And—with you as our partners—we will continue to do this.

Cheers, God bless, and good luck!

Kate Wendleton
New York City
http://www.FiveOClockClub.com

Acknowledgements

With appreciation to Richard Bayer, my husband and partner in business and in life. To three bright lights in our lives: Sara, Paul and Martin. And to the entire Dobbs Family for being dependable cheerleaders.

I appreciate all of The Five O'Clock Club members, old and new, some of whose stories are contained herein: Members provide feedback on our techniques, which allows our approach to evolve continually with the changing job market. Members also give us information for our database, so we can track trends and know what is going on.

I thank our branch heads and career consultants, who have brought this high-quality individual and group counseling program to other cities with enthusiasm and dedication to our members. Our consultants are a highly trained and dedicated group.

I thank the excellent staff of The Five O'Clock Club at our Headquarter's office, including the indispensable David Madison who heads up our national Guild of Five O'Clock Club career counselors. Special mention to Wendy Rothman, who wrote the research and bibliography sections in this series, was one of the original Five O'Clock Club counselors and started two of our branches. In addition, I would like to acknowledge Patricia Kelly, whose artwork, *Fruytagie*, hangs in our offices and appears in our publications—including this one.

We are all especially proud of Workforce America, our not-for-profit operation which runs The Five O'Clock Club program in Harlem and helps people move "from jobs to careers." After I started it and ran it for two years, it was taken over by Deborah Brown. When I met her seven years ago, I knew Deborah was the ideal person to head up this program. She has proven herself to be an intelligent, refined, selfless leader who has shown initiative, dedication and persistence beyond my wildest dreams. Her career plan is the model used in the "Advanced Career Planning" section of *Targeting the Job You Want*. Deborah's story is proof that planning works.

Since I came to New York in 1985, I have gotten a number of big breaks from people who believed in me. Edith Wurtzel at The New School for Social Research encouraged me to speak there. Three hundred and fifty people attended, and I later became director of their career center. Abe Fiss at Barnes & Noble agreed to carry my first self-published book in 1986, then my second, and kept reordering them for five years. Many, many others have befriended me, and have helped me to bring you what we have today.

Finally, my deepest appreciation goes to my trusted editor, Cordelia Jason, for her clarity, creativity, and caring in working on earlier editions of this work.

K.W.
New York City

Table of Contents

PART FIVE—The Five O'Clock Club Approach to Salary Negotiation: A Four-Step Strategy

PART SIX—Keeping It Going
After You've Gotten the Job You Want

Career and Job-Search Bibliography

(See our book *Targeting the Job You Want.*)

PART SEVEN—What is The Five O'Clock Club?
"America's Premier Career Counseling Network"

INTERVIEWING
and
SALARY NEGOTIATION

Introduction

We've all heard too many painful stories: out of work for over a year ... networking, mailings, search firms, ads—but can't get a job or even an assignment. Lots and lots of interviews but ...

At The Five O'Clock Club, we get impressive results. The average professional, manager, or executive who attends on a regular basis gets a job within ten to fifteen weeks. (Many had been looking for a year or more.) That's because they used the principles taught in this book series. As you will see, these techniques work at all levels—and for all types of people. They have even been used successfully by actors and actresses, and at least one orchestra conductor. Whatever your field, this book will give you the inside track.

When a job hunter finds a job, he reports to the group. Last week, a man reported that he had been unemployed for three years. His wife had a good job, he spent time with his kids, and he found a few temporary assignments, but he was essentially unemployed, and was trying very hard to get a job. After only four Five O'Clock Club sessions, he found a great one.

The week before, a woman spoke who had been unemployed for a year and a half; she had come to six sessions. Her first session had been a full year earlier, and she had decided to search on her own. After a year, she came back, attended five more sessions, and got a great job.

The week before that, a man who had been unemployed for six months before joining The Five O'Clock Club found a great job. In his four months with the Club, the group had helped him see how he was coming across in interviews (very stiff and preachy) and how to expand his job targets. Some people take longer because they are at the beginning of their search or because they have not searched in many years and need to learn this new skill.

Many job hunters think they have to lower their salary expectations because they are unemployed or have been job searching for a long time. You may have to lower your salary expectations for other reasons, but none of these three people did. Their unemployment did not affect their salary negotia-tions. In this book you will learn how to negotiate properly and increase your chances of getting what you deserve—whether you are employed or not.

The Five O'Clock Club techniques in this book work whether a job hunter is employed or unemployed. Most job hunters try to get interviews and then try to do well in them. They are skipping two important parts of the process, and are therefore probably not doing the two remaining parts very well. At The Five O'Clock Club, we consider all four parts to be important. They are:

- **Assessment:** Deciding what you want results in better job targets (see our book *Targeting the Job You Want*. Assessment also results in better résumés (see our book *Building a Great Résumé*).
- **Campaign Preparation:** Planning your campaign results in lots and lots of interviews in each job target (See our book *Getting Interviews*).
- **Interviewing:** Interviews result in an assessment of the *company's* needs.
- **Interview Follow-Up:** Follow-up after the interview results in job offers.

As you can see, job hunters who think that interviews lead to offers have skipped a step. Interviews lead to a better understanding of what the company wants. What you do *after* the interview leads to an offer.

Here are a few quick stories to get you started.

CASE STUDY: PHIL
Expanded his job hunting targets
—and went through the brick wall to get the job.

Phil had been earning hundreds of thousands of dollars a year as a senior executive in a large publishing company. When I met him, he had been job searching for a year, focusing on twenty-four publishing and health care companies in his geographic area. Given his level, his search was obviously not going to work: his target was too small. He needed to look into other industries and other geographic areas.

In addition, Phil needed a new attitude. He expected people to recognize his credentials and simply hire him—something that had always happened in the past. Now he needed to go

People can be divided into three groups:
those who make things happen,
those who watch things happen—
and those who wonder, What happened?
Anonymous

through the brick wall to get a job.

Phil found a job within three weeks after our meeting. He answered an ad in the paper for a job—not in publishing or health care—in another state. (It doesn't matter how you get the interview: through a search firm, an ad, networking, or direct contact.) He was called in for two interviews and then received a rejection letter: the company had decided against him.

But this time Phil wanted to fight for the job. He wrote to the president of the company and said there had obviously been a big mistake. The company reconsidered and hired him.

Job Hunter	Jobs/Assignments

Brick Wall

You have to be willing to go through the brick wall to get the jobs.

CASE STUDY: STEELWORKERS
Who gets hired?

A colleague of mine, Aaron Nierenberg, tells of a counselor who did a workshop for steelworkers a few years back when many of them were losing jobs. They were not of a mind to do résumés (many of them didn't even speak English), so the counselor concentrated on the most important part of the search process—follow-up.

The counselor asked, "How many of you have already contacted companies about getting a job?" Sixteen hands went up. "Your homework for tomorrow," he said, "is to *recontact* those companies and report back here." The next day, four workers had gotten jobs.

The explanation for this is simple. Look at it from the hiring manager's point of view. The steel industry was laying off thousands of workers, who went to other steel mills looking for work. Hun-

dreds of workers went to the hiring managers and said, "Have you got any work?" How could a manager easily decide which workers he should hire? But when a worker said, "I was here last week looking for work. Do you have anything now?" the manager then knew whom to select.

Much of the selection process is a self-selection process: the *job hunter* decides which companies he or she wants to work for, and behaves very differently toward those companies than toward others in which he or she is not interested.

Job hunters put most of their effort into getting interviews and doing brilliantly well in those interviews. Then they stop. Five O'Clock Club job hunters keep going and turn more interviews into offers. Don't follow up with a silly thank you note. Instead, *influence* the person. This book will give you a process for analyzing the interview so you can decide what to do next.

See People Two Levels Higher Than You Are

Norman had been searching for a job for over a year. He did what he had been told: he networked. By now he had met with almost 250 people! Yet he could not find a job. The problem: He was meeting with people at his own level. When he started meeting with higher-level people (through direct contact), he started seeing results. Within two months, he found a great job.

Most job hunters network incorrectly. In our book *Getting Interviews*, we tell you exactly how to network so you can get the most out of it. We also cover the other techniques for getting interviews: through search firms, answering ads, and directly contacting companies.

Take the Long View

The next job you take will not be your last. Where will you go after that one? When deciding between two or more possibilities, select the one that positions you best for the long term.

Christine is a good example. She had three job offers—which is what we like people to have. Two offers paid $10,000 more than the third one. Which job should she take?

Christine selected the one that positioned her

People are always blaming their circumstances for what they are. I don't believe in circumstances. The people who get on in this world are the people who get up and look for the circumstances they want, and if they can't find them, make them.
George Bernard Shaw

best for the long term—which happened to be the lower-paying job. She is now as happy as a person can be, getting tremendous experience and meeting lots of important people. After a few years, she could easily leave (if she wants) and get much more money than she ever would have gotten had she taken one of the other two positions.

Julio is a portfolio manager with strong connections to South America. He had five job offers and wondered which one he should take. I couldn't help him until I knew his long-term plans. Otherwise, his decision would be based strictly on the money or the kind of people at each company. We spent ten minutes working on his Forty-Year Vision, which is covered in *Targeting the Job You Want*. It turned out that he imagined himself working out of his house five to ten years down the road. Then, the decision-making process became easy. Only two of the companies would eventually allow him to work from home. He selected one of them. Had he selected one of the others, he would have had a problem in a few years.

Targeting the Job You Want helps you think about *your* long-term plan. Your next job is simply a step. You can plan that step and the ones after that. Job hunters are not powerless. They can do a lot to influence the hiring process and their own long-term careers.

A Changing Economy

Today, we know that doing a good job is not enough. Our career prospects can now change for reasons that have nothing to do with our personal job performance, but rather with the performance of our employers. It's a new economy—a world economy—and the changes are not going to slow down. Not only will things not return to the way they were, the amount of change will increase.

Government statistics show the impact of change on job hunters:

The average American has been in his or her job only four years.

The average American getting out of college today can expect to have five careers during his or her lifetime—that's not five jobs, but five separate careers! We will probably have twelve to fifteen jobs in the course of those five careers.

Ten years from now, half the working population will be in jobs that have not yet been invented. Let's make that more personal: ten years from now, half the people reading this book will be in jobs that do not exist today. That's okay. *Targeting the Job You Want* tells you where some of the new jobs are, but you'll have to do research as well.

Ten years from now, half the working population will be in non-traditional forms of employment. This means that half of us will not be working full-time, on payroll, for one employer—a wrenching change in our mindsets. Some of us may work two days a week on payroll for one employer, and three days a week for another. Or three days a week on payroll, with consulting or freelance work on the other days. Or we may be paid by one company that farms us out to another. The variations are endless—and changing.

The situation is unsettling—to say the least. However, we cannot fight it. In this time of dramatic change, few companies really know where they are heading, but some are learning what kind of workers they need: flexible, self-aware ones who continually improve their skills. Gone are the days when it was good enough for employees to simply do their assigned jobs well. America wants and needs a new kind of workforce.

Employees too are learning that they must take care of themselves and remain marketable so they are not dependent on one employer. They are proactively figuring out what they bring to the party, while finding out—and fitting into—the new directions their companies and industries are taking.

A New Definition of Job Hunting

Job hunting in our changing economy is a *continuous* process and requires a new definition. Job hunting now means continually becoming aware of market conditions both inside and outside of our present companies, and learning what we have to offer—to both markets. This new definition means we must develop new attitudes about our work lives, and new skills for doing well in a chang-

It is other people's experience that
makes the older man wiser than the younger man.
Yoruba Proverb

ing economy.

Today's economy requires job hunters to be more proactive, more sophisticated, and more willing to go through brick walls to get what they want. Employers no longer plan your career for you. You must look after yourself, and know what you want and how to get it.

Understanding How the Job-Hunting Market Works

Knowing why things work the way they do will give you flexibility and control over your job hunt. Knowing how the hiring system works will help you understand why things go right and why they go wrong—why certain things work and others don't. Then you can modify the system to fit your own needs, temperament, and the workings of the job market you are interested in.

It is overly simplistic to say that only one job-hunting system works. The job-selection process is more complicated than that. Employers can do what they want. You need to understand the process from their point of view. Then you can plan your own job hunt, in your own industry. You will learn how to compete in this market.

Always remember, the best jobs don't necessarily go to the most qualified people, but to the people who are the best job hunters. You'll increase your chances of finding the job you want by using a methodical job-hunting approach.

The Five O'Clock Club Coaching Approach

Our approach is methodical. Our counselors are the best. Five O'Clock Club counselors are full-time career coaches. Each one has met with hundreds of job hunters. Often we can pinpoint what is wrong with a person's search and turn it around. In this book, you will get that same information. Like our Five O'Clock Club job hunters, you will learn the techniques and hear the stories of other people so you can job hunt more effectively.

Sometimes we call our techniques the *Parachute* for the nineties. The original *Parachute* book (*What Color is Your Parachute?* by Richard Nelson Bolles, Ten Speed Press) was first published more than twenty years ago. It teaches first-time job hunters or career changers how to get jobs. Now we have a nation of skilled workers, managers, executives, and professionals who are out of work or unhappy in their jobs—people who used to be routinely wooed and solicited for their talents. Now these people have to do the selling. They need a very different and specific approach to finding jobs and changing careers.

How The Five O'Clock Club Works

The Five O'Clock Club provides both individual and group career counseling, including individual counseling in-person or by phone. On request, Club members are matched up with Five O'Clock Club career counselors who we think are appropriate for them.

The groups vary from place to place. Some groups are for professionals, managers, and executives. Others may focus on recent college graduates, for example, or blue-collar workers. Generally, half the people who attend are employed (and perhaps unhappy); half are unemployed. Members are from various industries and professions—usually difficult situations, or they wouldn't need us. The basic format is the same: the group meets every week for two hours. During the first hour, members hear a presentation on an important job hunting technique. These techniques are presented in this book. In between the first and second hours, those who have found jobs report on their searches, and we learn from what they did.

During the second hour, a career counselor leads the group of up to eight to ten job hunters in a strategy-planning session for each job hunter: how can this person move his or her search along? How can he get more interviews in his target market or turn those interviews into offers? Job hunters learn from the counselor and from the strategies other job hunters are pursuing. They get feedback on their own searches and critique the searches of others. They aim to get six to ten contacts in the works, and have three job offers.

Those who stick with the process find that it works. That process is presented in this book series.

PART ONE

THE CHANGING JOB-HUNTING PROCESS

AND CONTROLLING YOUR
JOB-SEARCH CAMPAIGN

If you only care enough for a result you will almost certainly obtain it. If you wish to be rich, you will be rich; if you wish to be learned, you will be learned; if you wish to be good, you will be good.
William James

The circumstances that surround a man's life are not important.
How that man responds to those circumstances is important.
His response is the ultimate determining factor between success and failure.
Booker T. Washington

Sometimes it's best if a man just spends a moment or two thinking. It is one of the toughest things he will ever do, and that's probably why so few bother to do it.
Alonzo Herndon
born a slave; died a millionaire;
Founder, Atlanta Life Insurance Company

The following chart outlines each part of the process. It's best to do every part, however quickly you may do it. Experienced job hunters pay attention to the details and do not skip a step.

The first part of the process is **assessment** (or evaluation). You evaluate yourself by doing the exercises in *Targeting the Job You Want*, and you evaluate your prospects by doing some preliminary research in the library or by talking to people.

Assessment consists of the following exercises:
- The Seven Stories Exercise
- Interests
- Values
- Satisfiers and Dissatisfiers
- Your Forty-Year Vision

If you are working privately with a career counselor, he or she may ask you to do a few additional exercises, such as a personality test.

Assessment results in :
- a listing of all the targets you think are worth exploring; and
- a résumé that makes you look appropriate to your first target (and may work with other targets as well).

Even if you don't do the entire assessment, the Seven Stories Exercise is especially important because it will help you develop an interesting résumé. Therefore, we have included that exercise in this book.

Research will help you figure out which of your targets:
- are a good fit for you; and
- offer some hope in terms of being a good market.

You can't have too many targets—as long as you rank them. Then, for *each one*, conduct a campaign to get interviews in that target area.

Phase I: Campaign Preparation
- Conduct research to develop a list of all the companies in your first target. Find out the names

The Five O'Clock Club®

Phases of the Job Search
and the results of each phase

ASSESSMENT

Consists of:
- The Seven Stories Exercise
- Interests
- Values
- Satisfiers and Dissatisfiers
- Your Forty-Year Plan

Results in:
- As many targets as you can think of
- A ranking of your targets
- A résumé that makes you look appropriate to your first target
- A plan for conducting your search

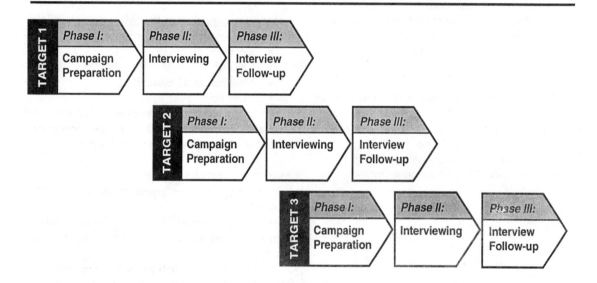

TARGET 1
Phase I: Campaign Preparation
Phase II: Interviewing
Phase III: Interview Follow-up

TARGET 2
Phase I: Campaign Preparation
Phase II: Interviewing
Phase III: Interview Follow-up

TARGET 3
Phase I: Campaign Preparation
Phase II: Interviewing
Phase III: Interview Follow-up

RESULTS

Phase I: Campaign Preparation.
Results in:

- ❏ Research (list of companies)
- ❏ Résumé
- ❏ Cover letter
- ❏ Plan for getting interviews
  - networking
  - direct contact
  - search firms
  - ads

Phase II: Interviewing.
Results in:

- ❏ Giving them information to keep them interested in you
- ❏ Getting information so you can "move it along"
- ❏ Plan for follow-up (You may do several in-depth follow-ups with each person)

Phase III: Follow-Up.
Results in:

- ❏ Aiming to have 6 to 10 things in the works, and

Job Offers!

---

*You ain't goin' nowhere . . . son.
You ought to go back to driving a truck.*
Jim Denny, Grand Ole Opry manager, firing Elvis Presley
after one performance. An interview on October 2, 1954.

of people you should contact in the appropriate departments in each of those companies.

• Develop your cover letter (Paragraph 1 is the opening; Paragraph 2 is a summary about yourself appropriate for this target; Paragraph 3 contains your bulleted accomplishments ("You may be interested in some of the things I've done"); Paragraph 4 is the close. (Lots of sample letters are in this book.)

• Develop your plan for getting **lots of interviews in this target**. You have four basic choices:

• Networking,
• Direct Contact,
• Search Firms,
• Ads.

You will read lots about each of these methods in the *Getting Interviews* book.

Phase II : Interviewing

Most people think interviews result in job offers. But there are usually a few intervening steps before a final offer is made. Interviews should result in getting and giving information.

Did you learn the issues important to each person with whom you met? What did they think were your strongest positives? Where are they in the hiring process? How many other people are they considering? How do you compare with those people? Why might they be reluctant to bring you on board, compared with the other candidates? How can you overcome the decision-makers' objections?

This is one of the most important and yet most overlooked parts of the job-search process. It is covered in extensive detail in this book.

Phase III: Follow-Up

Now that you have analyzed the interview, you can figure out how to follow up with each person with whom you interviewed. Aim to be following up with six to ten companies. Five job possibilities will fall away through no fault of your own.

What's more, with six to ten things going, you increase your chances of having three good offers to

choose from. You would be surprised: even in a tight market, job hunters are able to develop multiple offers.

When you are in the Interview Phase of Target 1, it's time to start Phase I of Target 2. This will give you more momentum and insure that you do not let things dry up. Keep both targets going, and then start Target 3.

Develop Your Unique Résumé

Read all of the case studies in *Building a Great Résumé*. You will learn a powerful new way of thinking about how to position yourself for the kinds of jobs you want. Each of the résumés in that book is for a unique person aiming at a specific target. Seeing how other people position themselves will help you think about what you want a prospective employer to know about you.

Now, it is best to go back to the first part of the process, assessment. In *Targeting the Job You Want*, you will read actual case studies that will show you how real people benefitted from doing the assessment, including the Forty-Year Vision.

However, if your targets are already defined, just keep reading.

Everyone should learn to do one thing supremely well because he likes it, and one thing supremely well because he detests it.
B. W. M. Young, Headmaster,
Charterhouse School

Life never leaves you stranded. If life hands you a problem, it also hands you the ability to overcome that problem. Are you ever tempted to blame the world for your failures and shortcomings? If so, I suggest you pause and reconsider. Does the problem lie with the world, or with you? Dare to dream.
Dennis Kimbro,
Think and Grow Rich: A Black Choice

How to Change Careers

*If an idea, I realized, were really
a valuable one, there must be
some way of realizing it.*
Elizabeth Blackwell
(the first woman to earn a medical degree)

---

*. . . civility is not a sign of weakness, and sincerity is
always subject to proof.*
John F. Kennedy
Inaugural Address, January 20, 1961

Ted had spent ten years in marketing and finance with a large cosmetics company. His dream was to work in the casino industry. He selected two job targets: one aimed at the cosmetics industry, and one aimed at his dream.

All things being equal, finding a job similar to your old one is quicker. A career change will probably take more time. What's more, the job hunting techniques are different for both.

Let's take Ted's case. The casino industry was small, focused in Atlantic City and Las Vegas. Everyone knew everyone else. The industry had its special jargon and personality. What chance did Ted have of breaking in?

Ted had another obstacle. His marketing and finance background made him difficult to categorize. His hard-won business skills became a problem.

It's Not Easy to Categorize Career Changers

The easier it is to categorize you, the easier it is for others to see where you fit in their organizations, and for you to find a job. Search firms, for example, generally will not handle career changers. They can more easily market those who want to stay in the same function in the same industry. Search firms that handled the casino industry would not handle Ted.

You Must Offer Proof of Your Interest and Competence

Many job changers essentially say to a prospective employer, "Give me a chance. You won't be sorry." They expect the employer to hire them on faith, and that's unrealistic. The employer has a lot to lose. First, you may lose interest in the new area after you are hired. Second, you may know so little about the new area that it turns out not to be what you had imagined. Third, you may not bring enough knowledge and skill to the job and fail—even though your desire may be sincere.

The hiring manager should not have to take those risks. It is the job hunter's obligation to prove that he or she is truly interested and capable.

HOW YOU AS A CAREER CHANGER CAN PROVE YOUR INTEREST AND CAPABILITY

- Read the industry's trade journals.
- Get to know the people in that industry or field.
- Join its organizations; attend the meetings.
- Be persistent.
- Show how your skills can be transferred.
- Write proposals.
- Be persistent.
- Take relevant courses, part-time jobs, or do volunteer work related to the new industry or skill area.
- Be persistent.

Ted, as a career changer, had to offer proof to make up for his lack of experience. One proof was that he had read the industry's trade newspapers for more than ten years. When he met people in his search, he could truthfully tell them that he had followed their careers. He could also say he had hope for himself because he knew that so many of them had come from outside the industry.

Another proof of his interest was that he had sought out so many casino management people in Atlantic City and Las Vegas. After a while, he ran into people he had met on previous occasions. Employers want people who are sincerely interested in their industry, their company, and the function the new hire will fill. Sincerity and persistence count, but they are usually not enough.

Another proof Ted offered was that he figured out how to apply his experience to the casino industry and its problems. Writing proposals to show how you would handle the job is one way to prove you are knowledgeable and interested in an area new to you. Some people prove their interest by taking courses, finding part-time jobs, or doing volunteer work to learn the new area and build marketable skills.

Ted initially decided to "wing it," and took trips to Atlantic City and Las Vegas hoping someone would hire him on the spot. That didn't work and took two months and some money. Then he began a serious job hunt—following the system which will be explained in the pages that follow. He felt he was doing fine, but the hunt was taking many months and he was not sure it would result in an offer.

After searching in the casino industry for six months, Ted began a campaign in his old field—the cosmetics industry. Predictably, he landed a job there quickly. Ted took this as a sign that he didn't have a chance in the new field. He lost sight of the fact that a career change is more difficult and takes longer.

Ted accepted the cosmetics position, but his friends encouraged him to continue his pursuit of a career in the casino industry—a small industry with relatively few openings compared with the larger cosmetics industry.

Shortly after he accepted the new position, someone from Las Vegas called him for an interview, and he got the job of his dreams. His efforts paid off because he had done a thorough campaign in the casino industry. It just took time.

Ted was not unusual in giving up on a career change. It can take a long time, and sometimes the pressure to get a paycheck will force people to take inappropriate jobs. That's life. Sometimes we have to do things we don't want. There's nothing wrong with that.

What *is* wrong is forgetting that you had a dream. What *is* wrong is expecting people to hire you on faith and hope, when what they deserve is proof that you're sincere and that hiring you has a good chance of working. *What is wrong is underestimating the effort it takes to make a career change.*

In the future, most people will have to change careers. Your future may hold an involuntary career change, as new technologies make old skills obsolete. Those same new technologies open up new career fields for those who are prepared and ready to change. Know what you're up against. Don't take shortcuts. And don't give up too early. Major career changes are normal today and may prove desirable or essential tomorrow.

For Other Techniques to Help You Change Careers, take at look at . . .

The following chapters in this book:
- Positioning Power for a Job Change
- Salary Negotiation: Power and Positioning (see especially "Case Study: Charlie—Negotiating a Career Change")

The following chapters in our book *Targeting the Job You Want*:
- Targeting the Jobs of the Future
- Case Studies: Targeting the Future
- Learning to Track Trends and Move Into a New Market
- Career Makeovers: Five Who Did It (case studies of ordinary people who followed the system and changed careers)

The following section in *Building a Great Résumé*:
- Résumés for Making a Career Change (Also see résumés and summaries for the industry or profession you are targeting.)

Stick with the optimists, Niftie.
It's going to be tough enough even if they're right.
James Reston

I knew that sweat was a lot of it.
I had a cot put in my cutting room. I would recut something maybe five times in a night and run it again and again and again. I just knew it was sweat.
I had no special touch or anything like that.
Robert Parrish,
Award-winning film editor-director
Quoted in *The New York Times*

*Man is not born to solve the problems of the universe,
but to find out what he has to do; and to restrain
himself within the limits of his comprehension.*
Goethe

Successful Job Hunting is a System

Working the system increases your chances of getting the job you want—faster. Working the system also helps relieve your natural anxiety about what you should be doing next.

The system is the same whether you are employed or unemployed, and even if you are not interested in changing jobs now. The system is the same whether you are looking for full- or part-time employment, consulting, or freelance work.

That's because job hunting in a changing economy means: *continuously becoming aware of market conditions inside as well as outside your present company. And learning what you have to offer—both inside and outside your company.*

The time to become aware of your opportunities is *not* when the pressure is on to find a new job, but *now.*

The Job-Hunting Process

You select or target a job market by selecting a geographic area you'd be willing to work in, an industry or company size (small, medium or large company), and a job or function within that industry. For example, you may want to be a pressman in the publishing industry in New Hampshire. That's your target market.

Then conduct a campaign for the sole purpose of getting interviews in your target area. A number of those interviews might eventually lead to acceptable job offers.

Job hunting seems to have dozens of equally important steps. There are résumés and cover letters to write, personal contacts to make, search firms to contact, ads to answer, notes to write, and so on. You can lose sight of what is most important.

There are only four main parts in a job-hunting campaign: targeting, getting interviews in each target, interviewing, and following up. Do your best and put your effort into those areas. Everything you do in a job hunt grows out of your targets, which lead to interviews and then to offers. If you have targeted well, can get interviews, are well prepared for them, and know how to turn inter-

Make it a rule of life never to regret and never to look back.
Regret is an appalling waste of energy; you can't build on it;
it's only good for wallowing in.
Katherine Mansfield

views into offers, you will be focused and less affected by mistakes in other areas of your search.

How Long Will a Job Search Take?

The length of each step in your search can vary considerably. For example, selecting the area in which you want to work (see *Targeting the Job You Want*) can be as simple as saying, "I want to be a controller in a small firm." Or it can be as complex as saying, "I want a position of leadership in a growing computer services business in any major U.S. city, where I can run my part of the operation—working with fast-paced but ethical people who are imaginative and leaders in their field. The job should lead to the position of partner."

The entire campaign can be very short. Let's say, for example, that:

- You have focused on a specific, realizable target.
- There are openings in the area that interests you.
- You know of someone in a position to hire you.
- You and the hiring manager "strike sparks" during the interview and it progresses naturally.

Start to finish could take a month or two.

The average job hunt does take longer. Statistics show that for professionals and middle managers, it takes an average of six months or more to find the job they want. As the previous chapter establishes, *career changers take longer.* And people currently employed usually take longer to find a new job because they often don't work as hard at the hunt.

It can take you longer than a month or two because, among other things:

- You may not be that clear about what you want.
- What you want may not be realistic.
- Maybe it *is* realistic, but there are no immediate openings.
- There may be openings, but you may not know where they are.
- You may hear of some openings, but may not know someone in a position to hire you.
- You may meet someone in a position to hire you, but the two of you don't hit it off.

Devote a large amount of time and energy to your search if you seriously intend to find a suitable job. A thorough search is so much work that the job you finally land will seem easy by comparison.

On the other hand, job hunting is like any other skill: You'll get better at it with practice. You'll learn the techniques, and you'll learn more about what's right for you. You'll become aware of what's happening in your chosen field, so that when you start a formal search it won't take so long.

The New Approach to Job Hunting

Keep up with changes in your company and your target area. To compete in today's competitive market, you must know:

- yourself
- the market—both inside and outside your company
- how to compete against "trained" job hunters.

Job Hunting—An Everyday Affair

Job hunting is no longer something that happens only when you want to change jobs. Do it informally *all the time* to stay sharp in your present position.

You should always be aware of what may adversely affect your present security. Don't expect your employer to tell you that the company or your department is heading in a different direction. Be ready when the time for change comes. Take advantage of changes so you can move your career in the direction *you* want it to go. Take control and "impose your own terms upon life."

In today's world, many people job-hunt virtually all the time. Years ago, at a time when U.S. corporations were more stable, I met an executive at a major pharmaceuticals company. He had been with that company thirty years, and planned to stay there until retirement.

Yet, while I was talking to him, he reached into his bottom drawer and pulled out an up-to-date résumé. He was not starting a new job hunt; he believed he should always have an up-to-date résumé and keep on looking—even though he had been working at the same company for thirty years! A good number of his job hunts were "successful" in that his outside exploration got him to his high

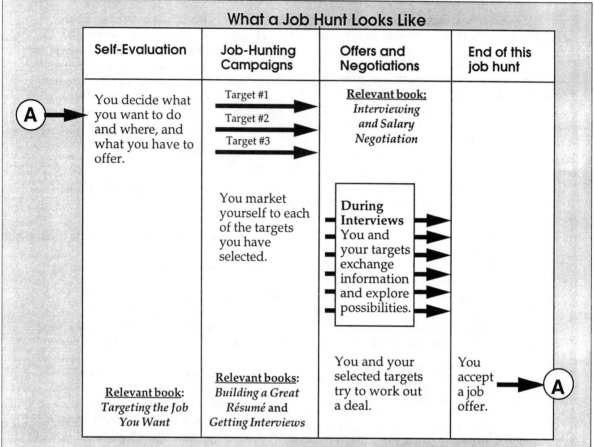

What a Job Hunt Looks Like

Self-Evaluation	Job-Hunting Campaigns	Offers and Negotiations	End of this job hunt
You decide what you want to do and where, and what you have to offer.	Target #1 Target #2 Target #3	**Relevant book:** *Interviewing and Salary Negotiation*	
	You market yourself to each of the targets you have selected.	**During Interviews** You and your targets exchange information and explore possibilities.	
Relevant book: *Targeting the Job You Want*	**Relevant books:** *Building a Great Résumé* and *Getting Interviews*	You and your selected targets try to work out a deal.	You accept a job offer.

Note: After you are in your new job for a while (such as six months, one year, two years), you will want to reevaluate your situation and make sure you are still on track. That's why this chart points back to the beginning after you've landed your job.

position in the same company.

Job hunting does not necessarily mean you want to change jobs now. Maybe you'll make your next actual job change a few years down the road. Or maybe someone will change your job for you—without asking. When are you going to start thinking about your next move?

Plan Your Next Move

Plan your career transitions—your moves from one job to the next—don't have them thrust upon you. First, know which job is right for you: a job in which you will excel and which you will feel satisfied doing. Then see how well your present job fits those desires. Don't leave your job for another one that is equally unsatisfying. On the other hand, don't remain in your current job out of inertia.

Career transitions are prompted by changes in a company—such as when it cuts back or introduces major technological or strategic changes—or by a change in you and your goals for your life. Be alert for a coming transition.

Our rate of progress is such that an individual human being, of ordinary length of life, will be called on to face novel situations which find no parallel in his past. The fixed person, for the fixed duties, who, in older societies was such a godsend, in the future will be a public danger.
Alfred North Whitehead

If You're Thinking About Changing Jobs

If you don't like your present job, don't leave yet. . . a good job hunt starts at home. Try to enrich your present job or move elsewhere in the company. Leave only after you are convinced that there is nothing there for you.

Whether you want to stay or leave, find out what your options are and what marketable skills you possess. Figure out what would make a good growth move for you.

One way to find out is to talk, on an informal basis, to people in other companies who are at least two levels higher than you are. They have an overview of the broad spectrum of job possibilities and are also in a position to hire you, or know others who might.

Another way to find out what is marketable is to look at the ads in the paper. You could get ideas for growing in your present position.

Let me give you an example. As soon as I accepted the job of vice president of operations for an advertising agency, I started clipping ads for V.P. of personnel, company controller, V.P. of finance, general manager —anything that would apply, even remotely, to my new position. The ads gave me ideas that neither my new employer nor I would have thought of.

I expanded the job and organized the categories of work I should be concentrating on.

These ads also told me the likelihood of being able to get one of those jobs. Even though I clipped lots of ads for V.P. of finance, I would never qualify because they required skills I did not have and was not interested in acquiring.

Ads also let you see who is hiring and what is in demand. Ads teach you the buzzwords of certain professions, and indicate how to tailor your résumé—just in case.

The fact that you're constantly job hunting can only be *good* for your present employer. It motivates you to do better, keeping your company more competitive than if you were not aware of what was happening outside.

The Practice of Job-Hunting Techniques

Job hunting is a specialized skill just as is public speaking or cooking a gourmet meal. You probably wouldn't, for example, get up to speak before an important audience without preparation and practice.

Job hunting takes planning to decide what your message is; some research; some thinking about your audience and how your message will sound to them; writing and rewriting résumés, letters, and interview presentations; and then some practice to hear how it all sounds.

Successful job hunting is a formal process. But once you know the basics, you can and should put your own personality into your presentations, just as you would in public speaking.

Follow the "rules" for job hunting the same way you would follow the "rules" for public speaking or cooking. As a wise beginner, do everything by the book. After you become skilled, you can deviate a bit—for the better—because you have mastered the basics. You will do what is right for you and the situation you are in. You can exercise sound judgment.

You will then be at the point where it flows. You will find that you are operating from an inner strength, and you'll feel what is important and what is not. It is *your* job hunt, and you are the one calling the shots. You will feel sure enough to do what is appropriate regardless of what some expert says. You will know when it is to your advantage to break the rules.

Don't develop a siege mentality. Practice job hunting now—even if you happen to enjoy what you're doing, and even if you want to continue in your present job. In fact, you will be more effective in your job if you become sharper about what is happening in the world.

The rules of the game keep changing and that's part of the game. Only those who change along with them will be allowed to continue to play.

Targeting: The Start of an Organized Search

To organize your search:

1) Brainstorm as many job targets as possible. You will not conduct a campaign aimed at all of them, but will have backup targets in case certain ones do not work out.

2) Identify three or four targets worthy of preliminary research.

3) Research each one enough to determine whether it is worth a full campaign. You can find this out through basic library research and a few networking interviews. This is your Preliminary Target Investigation.

4) If your research shows that a target now seems inappropriate, cross it off your list, and concentrate on the remaining targets. **As you continue to network and research, keep open to other possibilities that may be targets for you. Add those to your list of targets to research**.

As you add new targets, reprioritize your list so you are concentrating first on the targets that should be explored first. Do *not* haphazardly go after everything that comes your way.

5) If you decide the target is worth pursuing, conduct a full campaign to get interviews in that area:

- Develop your pitch.
- Develop your résumé.
- Develop a list of all the companies in the target area and the name of the person you want to contact in each company.

6) Then contact each company through networking, direct contact, ads, or search firms.

Serendipitous Leads

Make a methodical approach the basis of your search, but also keep yourself open to those serendipitous "lucky leads" outside of your target areas that may come your way. In general, it is a waste of your energy to go after single serendipitous leads. It is better to ask yourself if this lead warrants a new target. If it does, then decide where it should be ranked in your list of targets, and research it as you would any serious target.

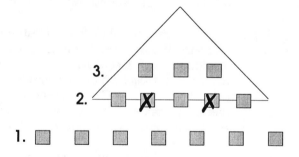

The boxes above represent different job targets. The triangle represents your job search. As you investigate targets, you will eliminate certain ones and spend more time on the remaining targets. You may research your targets by reading or by talking to people. The more you find out, the clearer your direction will become.

During Phase 1 of your search, you brainstormed lots of possible job targets, not caring whether or not they made sense.

During Phase 2, you conducted preliminary research to determine whether or not you should mount a full campaign aimed at these targets.

During Phase 3, you will focus on the targets that warrant a full campaign. This means you will do full research on each target, and consider using all of the techniques for getting interviews: networking, direct contact, search firms, and ads.

The
Five
O'Clock
Club®

How to
Control Your Campaign

Do not fear death so much,
but rather the inadequate life.
Bertolt Brecht

Your overall campaign can be managed with just a few important worksheets:

• Use the **Interview Record** for *every* meeting—both networking and job.

• Consider using the **Monthly Job-Hunting Calendar** to record your search activities—so it will be clear to you how much (or how little) you are doing. (See our book *Getting Interviews.*)

• The most important worksheet for controlling your search is the **Current List of My Active Contacts by Target**. At the beginning of your search, these will simply be networking contacts with whom you want to keep in touch. At that stage, your goal is to come up with six to ten contacts you want to recontact later.

Later, the quality of your list will change. Then the names will be prospective job possibilities that you are trying to move along.

If you have six to ten job possibilities "in the works," five of them will fall away through no fault of your own (because of job freezes or the hiring manager changing his or her mind about the kind of person wanted). Then you'll need to get more things in the works. With this critical mass of ongoing possible positions, you stand a chance of landing the kind of job you want.

Other Worksheets

The worksheets mentioned above are critical to the management of your search. Other worksheets guide specific parts of your search.

• In the beginning, the **Seven Stories Exercise** and **Your Forty-Year Vision** will help you select job targets that are appropriate for you (see our book *Targeting the Job You Want).*

• **Measuring Your Targets** will assure that you

have targets of a size that have a reasonable chance of working.

• Your **List of Companies to Contact** will help you organize whom you should contact in your search—either in person or some other way.

• The **Summary of What I Have/Want to Offer** will help you "position" yourself appropriately to each of your targets.

• **People to Contact in Each Target Area** is a way to get your search off to a quick start through networking or targeted mailings.

• The **Format of a Networking Interview** is your guide to properly managing the networking-type interviews you get through networking, targeted or direct mailings, or cold calls. (See our book *Getting Interviews.*)

• **The Follow-Up Checklist: Turing Job Interviews Into Offers** will help you assess the interview and decide what to do next. Your goal, after all, is to move the process along and see if you can create a job for yourself.

• Assessing whether you are at **Stage 1, 2 or 3** of your search will help you see where you really stand, rather than hoping for a job offer too soon.

Four-Step Salary Negotiation

• Are you keeping all four steps in mind?

• Are you **negotiating the job** to make it appropriate for you and for the hiring manager?

• Are you **paying attention to your competition**, what they have to offer and what you must do to outshine and outlast them? Are you aware that your competitors may not be real people, but may be in the mind of the hiring manager?

• Are you trying to postpone discussion of salary until after you **get the offer**?

The
Five
O'Clock
Club®

Current List of My
Active Contacts by Target

Make copies of this page for each target, and keep track of your active contacts in each target area. To see how well you are penetrating each target market, compare the total number of appropriate contacts in your market with the number you have actually contacted. Keep adding names to your list. Certain people will become inappropriate. Cross their names off. You should probably have some contact once every month or two with the people who remain on your list.

After your search is up and running, keep track of your contacts by the stage you are in for each one. This will tell you how well you are doing in your search, and will give you some idea of how likely it is for you to get an offer.

For Target _____:

Geographic area: _____
Industry or company size: _____
Position/Function: _____

	Name of Contact	Company	Position	Date of Last Contact	Targeted Date of Next Contact
1.					
2.					
3.					
4.					
5.					
6.					
7.					
8.					
9.					
10.					
11.					
12.					
13.					
14.					
15.					
16.					
17.					
18.					
19.					
20.					

Current List of Active Stage-1 Contacts:

Networking Contacts with whom you want to keep in touch

the beginning of a search

Measure the effectiveness of your search by listing the number of people with whom you are currently in contact on an ongoing basis, either by phone or mail, who are in a position to hire you or recommend that you be hired. The rule of thumb: If you are seriously job-hunting, **you should have six to ten active contacts going at one time**. **At the beginning of your search, these will simply be networking contacts with whom you want to keep in touch**. You are unlikely to get an offer at this stage. You are gathering information to find out how things work—getting your feet wet. You look like an outsider, and outsiders are rarely given a break. Keep adding names to your list because certain people will become inappropriate. Cross their names off. You should probably have some contact once a month with the people who remain on your list.

Because you have already developed targets for your search, please note below the target area for each contact, or note that it is serendipitous and does not fit in with any of your organized targets. This will help you see the progress you are making in each target area.

	Name of Contact	Company	Position	Date of Last Contact	Targeted Date of Next Contact	Target Area or Serend.
1.						
2.						
3.						
4.						
5.						
6.						
7.						
8.						
9.						
10.						
11.						
12.						
13.						
14.						
15.						
16.						
17.						
18.						
19.						
20.						

The
Five
O'Clock
Club®

Current List of Active Stage-2 Contacts:

The right people at the right levels in the right companies

the middle of a search

The nature of your "six to ten things in the works" changes over time. Instead of simply finding networking contacts to get your search started, you meet people who are closer to what you want.

Getting a job offer is not the way to test the quality of your campaign. A real test is when people say they'd want you—but not now. Do some people say: **"Boy, I wish I had an opening. I'd sure like to have someone like you here."**? Then you are interviewing well with the right people. All you need now are luck and timing to help you contact (and recontact) the right people when they also have a need.

If people are *not* saying they want you, find out why not. If you think you are in the right targets, talking to people at the right level, and are not early on in your search, you need feedback. Ask: "If you had an opening, would you consider hiring someone like me?" Find out what is wrong.

Become an insider—a competent person who can prove that he or she has somehow already done what the interviewer needs. *Prove* you can do the job, and that the interviewer is *not* taking a chance on you.

You still need six to ten contacts at this level whom you will recontact—perhaps once a month. Keep adding names to your list because certain people will become inappropriate. Cross their names off.

Name of Contact	Company	Position	Date of Last Contact	Targeted Date of Next Contact	Target Area or Serend.
1.					
2.					
3.					
4.					
5.					
6.					
7.					
8.					
9.					
10.					
11.					
12.					
13.					
14.					
15.					
16.					
17.					
18.					
19.					
20.					

The
Five
O'Clock
Club®

Current List of Active Stage-3 Contacts:
Moving along actual jobs or the possibility of creating a job
the final stages of a search

In this stage, you <u>uncover six to ten actual jobs (or the possibility of creating a job) to move along</u>. These job possibilities could come from *any* of your target areas or from serendipitous leads. Find a *lot* of people who would hire you if they could. If you have only one lead that could turn into an offer, you are likely to try to close too soon. Get more leads. You will be more attractive to the manager, will interview better, and will not lose momentum if your best lead falls apart. A good number of your job possibilities will fall away through no fault of your own (such as job freezes or major changes in the job requirements).

To get more leads, notice which targets are working and which are not. Make *additional* contacts in the targets that seem to be working, or develop new targets. <u>Recontact just about everyone you have met earlier in your search</u>. You want to develop more offers.

<u>Aim for three offers</u>: This is the stage of your search when you want them. When an offer comes during Stage 1 or Stage 2, you probably have not had a chance to develop momentum so you can get a number of offers. When choosing between offers, <u>select the job that positions you best for the long term</u>.

Name of Contact	Company	Position	Date of Last Contact	Targeted Date of Next Contact	Target Area or Serend.
1.					
2.					
3.					
4.					
5.					
6.					
7.					
8.					
9.					
10.					
11.					
12.					
13.					
14.					
15.					
16.					
17.					
18.					
19.					
20.					

Stuck in Your Search?
What to Do Next

Drive thy business, or it will drive thee.
Benjamin Franklin

---

*To laugh often and much; to win the respect
and the affection of children;
to earn the appreciation of honest critics and endure
the betrayal of false friends; to appreciate beauty; to
find the best in others; to leave the world a bit better—
whether by a healthy child, a garden patch
or a redeemed social condition;
to know even one life has breathed easier
because you have lived.
This is to have succeeded.*
Ralph Waldo Emerson

---

*I know God will not give me anything
I can't handle. I just wish He didn't
trust me so much.*
Mother Teresa

---

*Life moves on, whether we act as cowards or heroes.
Life has no other discipline to impose, if we would but
realize it, than to accept life unquestioningly. Everything we shut our eyes to, everything we run away
from, everything we deny, denigrate or despise, serves
to defeat us in the end. What seems nasty, painful,
evil, can become a source of beauty, joy and strength,
if faced with an open mind. Every moment is a golden
one for him who has the vision to recognize it as such.*
Henry Miller

How to Measure the Effectiveness of Your Search

Most job hunters say, "I'll know my search was good when I get a job." That's not a very good way to measure your search. You need to be able to tell as you go along whether you are heading in the right direction. There are a number of hints you can pick up along the way.

What Stage Are You In?

As you go along, the basic measurement tool to use in your search is this: "Do you have six to ten things in the works?" That is, are you talking to six to ten people on an ongoing basis who are in a position to hire you or recommend that you be hired?"

The quality of your contacts varies with where you are in your search.

• In the beginning of your search, you will speak to as many people as possible in your target market—regardless of the company for which they work. At this stage, you simply want market information. If you plan to stay in touch with them on an ongoing basis, they are Stage-1 contacts. To have any momentum going in the beginning of your search, keep in touch with six to ten people on an ongoing basis (every few months).

Over time, you will talk to more and more people who are Stage-1 contacts—perhaps 60 to 100 people during the course of your search. Some of those contacts will bubble up and become Stage-2 contacts.

• Stage-2 contacts are people who are the right people at the right level in the right jobs in the right companies in your targeted areas. They are senior to you, perhaps future hiring managers. Your goal is to have contact with six to ten of the right people on an ongoing basis. Then you have a full Stage-2 search going: You are in the middle of your search.

However, you will rarely get a good job offer at Stage 2. You aren't even talking to these people about real jobs at this point. You just want the right people to know you and remember you. And if one later happens to have a job opening, you still need to go after six to ten other job possibilities, because five will fall away through no fault of your own. If you do get an offer at Stage 2, you won't have many others with which to compare it. Keep in touch with your current Stage-1 contacts (using *networking* follow-ups), and develop additional Stage-1 contacts, so more will bubble up to Stage 2. Some of those will bubble up to Stage 3 (real job possibilities)—and then you're really cooking.

• You are in a full Stage-3 search when you are talking to six to ten people on an ongoing basis who actually have job openings or who have the possibility of creating a job for you. Then you have a number of opportunities that you can move along (using *job* follow-ups), and are in the best possible position to get the right job for you: the one that positions you best for the long term and the one that pays you what you are worth.

If you have six to ten possibilities in Stage 3, you have the chance of getting three offers. Remember, these do not have to be ideal jobs—some may even be disgusting. But an offer is an offer, and makes you more desirable in the market. You don't have to want to work at each of these places, but at least you will have a fallback position, and can honestly say, if appropriate, "I have a number of job offers, but there's no place I'd rather work than yours." With a number of offers in hand, you are less likely to be taken advantage of by a prospective employer who thinks you are desperate.

How's Your Search Going?

When I ask you how your search is going, I don't want to hear that a prospective employer really likes you. That's not a good measure of how well your search is going, because that one prospect could easily fall away: they may decide to hire no one, or decide to hire an accounting person instead of a marketing person. A lot can

happen that is beyond your control.

Instead I expect you to tell me how many things you have in the works. You would say, for example, "My search is going great. I have five Stage-1 contacts in the works. I'm just getting started."

Or you might say, "I have nine Stage-2 contacts, and three contacts in Stage 3." If you are an expert at this, you may even add: "I want more Stage-3 contacts, so my goal is to get thirty more in Stage 2. Right now, I'm digging up lots of new contacts, and keeping the other ones going. With my Stage-2 contacts, I'm generally doing networking follow-ups, and with my Stage-3 contacts, I'm generally doing job follow-ups."

That kind of talk is music to my ears.

It usually takes very little effort to get a few more things "in the works." Simply recontact your network, network into someone you haven't met with yet, directly contact someone, talk to a search firm, answer an ad. You will soon have more activity in your search.

What Job Hunters Do Wrong

In addition to looking at the *stage* of your overall search, it is also helpful to look at what can go wrong in each *phase* of your campaigns. Some job hunters err in their overall search approach or attitude. Then there are things that can go wrong in the Assessment Phase, or in the parts of your campaigns (in the Planning, Interviewing, or Follow-Up phases). We'll examine each of these to determine what you may be doing wrong, if anything.

The Overall Search: What Can Go Wrong?

Here are some problems that are general to the entire search:

• **Not spending enough time** on your search. If you are unemployed, you should be spending thirty-five hours a week on your search. If you are employed, spend fifteen hours a week to get some momentum going. If you spend only two or three hours a week on your job search, you may complain that you have been searching forever, when actually you have not even begun. If you are employed, you can do most of your work in the evenings and on weekends—research, write cover letters and follow-up letters. You can even schedule your meetings in the evenings or early mornings.

- **Not having enough fun**. Some job hunters—especially those who are unemployed—say they will start having fun after they get a job. But your search may take many months, and you are more likely to come across as desperate if you are not allowing yourself to have some fun. Having fun will make you seem like a more normal person on your interviews, and you'll feel better about yourself. The Five O'Clock Club formula is that you *must* have at least three hours of fun a week.

- **Not having six to ten things in the works**. See the beginning of this chapter about Stages 1, 2, and 3 of your search.

- **Talking to people who are at the wrong level**. At the beginning of your search, talk to peers just to gather information to decide whether a prospective target is worth a full campaign. When you have selected a few good targets, then talk to those who are higher level.

- **Trying to bypass the system**. Some job hunters feel they don't have time for this, and simply want to go on job interviews (usually through search firms or answering ads). Others want to skip the assessment process (see our book *Targeting the Job You Want*), or don't even do the Seven Stories Exercise. Their campaigns are weaker because they have no foundation.

At least touch on every step in the process. You will have a quicker and more productive search.

- **Lowering your salary expectations just because you have been unemployed awhile**. Even those who have been unemployed a year or two land jobs at market rates. They get what they are worth in the market because they have followed the system.

At The Five O'Clock Club, half the people who attend are employed; half are unemployed.

Many of those who are unemployed have been out of work for a year or two. Usually, they have been doing something wrong in their searches, and the counselor and their group can help them figure out what it is. When they get a job (which they almost certainly will if they stick with the system), they usually wind up getting something appropriate at an appropriate salary level.

Sometimes, if people really need money, we suggest that they take something inappropriate to earn some money, and continue to search while they are working.

- **Getting discouraged**. Half the battle is controlling your emotions. Jack had been unemployed one and a half years when he joined us. He seemed very agitated—almost angry—which happens when a person has been working at a job search for so long. I told him I was afraid that he might come across that way during interviews. He assured me (with irritation in his voice) that he was completely pleasant during the interview, but was simply letting his hair down in the group.

In career counseling, we have nothing to go on but the way the person acts in the group: The way you are in the group probably bears some resemblance to the way you are in the interview. We would recognize you as being the same person. Anyway, it's all we have to go on, so we have to point out to you what we see.

The next week, Jack still seemed angry. I asked the group what they thought, and of course they could see it too. It was easier for him to hear it from his peers, and, because he was a mature person, Jack listened to them.

The third week, Jack laughingly announced that he had had a lobotomy, and was a completely different person. He said he had changed his attitude, and that his interviews reflected this change.

The fourth week, he announced that he had had another lobotomy because he felt he still had room for improvement. He was a noticeably different person, and did not seem at all like someone who had been out of work a long time.

26

Quit now, you'll never make it.
If you disregard this advice, you'll be halfway there.
David Zucker

Jack read every day the books we use at The Five O'Clock Club, and provided very good insights to the other job hunters in our small group.

By the fifth week, Jack was almost acting like a co-counselor in the group. He had made great strides in his own search (with three Stage-3 contacts, and lots of Stage 2 contacts), and was able to astutely analyze the problems others were having. He was a wonderful contributor.

By the seventh week, Jack was close to a number of offers, and in the eighth week, Jack proudly addressed the large group and reported on his successful search. We were sorry to see him go.

By the way, Jack did not have to take a pay cut or a job that was beneath him. His prolonged search did not affect his salary negotiation.

Do what you need to do to keep your spirits up. Don't ask yourself if you feel like searching. Of course you don't. Just do it anyway. And act as if you enjoy it.

- **Not having support**. Looking for a job is a lonely business. A job hunter may "buddy" with another job hunter. They call each other every morning to talk about what they are each going to do that day and to review what they each accomplished the day before. Other job hunters join free emotional-support groups at places of worship. You may find that you need that help in addition to the job-search strategy you get at The Five O'Clock Club. Or you may find you would like to see a counselor privately to help you with specifics having to do with your search, such as your résumé, a review of your search, salary negotiation, or the follow-up to a very important job interview. Get the help you need.

- **Inflating in your own mind the time you have actually been searching**. You may feel as though you've been searching forever. But if you are searching only three hours a week, you have not yet begun. If at the end of a year, you finally start to put in the required 15 to 35 hours a week, you have just really started to search. Then when people ask how long you have been searching, the correct answer is "a few weeks." It's good to be honest with yourself about how long you have actually been searching.

During the Assessment Phase: What Can Go Wrong?

In the Assessment Phase you use our book, *Targeting the Job You Want*, to go through the exercises (The Seven Stories, Values, Forty-Year Vision, and so on), and select job targets (industries or companies of a certain size; the position you would like in each target; and the geographic area).

If you are not sure what you should do with your life, assessment is a time to explore—perhaps with the help of a career counselor. What can go wrong in this phase?

- **Selecting one or two targets too quickly**. Rather than exploring, a job hunter may pick a target, go after it, find out it doesn't work, and then not know what to do next. Instead, brainstorm as many targets as you can at the beginning of your search, rank them, and go after them in a methodical way.

- **Not being specific in selecting a target**. Some job hunters say, "I just want a job. I don't care what it is." You may not care, but the hiring team wants someone who cares about their specific industry and organization. In the beginning of your search, you want to explore, and stay calm while you are doing your research to find out what the likely targets are for you. If you don't have targets defined (such as "being a COBOL computer programmer in a medium-sized company in the Albuquerque area"), then you are still exploring, and that's okay. But it is not an organized search. And even when your search is organized and targeted, you will still have plenty of room for serendipitous leads.

- **Not doing the right research**. Read the extensive material Wendy Alfus Rothman wrote on research, including the annotated bibliography at the back of *Targeting the Job You Want*. Research is critical throughout your search, and separates those who follow The Five O'Clock Club method from other job hunters.

The thing always happens that you believe in; and the belief in a thing makes it happen.
Frank Lloyd Wright

If you want a quality, act as if you already had it. Try the "as if" technique.
William James

Instead of just "doing" research, why not learn to enjoy it and make it part of your life?

The better your research, the richer your targets will become—well defined rather than superficial—and the more knowledgeable you will sound to prospective employers. In addition, you will save a lot of time as you discover where the markets are and which ones are the best fit for you.

• **Not ranking your targets**. Some job hunters go after everything at once. For a more organized search, overlap your targets, but still conduct a condensed search focusing on each target and keeping them separate in your mind.

Take a look at the chart below, which shows a campaign aimed at each target (T1, T2, and T3). Yet the targets overlap to speed up the search.

Next, let's look at what can go wrong in the various phases of the campaign aimed at each target.

During the Preparation Phase: What Can Go Wrong?

In the Preparation Phase you use our book, *Getting Interviews*, to research companies and develop a list to target, to develop your cover letters, and to figure out how to get lots of meetings in your target market.

• **Relying on only one technique for getting interviews**. Consider using all four techniques for getting interviews: networking, direct contact, search firms, and ads. Even in fields where people like to talk to people, such as sales or human resources, though networking is easier, it is not thorough. It is a scattered approach.

Make a list of all the companies in your target area—say, 120 companies.
- Perhaps network into 20 of them;
- Do a targeted mailing into 20—it's just like networking: Use a letter with a follow-up phone call. Remember that you want to see this person whether or not he or she has a job opening;
- Talk to search firms (if appropriate); and
- Answer ads.
- You can also do a direct-mail campaign (no follow-up phone call) to the remaining 80 companies—just to be thorough so all the companies in your target area know that you exist and are looking.

• **Contacting the wrong person**. The human resources person is the wrong one unless you want a job in human resources. The right person is one or two levels higher than you are in the department or division in which you want to work. If you are very senior and want to work for the president, the right person for you to contact is the president or perhaps someone on the board. If you want to be the president, the right person is someone on the board, or whoever may influence the selection of the president.

• **Being positioned improperly**. If you are not positioned properly, you will not be able to get interviews. Write out your Two-Minute Pitch.

If you are distressed by anything external, the pain is not due to the thing itself, but to your estimate of it; and this you have the power to revoke at any moment.
Marcus Aurelius

In your small group, be sure to practice your pitch. Try role-playing. Tell the group who they are pretending to be, and ask them to critique you. You want to make sure you have your pitch down pat. Write it out.

- **Using skimpy cover letters**. We use a four-paragraph approach that is thorough. Most job hunters write paragraphs one and four, and skip the meat.
- **Having a weak or inappropriate résumé**. If your résumé doesn't speak for you in your absence, and tell them exactly who you are, your level, and what you bring to the party, develop one that helps you. We have a whole book on this topic—along with case studies of real live people. See our book *Building a Great Résumé*.
- **Skipping the research phase to develop a good list of target companies**. If you have a good list, you will get more out of every one of your networking contacts. Show your list of prospective companies to your contacts, ask them what they think of the companies on the list, who they suggest you should contact at the good companies, and ask, "May I use your name?"

During the Interviewing Phase: What Can Go Wrong?

- **Trying to close too soon**. When a company is interested in you, you may have the tendency, like most job hunters, to focus on that one possibility and hope you get an offer. Because everything depends on that one possibility, chances are that you will do something wrong—trying to force them to decide before they are ready.

Instead, get other things going while you keep an eye on the company you are already interested in. Ease the pressure on yourself and that company. Get your six to ten things in the works and you'll have a balanced search.

- **Being seen as an outsider**. It's okay to be an outsider when it is early in your search. However, to get offers, you must be seen as an insider. When you are an insider, higher-level networking contacts say, "I really wish I had an opening

because I would love to have someone like you on board." You are being well received, and this person counts as a Stage-2 contact. Keep in touch with him or her. Find lots more. It's only a matter of time until you get a job: if the target you picked is a good one; if you contact more and more people who say the same thing; and if you keep in touch with those whom you already met.

- **Not using the worksheets**. Fill out What I Have/Want to Offer. This will help you position yourself to each targeted area. Use one for each of your targets. Make a zillion copies of the Interview Record. Fill one out every time you go on an interview. Note to whom you spoke, to whom they referred you, their important issues, and so on. Two weeks later you may not remember what you discussed.

If you are having a terrific search, you may meet with five to fifteen people each week. Keep track of them with your Interview Record. Some people keep the records in a three-ring binder, alphabetically or by industry or target. Every time they write a follow-up letter, they attach a copy of that letter to the Interview Record. They cross-reference the information, and become very methodical.

That way, when you conduct your networking follow-ups every two months, you will have the notes from your last discussion, and copies of the letters you had sent earlier.

Other things that can go wrong in the Interviewing Phase include:

- Not thinking like a consultant.
- Not looking or acting like the level for which you are searching.
- Not seeing the interview as only the beginning of the process.
- Not getting information/giving information to move it along. "Where are you in the hiring process?" "How many other people are you talking to?" "How do I compare with them?" Be impersonal in the way you ask these questions so you can find out about your competition.
- Not preparing for the interview by having a 3x5 card or finding out with whom you will be

meeting.

- Not being in sync with their timing (trying to close too soon or not moving quickly enough).
- Not listening to what is really going on.

During the Follow-Up Phase: What Can Go Wrong?

In addition to targeting, follow-up is the most important reason Five O'Clock Clubbers land jobs quickly. This is the brainiest part of the process. Notice that the earlier diagram showed the three parts as equal: Preparation, Interviewing, and Follow-Ups. Spend an equal amount of time on each.

Study thoroughly those parts of this book. Some of the obvious things that go wrong include:

- **Taking the first offer**. Try to get three offers at the same time. Then select the one that positions you best for the long run.
- **Not recontacting your contacts**. If you have been in search awhile, the most important action you can take to develop new momentum is to recontact those with whom you have already met—perhaps every two to three months. That way they have a better chance of thinking of you when they come across news that may help you in your search.

Tell them, "It's been awhile since we've met, and I am having a very interesting time. My search has taken a slightly different direction, and I now find there is a lot of activity in the roof-repair market, which I am currently exploring. You were such a help to me before that I would like to call you again to find out what is going on at your end, and to tell you a little about what I've been doing." However you do it, recontact your contacts.

- **Not studying the books**. Follow-up is covered in great detail in this book. Study it and spend the time it takes to think through what you can do next to move along the *job* contacts you have made. While those you have networked with should be contacted every few months, job follow-up is more complicated.

- **Stating your salary requirements too soon**. The discussion of salary negotiation in this book is another thing you should read thoroughly *at the beginning of your search*. Salary negotiation starts with the way you position yourself at your very first meeting.

- **Not reassessing where you stand in your search.** Let's say you have been in search awhile, and would like to know where you stand. Take all of the contacts you have in the works (people you are in touch with on a regular basis), and divide them up into Stage 1, Stage 2, or Stage 3 contacts. You will probably have a ratio of 60 Stage 1 to 20 Stage 2 to 6 Stage 3. Therefore, to increase the number of contacts you have in Stage 3, your only recourse is to increase the number of contacts you have in Stage 1. Some will bubble up to Stage 2, and others to Stage 3.

Now that we've taken a break from your search to assess how you are doing, it's time to get back to work. Read on!

PART TWO

PREPARING FOR THE INTERVIEW

DON'T SKIP THIS STEP

Positioning Power for a Job Change

*Greatness is not measured by what a man or woman
accomplishes, but by the opposition
he or she has overcome . . . .*
Dr. Dorothy Height, President,
National Council of Negro Women

Feel stuck in your present position? Peel off your old label, slap on a new one, and position yourself for something different.

Whether you're a branch manager who wants to go into commercial lending, or an operations person who dreams of being a trainer, the challenge you face is the same: You have to convince people that, even though you don't have experience, you can handle the new position.

It's a little like show biz: You play the same role for years and then you get typecast. It can be difficult for people to believe that you can play a different role. To move on to new challenges, you have to negotiate into the new job by offering seemingly unrelated skills as an added benefit to the employer. The key to these negotiations is "positioning" yourself.

Positioning

Simply put, positioning yourself means stating your skills and qualities in a way that makes it easy for the prospective employer to see you in the position that is open or in other positions down the road.

You may want to stay in your present company. In that case, you are positioning yourself to the person in charge of hiring for the particular department you want to enter. Or, you may want to go to a new company or even a new industry. In this case, you are positioning yourself to a new employer. Either way, the steps are the same:

1) Determine what skills and qualities your prospective employer wants.

2) Search your background to see where you have demonstrated skills and qualities that would apply.

3) Write a summary at the top of your résumé to position yourself.

4) Use the same summary to sell yourself in an interview.

Your summary says it all. It should sell your ability, experience, and personality. It brings together all your accomplishments.

The rest of your résumé should support your summary. For example, if the summary says that you're a top-notch marketer, the résumé had better support that. It's completely within your control to tell whatever story you want to tell. You can emphasize certain parts of your background and deemphasize others.

**You can get typecast.
To move on, you have to negotiate
into the new job . . . by "positioning" yourself.**

Thinking through your summary is not easy, but it focuses your entire job hunt. It forces you to clarify the sales pitch you will use in interviews.

However, a summary that positions them is *not* what many people put on their résumés. They say they want "a challenging job in a progressive and growth-oriented company that uses all my strengths and abilities." That doesn't say anything at all, and it doesn't do you any good.

Let's consider a few examples of summaries that *will* work for you:

Pursuing the Dream Job

Jane, a client-relationship manager at a major bank, has handled high-net-worth clients for more than twenty years. She is taking early retirement and thinking about a second career. Two directions interest her: a job similar to what she has done but in a smaller bank; or, the job of her dreams—working as one of the top administrative people for a high-net-worth family (such as the Rockefellers), handling their business office and perhaps doing some of the things that involve her hobbies over the years: staffing and decorating.

If Jane were to continue on her current career path and go for a position as a relationship manager at a smaller bank, she would highlight the years she has worked at the bank. Her summary, if used in her résumé, would look like this:

Over 20 years handling all aspects of fiduciary relationships for PremierBank's private banking clients. Successfully increased revenue through new business efforts, client cultivation, and account assessment. Consistently achieved fee increases. Received regular bonus awards.

However, to pursue her dream job, Jane's regular résumé won't do. She has to reposition herself to show that her experience fits what her prospective employer needs. Her summary would read like this:

Administrative manager with broad experience in running operations. In-depth work with accountants, lawyers, agents, and so on. Over 20 years' experience handling all aspects of fiduciary relationships for PremierBank's private banking clients (overall net worth of $800 million). Expert in all financial arrangements (trust and estate accounts, asset management, non-profit, and tenant shareholder negotiations).

Her résumé would also focus on her work *outside* of PremierBank because these activities would interest her prospective employer: first, her work with the high-class apartment building of which she was president for fourteen years, and then the post she held for ten years as treasurer of a nonprofit organization. Finally, Jane would highlight the work she had done at PremierBank that would be of interest to her prospective employer, such as the account on which she saved a client $300,000 in taxes.

Ready to Take Charge

Robert had worked in every area of benefits administration. Now he would like to head up the entire benefits administration area—a move to management. His summary:

14 years' experience in design and administration of all areas of employee benefit plans, including five years with Borgash Benefits Consultants. Advised some of the largest and most prestigious companies in the country. Excellent training and communications skills. MBA in Finance. An effective manager who delivers consistent results.

From Supporting to Selling

Jack wants to move into sales after being in marketing support. He lacked a summary on former résumés. Therefore people saw him as a marketing support person rather than a salesperson—because his most recent job was in marketing support. He has been an executive in the sales promotion area, so his summary stresses his internal sales and marketing as well as his management experience:

10 years' progressive sales, marketing and managerial experience. Devise superior marketing strategies through qualitative analysis and product repositioning. Skillful at completing the difficult internal sale, coupled with the ability to attract business and retain clients. Built strong relationships with the top consulting firms. A team player with an enthusiastic approach to top-level challenges.

Notice how he packages his experience running a marketing department as sales. His pitch will be, "It's even more difficult to sell inside because, in order to keep my job, I have to get other people in my company to use my marketing services. I have to do a good job, or they won't use me again."

If you do not have a summary, then, by default, you are positioned by the last job you held. In Jack's case, the employer would receive the new résumé and say, "Ah-ha! Just what we need—a salesperson!"

Making a Career Change

Elliott had been in sports marketing years ago, and had enjoyed it tremendously. However, he had spent the past four years in the mortgage industry, and was having a hard time getting back into sports marketing.

The sports people saw him as a career changer—and they saw him as a mortgage man. Even when he explained that marketing mortgages is the same as marketing sports, people did not believe him. He was being positioned by his most recent experience, which was handicapping him.

When a job hunter wants to change industries—or go back to an old industry—he cannot let his most recent position act as a handicap. For example, if a person has always been in pharmaceuticals marketing, and now wants to do marketing in another industry, the résumé should be rewritten to make it generic marketing, and most references to pharmaceuticals should be removed.

In Elliott's case, the summary in the new résumé helps a great deal to bring his old work experience right to the top of the résumé. In addition, Elliott has removed the word "mortgage" from the description of his most recent job, his title at the mortgage company now stands out more than the company name, and he has gotten rid of company and industry jargon, such as the job title of segment director, because it is not something easily understood outside of his company.

Notice that the description of what Elliott did for the mortgage business is now written generically—it can apply to the marketing of *any* product. With his new résumé, Elliott had no trouble speaking to people in the sports industry. They no longer saw his most recent experience as a handicap, and he soon had a terrific job as head of marketing for a prestigious sporting-goods company.

If you want to move into a new industry or profession, state what you did generically so people will not see you as tied to the old.

Bring Something to the Party

When it comes down to negotiating yourself into a new position, seemingly unrelated skills from former positions may actually help you get the job.

For example, some of my background had been in accounting and computers when I decided to go into counseling. My CFO (chief financial officer) experience helped me ease into that career. I applied at a ninety-person career counseling company and agreed to be their CFO for a while—provided I was also assigned clients to counsel. They wanted a cost-accounting system, so my ability to do that for them was what I "brought to the party." I was willing to give the company something they wanted (my business experience) in exchange for doing something I really wanted to do (counseling executives).

Combining the new with the old, rather than jumping feet first into something completely new, is often the best way to move your career in a different direction. You gain the experience you need in the new field without having to enter at the entry level. Equally important, it is less stressful because you are using some of your old strengths while you build new ones.

Coming from a background different from the field you are targeting can also give you a bargaining chip. If you are looking at an area where you have no experience, you will almost certainly be competing with people who do have experience. You can separate yourself from the competition by saying, "I'm different. I have the skills to do this job, and I can also do other things that these people can't do." It works!

Our book, *Building a Great Résumé*, contains dozens and dozens of additional positioning (summary) statements. In addition, you will see how the positioning statements are used to set the tone for the rest of the résumé.

**Elliott's positioning (summary) statement
is on the next page.**

Think like a duchess, act like a duchess, talk like a duchess,
and one day you will be a duchess!
Henry Higgins to Eliza Doolittle in
George Bernard Shaw's *Pygmalion*

"Before" Résumé

Elliott Jones

421 Morton Street

Chase Fortune, KY 23097

Sears Mortgage Company   1994 - present
Vice President, Segment Director, Shelter Business
- Director of $4.6-billion residential-mortgage business for the largest mortgage lender in the nation.
- Organized and established regional marketing division for largest mortgage lender in nation, a business which included first and second mortgages, and mortgage life insurance.

SportsLife Magazine   1991-1994
Publisher and Editor
- Published and edited the largest consumer health and fitness magazine and increased circulation 175%.

and so on. . .

"After" Résumé

Elliott Jones

421 Morton Street

Chase Fortune, KY 23097

Summary of Qualifications

Fifteen-plus years of domestic and international marketing management experience in the <u>leisure/sporting goods industry</u>; multi-brand expertise specializing in marketing, new business development, strategic planning, and market research.

Proven record of identifying customer segments, developing differentiable product platforms, communication strategies, sales management, share growth, and profit generation.

Business Experience

Sears Mortgage Company   1994 - present
<u>**VICE PRESIDENT, BUSINESS DIRECTOR**</u>
Residential Real Estate Business

- Business Director of a $4.6-billion business. Managed strategic planning, marketing, product development, and compliance.

- Consolidated four regional business entities into one; doubled product offerings. Grew market share 150 basis points and solidified #1 market position.

- Developed and executed nationally recognized consumer and trade advertising, public relations, and direct-response programs.

- Structured a product development process which integrated product introductions into the operations and sales segments of the business.

- Organized and established regional marketing division for largest mortgage lender in nation, a business which included first and second mortgages, and mortgage life insurance.

SPORTSLIFE MAGAZINE   1991-1994
<u>**Publisher and Editor**</u>

- Published and edited the largest consumer health and fitness magazine and increased circulation 175%.
and so on. . .

36

Your Two-Minute Pitch:
The Keystone of Your Search

> ## If your pitch
> ## —the way you position yourself—
> ## is wrong, everything else about your
> ## search is wrong.

Your Two-Minute Pitch is the backbone of your search. You'll use it in job and net-working interviews, and in your cover letters. You'll be ready when someone calls and says, "So tell me about yourself."

Your résumé summary statement could serve as the starting point for your pitch. Keep in mind:

- to whom you are pitching
- what they are interested in
- who your likely competitors are
- and what you bring to the party that your competitors do not.

In your pitch, you are *not* trying to tell your life story. Instead:

- Let this person know that you are competent and interested in the area in which he or she is interested.
  - Say things that are relevant.
  - Come across at the right level.

Think about your target audience and what you want to say to them. Examine your background to find things that fit.

My Basic Pitch—Target 1

Here's what my pitch was, a number of years ago, to someone interested in my counseling back-ground:

"For over ten years, I've been counseling people who are in the $40,000 to $600,000 range. I run The Five O'Clock Club, which is a career-development group. I also started and am in charge of The New School's career-development program, where we have over fifteen faculty members.

"I spent three years at a major outplacement firm. There I was regularly assigned the most difficult cases—those who had been unemployed a year or more. All of them had jobs within three months.

"I counsel executives in my private practice and also for a major corporation. And I have my M.B.A. in Behavioral Science.

"You can see that counseling is my life, and I'm excited about the situation in your company be-cause . . ."

Tailoring the Pitch

This is my basic counseling pitch, but I have to **tailor it to suit the situation**.

For example, for a pitch for a job counseling executives at Citibank, I added that I had worked many years for major corporations (such as . . .) and understood how corporations worked.

What else would they want to know? That I could work with their kind of employees. So I told them, "I like the kind of employees you have—sharp, aggressive—I like those kinds of people." I wanted to let them know that I knew their reputation.

My Basic Pitch—Target 2

I'll have more to say about pitching myself to a specific company, but let's first take a look at an-other way I could pitch myself. Remember, if my pitch is wrong, everything else is wrong.

"I have over twenty years of business-manage-ment experience spanning a variety of areas.

"I started out in computers—doing computer programming on very complex projects. Then I was a systems analyst, and finally a trainer of program-mers, analysts, and managers.

"Then I went into advertising management, managing a staff of thirteen artists, writers, and others. We developed ad campaigns, did public relations, and so on.

"After that, I went into small-business manage-ment, serving as CFO and specializing in turning around small service companies that were in dire financial straits—companies of fifty to a hundred professional employees. In those positions, I managed the accounting and control functions and other administrative areas such as computers, research, public relations, and so on. I also have my M.B.A.

"The reason I wanted to talk to you today is that

I want to get back into business management."

You can see that this is a good pitch if indeed I want to get back into business management, but a terrible pitch if I want to counsel executives.

Both pitches are true about me. But each pitch is tailored to my target market. Notice, for example, that in one pitch I mention I have an M.B.A. in Behavioral Science, and in the other pitch I simply say I have an M.B.A.

You too have to think through what you want to say to the market you are targeting—just as you did when you were developing the summary statement on your résumé.

What's Wrong with This Pitch?

Take a look at the beginning of my client's pitch, and see if you can tell what's wrong.

"I have eighteen years' experience in education and training: in developing training programs, in running training centers, etc."

What's wrong with this pitch? We can't know until we know to whom he is talking. It turns out that the pitch was wrong because the interviewer was not interested in training, but in personal computers. How much did my client know about PCs? A lot. "Why, I can make PCs dance," he said. "The only problem is that the hiring manager would probably want someone who could network them together, and I've never done that."

"*Can* you do that?" I asked.

"Of course I can do it," he replied.

"Then go *do* it," I said, "so you can tell her you have already done it. Network together the computers you have at home. And join a group that specializes in that. Ask one of the people if you can go along and help him or her network computers together."

Here's the pitch one week later:

"I have eighteen years' experience in computers, specializing in PCs. I have built PCs from scratch, and I've done software and applications programming on PCs. I also understand how important networking is. I've even networked together the PCs I have at home, and I belong to a group of PC experts, so I always know whom to talk to when tricky things come up. I can do anything that needs to be done with PCs. I can make PCs dance!

"I'm excited about talking to you because I know your shop relies on PCs."

Do you see how a pitch has to be tailored to each specific situation?

More Tailoring in the Interview

Now, let's get back to my pitch to a specific company. In my two-minute counseling pitch, I laid the groundwork, but that's not enough.

At Citibank, for example, what were the hiring manager's specific needs, and who was my competition? What extra could I bring to the party?

I assumed management would not need someone with my counseling credentials—all they needed was a good counselor. So I toned down my Two-Minute Pitch. Now I needed to find some other competitive advantage.

Here's how the conversation went:

Kate: "Are there other things you would want the new person to do besides counseling? Some special projects?"

Manager: "No, that's all. It's a counseling position, and the person will be counseling executives all day."

Kate: "But what you're really doing is running a small business. Are there things you feel frustrated about that you would like someone to be able to handle?"

Manager: "Well . . . actually there is something. [It didn't matter to me what she said next. I knew it would be my competitive advantage because obviously she had not told anyone else.]

"I don't like the look of the materials we have here. They aren't professional enough. I'd like to have our own logo and our own look."

Kate: "Well, you are talking to the right person. It just so happens that I have an advertising background and I was responsible for corporate literature. I'd like to bring in some of my work to show you."

Her eyes lit up. Finally— someone to take over

this ugly job of redoing the literature.

Know Something About Them

When you go for an interview, and they immediately say: "Tell me about yourself," how will you know how to position yourself? You don't want to bound into a standard Two-Minute Pitch unless you feel that you know something about them.

If you don't know anything at all about them or the job, you may say: "I'd be happy to tell you about myself, but could you first tell me a little about the kind of job we're talking about?"

What Point Are You Trying to Make?

Most people write their Two-Minute Pitch and rehearse it in front of a mirror. As you are listening to yourself, think: What *point* am I trying to make? What impression do I hope they'll get about me?

I was listening to a client's pitch, and could not understand the point this executive woman was trying to make. After she had finished:

Kate: "I don't get it. What point are you trying to make?"

Client: "Look, I want them to know that I have twenty years' experience in capital markets, whether it's in aerospace or petroleum, metals and mining, or real estate. *My experience is in capital markets.*"

Kate: "That's a great pitch. Why don't you just tell them exactly that up front?"

They Won't "Get It" on Their Own, So Just Tell Them.

Most job hunters think: I'll just tell them my background, and they'll see how it fits in with their needs. But they probably won't see.

Don't expect the hiring team to figure out something about you. If you have a conclusion you'd like them to reach about you, tell them what it is.

If you want them to see how all of your jobs have somehow been involved in international, say,

"All of my jobs have somehow been involved in international." Isn't that easy?

If you want them to notice that you have always been willing to move wherever the company wanted you to move, then say just that. If you want them to know that you have done things treasury executives rarely do, then tell them that.

If you want them to see that you have developed intensive product knowledge while handling various operations areas, tell them that. Do you want them to know that FORTRAN is your favorite language? Then don't say, "I have five years of FORTRAN experience." That's not your point. Do you want them to know that you can make computers dance? Tell them. Don't make them figure it out for themselves. They won't.

Make your message so clear that if someone stops them and says, "Tell me about John," they will know what to tell the other person about you.

Communicating Your Pitch

Many job hunters try to cram everything they can into their Two-Minute Pitch, but people can't hear it. Think about those who are considered the great communicators today. We judge communicators very differently from the way we did in the past, when the Winston Churchill type was ideal. Today, our standards are based on the medium of TV. The best communicators speak on a personal level—the way people talk on TV. Whether you are addressing a big audience or are on a job interview, cultivate a TV style—a friendly, one-on-one conversational style—not a "listing of what I've done" style.

The interviewer is assessing what it would be like to work with you. Make your pitch understandable. Before people go on TV, they decide the three major points they want to make—what they want the audience to remember.

What do you want your "audience" to remember about you? Polish both your Two-Minute Pitch and the two or three accomplishments that would interest this person. Prepare your pitch about each accomplishment the same way you prepared your Two-Minute Pitch. For example, don't say,

You can have anything you want if you want it desperately enough.
You must want it with an inner exuberance that erupts through the skin
and joins the energy that created the world.
Sheilah Graham, *The Rest of the Story*

"I started out in this job as a trainer, where I traveled to x and y and worked on special projects, etc."—if what you really want them to know is "That was a great assignment. My programs accounted for more than two thirds of the company's revenue." Use a conversational tone. Speak the way you would normally speak.

Many job hunters have pitches that are too heavy in content. Let's return to the woman executive we were discussing:

"I have twenty years' experience in capital markets in airlines, real estate and petroleum, metals and mining—assessing customers' and prospects' financial requirements based on the industry's point within the business cycle as well as the specific company's. I assess client credit, etc."

People can't listen to that. It's too dense. It needs some filler around the important words to resemble the way people really talk:

"I have twenty years' experience in capital markets—capital markets has always been my chief interest. I had this experience in three different areas, but the area where I spent the most time was in the airlines. I was also most recently involved in petroleum, metals and mining, and earlier on in my career, I was involved in real estate."

The new pitch is more conversational than a list, or simply getting all the facts out.

Two Minutes Is a Long Time.
Show Enthusiasm.

In this TV society, people are used to fifteen-second sound bites on the news. As the communicator, you have to engage the listener. Reinforce your main points. Don't say too many things. Sound enthusiastic.

If you are a boring person, the very least you can do is sit forward in your chair. I once did a magazine article on who got jobs and who got to keep them. I talked to the deans of business and engineering schools.

I learned that the person most likely to get the job was the one who sounded enthusiastic. And the one who got to keep the job was the enthusiastic one—even over people who were more qualified. Employers decided to keep someone who was willing to pitch in and do anything to help the company.

Even more interesting to me is that this same thing is true for senior executives. In my line of work, I sometimes have the opportunity to follow up when someone doesn't get a job. I am amazed by the number of times I am told (about people making from $150,000 to $600,000), that the applicant lacked enthusiasm:

"He was managing 1,300 people, and I don't know how he did it. He just doesn't sound enthusiastic. How could he motivate his troops if he can't motivate me? Anyway, I don't know that he really wants the job. He didn't sound interested."

Display enthusiasm. If you really want this job, act like it. It does not hurt your salary negotiation prospects.

A very large amount of human suffering and frustration is caused by the fact that many men and women are not content to be the sort of beings that God had made them, but try to persuade themselves that they are really beings of some different kind.
Eric Mascall,
The Importance of Being Human

You must know:
- to whom you are pitching; you have to know something about them.
- what they ideally would want in a candidate.
- what they are interested in.
- who your likely competitors are.
- what you bring to the party that they do not.

For Target 1:

Geographic area: _____

Industry or company size: _____

Position/Function: _____

1. What is the most important thing I want this target to know about me? (This is where you position yourself. If they know nothing else about you, this is what you want them to know.)

_____

2. What is the second most important thing I want this target to know about me? (This could support and/or broaden your introductory statement.) _____

_____

_____

3. Key selling points: statements/accomplishments that support/**prove** the first two statements:

1. _____
2. _____
3. _____
4. _____
5. _____

Statement of why they should be interested in me/what separates me from my competition:

_____

_____

_____

_____

Other key selling points that may apply even indirectly to this industry or position:

_____

_____

_____

Any objection I'm afraid the interviewer may bring up, and how I will handle it:

_____

Summary of What I Have/
Want to Offer—Target 2
To Help Me Develop My Pitch to That Target

You must know:
- to whom you are pitching; you have to know something about them.
- what they ideally would want in a candidate.
- what they are interested in.
- who your likely competitors are.
- what you bring to the party that they do not.

For Target 2:

Geographic area: _____

Industry or company size: _____

Position/Function: _____

1. What is the most important thing I want this target to know about me? (This is where you position yourself. If they know nothing else about you, this is what you want them to know.)

_____

2. What is the second most important thing I want this target to know about me? (This could support and/or broaden your introductory statement.) _____

_____

_____

3. Key selling points: statements/accomplishments that support/**prove** the first two statements:

1. _____
2. _____
3. _____
4. _____
5. _____

Statement of why they should be interested in me/what separates me from my competition:

_____

_____

_____

_____

Other key selling points that may apply even indirectly to this industry or position:

_____

_____

_____

Any objection I'm afraid the interviewer may bring up, and how I will handle it:

_____

The
Five
O'Clock
Club®

Summary of What I Have/
Want to Offer—Target 3
To Help Me Develop My Pitch to That Target

You must know:
- to whom you are pitching; you have to know something about them.
- what they ideally would want in a candidate.
- what they are interested in.
- who your likely competitors are.
- what you bring to the party that they do not.

For Target 3:

Geographic area: _____

Industry or company size: _____

Position/Function: _____

1. What is the most important thing I want this target to know about me? (This is where you position yourself. If they know nothing else about you, this is what you want them to know.)

_____

2. What is the second most important thing I want this target to know about me? (This could support and/or broaden your introductory statement.) _____

_____

_____

3. Key selling points: statements/accomplishments that support/**prove** the first two statements:

1. _____

2. _____

3. _____

4. _____

5. _____

Statement of why they should be interested in me/what separates me from my competition:

_____

_____

_____

_____

Other key selling points that may apply even indirectly to this industry or position:

_____

_____

_____

Any objection I'm afraid the interviewer may bring up, and how I will handle it:

_____

Hints for Seemingly Low-Key People

In this country, we often think that people who are openly assertive, forceful, and dynamic are more able to get work done through others than those who are thoughtful, persistent—and perhaps relentless. These seemingly low-key, quiet types may have their abilities undervalued and their working style misunderstood. The hiring team may incorrectly see them as unable to make a strong impression on a customer, sell their ideas internally, or push projects through. They may even seem less intelligent than they actually are. Sometimes these people do not get the jobs they deserve because the interviewer is not able to see the full force of their personality at the interview itself.

If you are a low-key person, you may come across as more meek in the interview than you have been in your jobs. So be sure to sit forward in your seat, use more hand gestures than may be usual for you, and constantly put active, dynamic words into your conversation. Help the hiring team to understand your true style on the job. For example:

"I aggressively promoted products."

"I inspire and motivate people to go beyond whatever goals are set."

"Despite my low-key demeanor, I'm seen as a person who is relentless in meeting goals through others."

"I'm able to sell to anyone by using a low-key approach that disarms people."

"Once I am on the job, people see me as someone to be reckoned with, and I am able to convince them to do what needs to be done."

Make sure the hiring team sees you the way you really are on the job, and also sees the benefit of having someone with your style.

Darest thou, now O soul,
Walk out with me toward
the unknown region
Where neither ground is
for the feet nor any path to follow?
Walt Whitman

It's Not Necessarily Easier to Get a Lower-Level Job

When job hunters have problems finding a job at their current level, they often want to lower their sights. They think, I'll take a job two levels lower than the one I just had. But there is competition at that level, too.

Recently, a man was forced into early retirement after having been president of a major chain of retail stores. He didn't need much money, and he simply wanted to work at an easy job. He admired The Five O'Clock Club and asked if he could do junior-level office work for a modest salary. He said he was willing to run errands, stuff envelopes, and do other mundane assignments. He assumed that we would be eager to hire him for that job, because he was such a bargain.

But many people wanted that office-administration position, and most were more qualified for the job than he was. The other candidates knew how to use computers, would be better at taking phone messages and following up than he would have been, and had actually had experience doing those tasks.

If you honestly want a lower-level job, present a logical rationale to the hiring team, and think about your competition exactly the same way you would if you were going after a job at your most recent level.

One of the best ways to properly evaluate and adapt to the many environmental stresses of life is to view them as normal. The adversity and failures in our lives, if adapted to and viewed as normal corrective feedback to use to get back on target, serve to develop in us an immunity against anxiety, depression, and the adverse responses to stress.
Instead of tackling the most important priorities that would make us successful and effective in life, we prefer the path of least resistance and do things simply that will relieve our tension, such as shuffling papers and majoring in minors.
Denis Waitley

The
Five
O'Clock
Club®

How to Handle Your References

by Wendy Alfus Rothman

In an exploratory meeting, the ball ends up in the savvy manager's court, which is exactly the intent. An observant manager also gains valuable information about the political lay of the land from such a meeting.

The manager should come out with a good sense of how hard a sell the idea is going to be. A great number of objections indicate a tough road but still can be used to develop strategy. Every objection or reservation shows a concern that needs to be taken into account or an agenda item of the manager who is objecting.
Joel M. DeLuca, Ph.D., *Political Savvy*

References are often the last thing you think about during your job search—literally. You expect to be asked for references at the very end of the process, almost as an afterthought. It just doesn't seem that important early on. And after all, you're busy enough thinking about the hiring manager's issues, the company's problems, your own strategy, and the pluses and minuses of your competition. Those are the things that really matter. References are just meant to cement the deal, once the decision to extend an offer has been made. Right?

Wrong. References are not a casual component stuck on at the end of a carefully thought-out job search. Rather, they are another strategic tool that can significantly impact the results of your search, and all of your career management. And while you certainly don't want to give out your references too soon in the interviewing cycle, you absolutely do want to be planning them and preparing them from the very beginning in Phase 1 of your search.

There is a method of handling references—things to pay attention to and situations to watch out for. Let's go through ten basic rules of references.

Rule #1.
Don't give out your references too soon.
Wait until the hiring company is absolutely ready to extend an offer to you before you allow them to make those contacts.

The people you use as references are very busy. They are doing you a favor every time they answer one of these requests. If the request does not end up leading to a serious job offer, you have unwittingly played a game of the Boy Who Cried Wolf. When the company that is serious about making an offer calls, your references may very well not be willing to extend themselves yet another time. And when they get a lot of calls, they may begin to wonder, "What's wrong with Shirley? Why doesn't she have a job by now?"

Rule #2.
Make sure you understand the issues that need to be addressed.
Often the hiring manager asks for references to check out a nagging doubt he or she may have about you. Perhaps there is an unvoiced concern or undisclosed objection. If a question does exist, it will be within a framework of three categories. The first is whether or not you have the qualifications—the skills and abilities—to get the job done. The second is whether or not you are motivated to get the job done. Do you really want the job? And the third is whether or not you fit into the culture and personality of the hiring company.

It is your responsibility to decide which of these three categories is the one in question when you are asked for a reference. Then choose a person who can address the appropriate issues. After all, your references can support your case, but they cannot create it for you.

So be sure to have your references prepared for each of the three categories. This framework can help you provide better references, and it provides something more: Thinking about your skills, motivation and fit can lead to significant insights about whether the company you are considering is really a place where you will be happy and productive.

Rule #3.

Help your references to help you by providing them with a script.

There are many reasons you want to prepare a script for your references, and even help them rehearse their lines.

One is that it takes time and skill to prepare an eloquent reference, and many people simply do not have the time or the talent. Offer to assist your references with a script of the points you would like them to cover. Provide specific supporting examples. They will appreciate your taking the time to help them help you.

A second reason to provide a script is that your references may not know what they should say to help your case unless you tell them. Even well-meaning people can actually give counterproductive kudos, if they do not know what concerns the hiring manager has about you, or what issues surround your potential new job. It won't help you land a management position if your reference gives accolades about your ability to take supervision.

Still another reason for scripts is the problem of the reference who fired you, or with whom you have had a difference of opinion. Often, these people would provide you with some sort of reference, but they really don't know what to say that would be sincere yet not too negative. A script provides a more positive response for those who would have been inclined to give you a negative reference. Otherwise, these people can wreak havoc on a potential offer.

If you provide a script, it should include several components.

It should have **a statement of your major strengths**, as well as **examples of those strengths**, tailored to the requirements for the position you want to be offered. Tell your reference the job you are going after and what the new company is looking for. Remind the person of the work you did for him or her that would be of interest to the new company. Let the person know the issues the new company may want to cover.

Your script should also have a prepared response to the question, **"Tell me about some areas for improvement—some weaknesses."** Always try to use a strength to illustrate your area of weakness. For example, you might say something like, "Sometimes I expect too much from the people who report to me—I expect them to be as dedicated as I am." Now, that's not too terrible a weakness! Be sure your reference is prepared for this question, but remind him or her to offer the response only if the question is asked.

You also want to **have a response ready regarding your reason for leaving your prior company**. Again, this needs to be framed positively, and should always be based on the truth. You can often work out an explanation that fits into your long-term plan. ("The company's goals and my career goals are moving in two different directions.") Clearly, you need to think this through and prepare it in advance with your reference.

Rule #4.
Select your references strategically.

From the beginning of your search, think about who might be potential references for each of your targets. Understand what issues are important to your target, and understand what your strengths and weaknesses are in each unique situation. Select references who can support your case to overcome potential obstacles. You may well find that you have different references for each of your targets.

Stage your references so that the hiring company talks to your best ones first. If Bill Good is a better reference than Sally Rough, tell your prospective employer that Sally is tied up in meetings for two weeks, and that Bill is available immediately.

If you do this, be sure to call Sally and tell her that you would like her to be a backup reference. Explain that because you do not expect her to have to provide a primary reference, you indicated that her schedule was very tight for the next few weeks. That way, Sally doesn't feel put

46

---

on the spot, and there are no surprises if the new company does make a call.

Rule #5.
Ask your references to follow up with you.

You need to know whether someone was called. Ask your references to let you know when they are contacted. If you have given out three names and none of them has been called within two to three weeks, you are probably not as close to an offer as you think. Call the hiring company and try to uncover any possible hidden objections.

Rule #6.
Be sure you follow up with your references.

Let your references know whether you take the new job, and what you will be doing. Let them know how they helped you, even if you decided not to take the position. This is a great opportunity to keep your network alive and well.

Rule #7.
Reciprocate in any way that you can.

People do not like to feel as though they have been taken advantage of. It is always appropriate to ask whether there is any way that you can be of assistance to the person who has helped you, or even has just agreed to help you. This kind of give-and-take is what networking is all about. Staying in touch with your references is exactly the way you develop long-term relationships.

Rule #8.
Develop references as you develop your network—over the long term.

When you call people to ask whether they will give you references, several things happen.
- You let them know that you are looking for a new position without putting them on the spot by asking for a job.
- You can ask for their opinion about the company in which you are interested, and in so doing learn more. Your references may also have ideas about other companies that would be worth pursuing.

- You let them know that other people are interested in you. It's more likely that people will help you if they know that other professionals are interested in you as well.
- You remind them of your sterling qualities without sounding too much like a braggadocio.
- You flatter them by asking for their help—something people usually love to give.
- You also stay current regarding the whereabouts of your references. This is very important because you eliminate the problem of not being able to locate a particular person who could provide the perfect reference when you need it.

Rule #9.
Settle on a mutually agreeable story if you are being fired or if you have had problems with your direct manager. If this is impossible, think of a substitute reference.

A hiring manager will absolutely want to talk to your immediate boss, or want to know why he or she can't. Scripting will certainly help in this situation (See Rule #3).

I do not recommend fabricating stories. Often what you need to do is determine what the positives really are about why you left your position. If you didn't get along with your boss, you probably had a difference in management style. Perhaps your style is more like the style of the company you are now interested in. Present this as a positive to both the hiring person and the prior boss. Point out that you have learned from your past where you fit and where you don't, and that is why you are so excited about this new opportunity. You see it as a much more appropriate match.

Sometimes it is very difficult to avoid saying something bad about a prior company or manager, yet bad-mouthing companies is viewed as quite unprofessional. If you are asked to give as a reference the name of a former boss with whom you really clashed, don't say how terrible he or she was. Try saying something like this:

"I'll be happy to give you Susan's phone

The heights by great men reached and kept
Were not attained by sudden flight,
But they, while their companions slept,
Were toiling upward in the night.

Henry Wadsworth Longfellow

number—I agree you should call her, since I did work for her for two years. I'm sure she will be able to share pertinent information about my management style. Let me remind you that one of the main reasons I am excited about the opportunity with your company is the motivating and enthusiastic attitude of the senior management team which, as we discussed, was not the case in my last job. I think Susan embodies their more stand-offish style, so please keep that in mind when you speak with her."

If there is no way you can risk giving your boss's name as a reference, be prepared with names of peers, subordinates, or your boss's boss as stand-in references.

Rule #10.
DO NOT LIE.

Do not make up names of people who you once worked for who have now "moved far, far away." Do not create fictitious companies that have now "gone out of business." Do not make up degrees and universities attended. Somehow, some way, it will come back to haunt you. And it is so unnecessary!

There are many stories of people who have a brilliant track record with ten or fifteen years' experience. Then they go after a new job, and lie about having a B.A. They get caught and then are rejected for a terrific job.

Usually the truth is that the degree (or whatever the issue is) was not that critical a component of the job requirements. And even if it were, you need to understand how this requirement relates to job performance. Explore the reasons behind the criteria a company establishes as prerequisites for employment and deal with your shortfalls directly.

If you keep these ten rules in mind, your references will support your job search—not sabotage it. In addition, you will have renewed valuable professional alliances that will continue to serve you throughout your career.

Reference Case Studies

CASE STUDY: CHARLEY
Don't Give Out Your References Too Soon

Charley was having a very difficult search. He had several problems: He was working, so his time was limited. He couldn't clarify his targets, so his efforts were haphazard and unfocused. He couldn't put a pitch together, and yet he insisted on doing his search his own way. It simply wasn't working. He couldn't get any momentum going, and he was getting more and more frustrated.

Naturally, he was elated when he finally managed to get an actual job interview with a small company in market research, for a sales position. He thought he liked the industry, although he had no idea why the industry might need his skills. He knew even less about the company with which he was to interview, except that they apparently had a job opening.

Nevertheless, he hoped the hiring manager would like him, that he would get an offer, and that he could short-cut the entire search process.

He and the hiring manager, Sheila, met offsite, so Charley did not have the benefit of gaining insights by seeing the company. He had no idea what the flow of traffic was in and out of the location, what the other employees looked like, whether the environment was busy or slow, clean or dirty, corporate or relaxed. He and Sheila talked for close to two hours, but their conversation was primarily about Charley, his lifestyle, his values and his career objectives.

Now, to the trained participant at The Five O'Clock Club, Charley was obviously making a lot of mistakes. He hadn't picked a target, he had not developed a search campaign strategy, he had done no research into this industry or this company, he knew absolutely nothing about their issues or concerns. He surely did not know who his competition was or why the job was open in the first place, how many other people had been interviewed, and who the real decision-

*Know how to ask. There is nothing more difficult
for some people. Nor for others, easier.*
Baltasar Gracian, *The Art of Worldly Wisdom*

makers were. Still, after the two hours, Sheila asked Charley for his references.

Why would she do that? Charley didn't know if Sheila questioned his skills, motivation or fit. Perhaps the job was impossible to fill, and she simply needed a body. Charley would fit the bill, as long as his references were reasonable. On the other hand, perhaps she really did think he was talented. Charley had no idea. Nor did he have any idea whether he would like the job—he hadn't even seen the office building yet, let alone talked to the people inside with whom he would be spending every day! But Charley wanted the process to be over with, and so he hoped for the best and gave Sheila his references.

Charley called me the next day to express a tiny bit of concern: One of the references he had given might not support the job title Charley claimed to have had, and he wanted to know whether he should call that person, and what he might say. He realized that he would have to explain to his reference what this new opportunity was all about, and how excited he was about it. When I asked him to tell me what he would say in this regard, Charley realized that he couldn't say anything—he had no idea what this opportunity was about at all! How could he ask his reference to support his strengths, when he didn't know what would be expected from him on the job?

Charley started to panic—what could he do? He had already given out the name of his reference. He was sure he would be caught in a foolish lie. He was afraid he might lose an offer from a company he wasn't even sure he wanted to work for in the first place.

As we strategized, Charley calmed down. This wasn't the only company in the world. The job title he had used was not so different from the one he actually had. Nothing catastrophic was going to happen. But he did need to refocus his attention on what the real issues were. And there was obviously a lot more information that he needed that had nothing whatsoever to do with his references.

Rather than call those references to discuss a job he knew nothing about and appear totally foolish, Charley decided to call Sheila instead. He explained that he had been so interested in their conversation, it was only after reflection that he realized there was much they both still needed to know about each other.

"I don't think either one of us is ready yet to seriously discuss an offer, and so I think it is premature to contact my references. After all, they are busy people and so are you. Why don't we get together again in your office and talk more specifically about some of the challenges you are facing and how I might be able to fit in to the company. Then, I can be sure that my references are appropriate and that the move is the right one for both of us."

Well, Sheila saw Charley again, but it turned out that she was not at all interested in him and hadn't been from the beginning of their first meeting. She felt that a good salesperson should control the conversation much more than Charley had. She felt that he should have done much more of the questioning, and tried to understand her needs and the goals of the organization. She had been very disappointed in his lack of assertive questioning, and assumed it was due to a lack of experience. Sheila had asked for his references, thinking that his prior bosses would be at the right level for the job she had in mind. She was hoping to recruit them directly, while pretending to call for a reference!

By identifying the objections Sheila had, Charley was able to clarify the strengths he needed to discuss if he were to pursue the bigger target of all market research firms in his geographic area. He began to understand how to position himself in order to be a more attractive sales candidate.

He called his references, but it was not to discuss his old job titles. It was to talk about what traits and skills they felt were important in the industry, and to solicit their views on several different companies. In other words, he used this as an opportunity to do real Phase 1 exploration

Courage is doing what you are afraid to do.
There can be no courage unless you're scared.
Eddie Rickenbacker

and research. They were happy to share their knowledge with him; Charley sent them sales leads and kept them informed of his progress.

When the time came for a good offer, Charley knew just which references to use. In fact, the job offer came from a lead generated by one of those references!

Charley ended up taking a position with a larger market research firm after a five-month, focused job search. One and a half years after he started, his company bought the firm Sheila had worked for, and they ended up at the same company after all. Except that by the time it happened, Charley had been promoted to sales manager, and Sheila was working for him!

The references that he had contacted for advice and assistance remained close professional allies, and Charley stays in touch with them to this day, sharing information and industry insights.

CASE STUDY: MITCHELL
Preparing Your References

Mitchell had been an independent financial planning consultant to small businesses for several years, and was now looking to get back into a corporate environment.

He had targeted several boutique investment firms. His qualifications were outstanding and his case was strong. He had several interviews and always got to the last round . . . and then came in second.

Mitch was puzzled. He knew he came on strong initially, but after that, something was happening that was making him lose the final offers. He needed to find out what it was and correct it. Together we examined what was happening during his last meetings—what he said and what the companies were saying. It turned out that in five out of six instances, he had been asked for references. Right after that, someone else was being offered the job. We decided to examine those references.

They were not the same as those of most people. Since Mitch had been in his own consult-ing practice for several years, he did not have the typical managers and bosses available for reference. Instead, he was using the presidents and other officers of the companies that were his current and past clients. That seemed okay.

He had called and asked them if they would be willing to serve as references and explained the requirements of each position he was interested in. Each of them assured Mitch that they would provide accolades regarding his professionalism, his financial knowledge, and his skill. "My references are great," he told me. "It couldn't be that."

Nevertheless, something was happening, so I asked Mitch to double check. He reviewed his interview notes from the last company he had been interviewing with. One of the concerns he had written down was that the hiring manager was apparently nervous about bringing someone on board who had been independent for so long. He was afraid that the person might be "unmanageable, too independent, and not a team player."

Mitch thought that he had addressed this issue by verbally reassuring the manager that he was a strong participant in group efforts, but when Mitch followed up he learned that the company had gone with another candidate who was actually *less* qualified than Mitchell. Interestingly enough, the person who did land the job had worked as a project leader in a self-managing team.

Mitch knew he was onto something. He guessed that this team-orientation objection was not an isolated occurrence, and that probably it was a significant factor in all of his rejections. Perhaps people were afraid that he really had been independent for too long, and would be difficult to manage.

What could Mitchell say on his own behalf when it wasn't his ability that was in question—it was his willingness to be a team player? He didn't *have* team members to call on since he worked on his own. Or did he?

Mitchell thought about what he did when he was working for his clients. He had to work with

*Language reflects social reality, and the reality of the pre-nineteenth-century
world was that people did not "have" jobs in the fixed and unitary sense;
they "did" jobs in the form of a constantly changing string of tasks.*
William Bridges, *JobShift: How to Prosper in a Workplace Without Jobs*

managers, owners, employees, their banks and loan officers, their insurance agents and accountants. All of these people had different agendas, and different strengths and weaknesses—just like members of work teams. Mitch's position as a consultant was very much like that of the team leader: He didn't make the actual decisions, but rather mobilized divergent groups into action, around a common goal.

Put that way, he had a lot more than verbal reassurance of his teamwork. He had hard evidence of his willingness to be part of a group rather than stand alone.

He called his clients and explained what he needed them to discuss about his work habits when called to provide a reference—not to discuss his financial-planning ability (which had never been in question), but to talk about his ability to cooperate as a team member, to take direction and supervision, and to be a collaborative group player. He selected one of each of the professionals he had worked with, and reminded them of specific instances that they could refer back to.

The end of this story should be that Mitch used these references, and turned his next three interviews into job offers. In fact, that is exactly what happened. The twist on this case study however, is that after contacting all those people for references, they were reminded of what a terrific guy Mitchell really was, and they all actually gave him *more* leads that turned into more consulting opportunities. Mitchell ended up staying in his own consulting firm, expanding his practice, and hiring an associate—starting his *own* team!

Not only can references help you overcome objections and position you for an offer, sometimes they can generate new offers themselves.

Remember that a job offer is made through *effective follow-up*. By contacting your references, you are both networking <u>and</u> following up at the same time. Look at what happened to Phillip.

CASE STUDY: PHILLIP
*Following Up with References
Can Lead to New Job Offers*

Phil had worked as a product manager for a pharmaceutical company in New Jersey for six months before his mother became ill. He had to return home to take care of her, and home was in Denver, Colorado. At first, his boss, Ray, granted him a leave of absence. It soon became clear that Phil's stay in Denver would be prolonged, and Raymond had no choice but to hire someone new. It was unfortunate and neither party wanted the relationship to end, but it just couldn't be helped. Ray found another project manager, and Phil found project work in Denver. The two lost touch as they went on with their lives and careers.

Thirteen months later, Phil's mother was fully recovered and he decided to return to New Jersey. He began a job search and interviewed at several pharmaceutical firms. One company was ready to extend an offer to him, and Claire (the hiring manager) asked for his references. Phil thought of Ray, since they had enjoyed an excellent professional relationship and it was also his last business contact in New Jersey.

Claire called Ray. He was delighted to hear that Phil had returned to the area. The reference he provided was outstanding, and started Ray thinking . . .

Claire called Phil the following day to arrange a time for him to come in and receive a formal offer. Phil was thrilled, but had actually changed his mind about the job! It turned out that Ray, after receiving Claire's phone call, decided to call Phil himself. Ray had been searching for a project director, and Phil was a natural choice. It seemed so obvious that Ray should think of Phil himself, but if he hadn't been called to provide a reference, the two might never have hooked up once again.

Both Mitch and Phil had good references. Not everyone is so fortunate. What happens if your references are somewhat less than laudatory?

CASE STUDY: SUSAN
Handling Negative References

Susan was going to get an offer to be a production coordinator for a company in teleconferencing technologies. She had been searching for this position for four months, after being fired from her prior company—a long-distance carrier where she had been a director of creative services.

Her prior boss had let Susan go primarily because of a "fit" issue. Susan was a creative person and preferred to work fairly autonomously. Her boss was a very structured person who checked everyone's work on an hourly basis, and ruled with an iron fist.

One day Susan and this boss had an argument; the manager berated Susan in front of her peers, and Susan retaliated by complaining to the senior vice president, who was annoyed by this petty problem, and felt it to be an inappropriate communication. He told Susan's boss that he did not want to bothered with these kinds of issues, and to "handle any insubordination appropriately." Susan was fired. These are not the circumstances under which you want to give a reference!

Susan realized this was an opportunity to find a place where she really did fit, and so she built this experience into her job search. During her interviews, when people asked her why she was looking, she told them that she wanted to work in a different environment. More specifically, she wanted to a part of a company that wanted independent but responsible people—people who were trusted to complete projects on time without requiring a great deal of supervision. She let her prospects know that her prior company was very hierarchical, and that she frankly did not fit in; that she had in fact left because of a culture fit.

When asked for references, Susan reiterated the circumstances that had prompted her to look for a new position in the first place. "My manager will feel that I was too independent and that I didn't work well in a corporate hierarchy. As we've already discussed, I would agree with that assessment! I believe that is also the reason we get along so well. I'm sure you will find that my prior manager has no complaint whatsoever with my performance and ability."

Susan also called the person who had fired her. She informed him that he would be getting a reference phone call, and told him what she had already told her prospective employers. "When they call, I don't want you to be in an uncomfortable position, nor do I want to lose the job opportunity. Perhaps you could tell them that you are about to go into a meeting, but can talk for a few moments. I thought you could say that we did in fact have a cultural fit problem, primarily because your company is quite structured and I am not. However my work performance was always satisfactory, and given the right personality variable you would recommend me for a position. Then if they want to continue the conversation, you can always say you have to go into your meeting."

Susan was uncomfortable making that call, but her former employer was happy to receive it. He had no interest in Susan's remaining unemployed, but he never would have known what to say on such a call.

Susan received the offer, ultimately she made amends with her former employer, and she found a position with a company where she truly did fit!

Wendy Alfus Rothman is managing director at Advantage Human Resourcing, Inc., a member of The Employment Roundtable, and one of the original counselors at The Five O'Clock Club.

The first principle of ethical power is Purpose. . . .
By purpose, I mean your objective or intention—
something toward which you are always striving.
Purpose is something bigger. It is the picture
you have of yourself—the kind of person you want to
be or the kind of life you want to lead.
Kenneth Blanchard and Norman Vincent Peale,
The Power of Ethical Management

How to Handle Rejection Letters

*In nature, there are neither rewards nor punishments—
there are consequences.*—Robert Green Ingersoll

Companies generally send the same rejection letter to everyone—complimenting the applicant on his or her credentials and offering regret that there are no appropriate openings at that time. A rejection letter is truly a rejection only when it follows an interview.

Rejection Letters in Response to a Direct-Mail Campaign

If you received a respectable number of responses (meetings) from your campaign, try another campaign of the remaining companies in a few months. Direct marketers say you should then expect approximately half the response you got with your first mailing. As an alternative, network into the companies that interest you, contact someone else in the same firm, or use a targeted mailing approach.

If the response rate from your mailing was poor, you picked the wrong market for what you have to offer, or the package you sent was lacking. Chances are, you were not as knowledgeable about this market as you thought. Research or network to learn more, or network to find out what was wrong with your package.

Rejection Letter in Response to an Ad

This is par for the course. The company probably received a thousand résumés. Or perhaps the ad was not for a legitimate opening.

If a company name was listed, network in, do a targeted mailing to someone who could be close to the hiring manager, or contact a search firm that handles the type of position mentioned. (See the chapter in our book *Getting Interviews:* "What to Do When You Know There's a Job Opening.") Your résumé was probably rejected by someone other than the hiring manager, so it's worth further effort if you're interested in the position. Some companies have a policy of immediately sending out rejection letters to everyone. Then they call those people they're interested in—even though the applicants have already been "rejected." For companies that always send rejection letters, this approach saves time.

Rejection Letter in Response to a Networking Contact You Tried to Make

The person did not understand that what you wanted was information. If many people respond to you this way, reassess your approach to networking.

Rejection Letter Following a Job Interview

This is a true rejection letter. It used to be that it took seven job interviews to get one offer. That figure may now be higher. If you are still interested in the company, don't give up. (Read what Michael did in the chapter "Following Up When There Is No Immediate Job.")

Lessons to Learn

When you get a rejection note in response to an interview, think about it. How interested are you in that firm? Did you hit it off with the interviewer? If you think there was some mutual interest, see if there might be other jobs with the company later—perhaps in another department. Or perhaps the person hired instead of you might not work out. Keep in touch. People rarely do, but we all like to hire people who truly want to work for us.

Case Study: Stan
Turning a Rejection Into an Offer

Stan was told an offer was being made to another candidate. He was crushed, but he immediately dashed off a letter to the hiring manager and hand-delivered it. A brief letter, it said, in part:

> I was disappointed to hear that you have offered the position to someone else. I truly believe I am right for the position, and wish you would keep me in mind anyway. You never know—something could happen to the new person, and you may need a replacement. Please consider me no matter when this may occur, because I believe I belong at your institution.

The next day, Stan received a call with an offer. Some people may think the offer to the other candidate fell through. However, I believe Stan's letter influenced the hiring manager. When he saw the letter, he thought to himself, We're offering the position to the wrong person! and he allowed the negotiation with the other candidate to lapse.

PART THREE

THE FIVE O'CLOCK CLUB APPROACH TO INTERVIEWING

THINKING LIKE A CONSULTANT

*Just know your lines and
don't bump into the furniture.*
Spencer Tracy's advice on acting

Make yourself necessary to someone.
Ralph Waldo Emerson

---

*I have always tried to be true to myself,
to pick those battles I felt were important.*
Arthur Ashe

An interview is not simply a conversation; it's show time, folks. You will be competing against people who are well-rehearsed and know their lines.

Develop Your Lines

In an interview, an inability to express yourself clearly is worse than a lack of experience. Refine your sales pitch by listing on a 3 x 5 card:

- the main reason the employer would want to hire you;
- what you have to offer in the way of experience, credentials, and personality;
- two key accomplishments to support your interest in this position;
- an answer to what you think might be the employer's main objection to you, if any;
- a statement of why you would want to work for this company.

Keep this card in your pocket or purse and review it just before going in for the interview so that you will know your lines.

Look and Act the Part

Remember, this is show biz. Even if you don't feel self-confident, act as if you do. If you come in looking defeated, like a loser, why would anyone want to hire you? *Act* as if you are successful and feel good about yourself, and you will increase your chances of actually *feeling* that way. Enthusiasm counts. Every manager is receptive to someone who is sincerely interested in the company and the position.

During the Interview
—Play the Part of a Consultant

Pretend for a minute that you own a small consulting company. When you first meet a prospective client, you want to probe to better understand the problems this person is facing. If the client has no problems, or if you cannot solve them, there is no place for you.

You are also there to sell your company. Therefore, as the manager talks about company problems, you reveal your own company's experience and credentials by asking questions or by telling

The people you want to reach, whether they're your coworkers, your boss or an organizational president, should be viewed as distinct target audiences that require different approaches and strategies.

Jeffrey P. Davidson, *Management World*, September/October, 1987

how you have handled similar situations. You want to see how your company fits in with this company.

If the conversation goes astray, lead it back to the topics on your 3 x 5 card—the work you would do for them and your abilities. That way, you can make your points in context.

It is your responsibility to reassure the hiring manager that everything will work out. The manager does not want to be embarrassed later by discovering he's made a hiring mistake. It is almost as if you are patting the manager on the arm and saying, "There, there. Everything will be just fine. You can count on me."

> *If the interviewer has no problems, or if you cannot solve them, there is no place for you.*

You must display self-confidence in your ability to handle the position. If you are not confident, why should the hiring manager take a chance on you? If you want the job, take a stand and say that you believe it will work.

If you are asked how you would handle a situation, reassure the manager that even though you do not know specifically what you would do (because, after all, you are not on the job yet), you know you can figure it out because:

• It won't be a problem. I'm good at these things.

• I'm very resourceful. Here's what I did as company controller...

• I've been in that situation before. I can handle your situation even though I don't know the specifics.

Let the manager air his or her doubts about you. If you are told what these reservations are, you can reassure the manager right then, or you can mull it over later and reassure the manager in writing.

Do not appear to be "shopping around." Be sincerely interested in this particular company—at least during the interview.

Follow up on your meetings. Address the important issues, stress your interest and enthusiasm for the job, and state your major selling points—especially since you now know what is of interest to the interviewer.

Questions You Might Ask in an Interview

You are there not only to answer the interviewer's questions, but also to make sure you get the information you need. Ask questions that are appropriate. What do you really want to know? Here are a few to get you thinking in the right direction:

QUESTIONS TO ASK PERSONNEL

• Can you tell me more about the responsibilities of the job?
• What skills do you think would be most critical for this job?
• Is there a current organization chart available for this area?
• What happened to the person who held this job before?
• What kinds of people are most successful in this area?
• What do you see as the department's strengths and weaknesses?

QUESTIONS TO ASK MANAGERS (AND PERHAPS PEERS)

• What are the key responsibilities of the job?
• What is the most important part of the job?
• What is the first problem that would need the attention of the person you hire?
• What other problems need attention now? Over the next six months?
• How has this job been performed in the past?
• Are there other things you would like someone to do that are not a formal part of the job?
• What would you like to be able to say about the new hire one year from now?
• What significant changes do you see in the future?
• May I ask what your background is?
• What do you find most satisfying about working here? Most frustrating?
• How would you describe your management style?
• How is the department organized?
• May I meet the other people who work in the area?
• How is one's performance evaluated? By whom? How often?
• What skills are in short supply here?

The world is moving so fast these days that the man who says it can't be done is generally interrupted by someone doing it.
Harry Emerson Fosdick

> **Follow-up will dramatically increase the number of job offers you get. It is one of the most powerful tools you have to influence the situation.**

> **Be sure to record every networking and job interview on the Interview Record.**

Get a Job Offer

To take what there is and use it, without waiting forever in vain for the preconceived—to dig deep into the actual and get something out of that —this doubtless is the right way to live.
Henry James

Sincerely intend to turn each interview into a solid job offer. Do your best to make the position and the pay into something acceptable. Make the most of each interview. Negotiate changes in the job itself. Suggest additional things you can do for the company—jobs often can be upgraded a level or two. Or perhaps the manager could refer you to another area of the company. You should make every effort to turn an interview into a reasonable job offer.

- This is an opportunity to practice your negotiation skills and increase the number of interviews you turn into offers. You can always turn the job down later.
- Getting job offers helps your self-esteem. You can say you received a number of offers, but they didn't seem right for you. This puts you in a stronger negotiating position.
- Even if you turn down an offer, stay friendly with the hiring manager. This may lead to another offer later that is more appropriate.
- When you get an offer you are not sure about, say that you have a few other things you must attend to, but will get back to them in a week. Then contact other companies that were of real interest to you. Tell them you have received an offer but were hoping to work something out with them. They may tell you to take the other offer—or they may consider you more seriously because the other offer makes you more valuable. Sometimes knowing you got another offer is the only thing that will make a company act.

Do Your Homework

Before the interview, research the company and the industry. If you're asked why you are interested in them, you will have your answer. Do library research. Call the company's public relations department and ask for literature or an annual report. Ask others about the company. Show up early and read company literature in the reception area, talk to the receptionist, and observe the people. Get a feel for the place.

The Rehearsal

It may sound like a contradiction, but you achieve spontaneity on the set through preparation of the dialogue at home. As you prepare, find ways of making your responses seem newly minted, not preprogrammed.
Michael Caine, *Acting in Film*

Even experienced job hunters need practice. Each interview smooths out your presentation and responses. As you get better, your self-confidence grows.

By now, you've had networking or information-gathering interviews. You will have practiced talking about yourself and will have information about your area of interest and the possibilities for someone like you.

When I was unemployed, I had lots of interviews, but I was not doing well in them. I was under so much stress that I kept talking about what *I* wanted to do rather than what I could do *for the company*. I knew better, but I could not think straight. An old friend, who belongs to The Five O'Clock Club, helped me develop my "lines" for my 3 x 5 card. Then we practiced. After that, my interviews went well.

- You may be surprised: Perhaps what you originally found objectionable can be changed to your liking. If you end the process too early, you lose the possibility of changing the situation to suit you. Having a job created especially for you is the best outcome.

Coming in As a Freelancer or Consultant

Some job hunters are willing to work for a company as a freelancer or consultant and hope the company will later put them on the payroll. This rarely happens. If you are doing a great job for little money, the company has no incentive to change that arrangement. If you want to be "on salary," consult only if you are sure you have the self-discipline to continue job hunting after you start consulting.

You can parlay a consulting assignment into a full-time job at a decent salary if you do outstanding work on the assignment, and get a decent offer somewhere else. Then tell your manager that you enjoy what you are doing and would like to be a salaried employee—but have received another job offer. You would prefer working for his company, but this temporary arrangement is not what you want.

Aiming for the Second Job Out

Sometimes the job you really want is too big a step for you right now. Instead of trying to get it in one move, go for it in two moves. Make your next job one that will qualify you for the job you really want.

What Do You Really Want?

*I am proud of the fact that I
never invented weapons to kill.*
Thomas A. Edison

If I had known, I should have become a watchmaker.
Albert Einstein,
on his role in making the atomic bomb possible.

To get ahead, many people compromise what they want. A lot of compromising can result in material success but also feelings of self-betrayal and not knowing who you really are.

It can be difficult to hold on to your values and live the kind of life that is right for you. You may feel there is no hope for change. If you are really

honest, you may discover that you have tried very little to make changes. Ask yourself what you have done to improve your situation.

Deciding where you want to work is a complex problem. Many unhappy professionals, managers, and executives admit they made a mistake in deciding to work for their present companies. They think they should have done more research and more thinking before they took the job.

The stress of job hunting can impair your judgment. You may make a decision without enough information simply because you want to "get a job." Ego can also be involved: you want to get an offer quickly so you can tell others and yourself that you are worth something. Or you may deceive yourself into thinking you have enough information. Even if you are normally a good decision-maker, you can short-circuit the decision-making process when it comes to your own career.

You will make better decisions when you are not deciding under pressure. Start now to see what your options are. Then you already will have thought them through in case you have to make a move quickly later.

Objectively evaluate the information you come up with, and develop contingency plans. Decide whether to leave your present position, and evaluate new opportunities. List the pros and cons of each possibility for you and those close to you.

You may decide, for example, that a certain position is higher level, higher paying, and more prestigious, but you will have less time for your family, and the job will make demands on your income because you will have to take on a more expensive lifestyle. You may even decide that you don't like the kind of work, the conditions, or the people, or that your lack of leisure time will push you farther away from the way you want to live.

Depending on your values, the job may be worth it or not. If you list the pros and cons, you are more likely to adhere to your decision and have fewer regrets. You are more likely to weigh the tradeoffs, and perhaps think of other alternatives. You will decide what is important to you. You will have fewer negative surprises later, and will be warned of areas where you may need more infor-

A man should always consider how much he has more than he wants,
and how much more unhappy he might be than he really is.
Joseph Addison

mation. You will make better decisions and have more realistic expectations about the future.

What If Your Interviews Are Not Turning into Job Offers?

If one man says to thee, "Thou art a donkey," pay no heed. If two speak thus, purchase a saddle.
The Talmud

Listen to gather better information. You may find that your target market is declining, or that you don't have the required background, or whatever. One of my clients kept saying that managers insulted her. If you have the same experiences again and again, find out what you are doing wrong.

Perhaps you are unconsciously turning people down. A job hunter may make unreasonable demands because, deep inside, he or she knows there are things dramatically wrong with a situation. The requests for more money or a better title are really to make up for the unacceptable working conditions. Then the company rejects the applicant. One job hunter thought he was turned down for the job. In reality, *he* turned down the job. He did not let an offer happen because he knew the job was not right, and he made it fall through. There is nothing wrong with this—so long as he knows he could have had a job offer if he had wanted one.

Job hunters are under tremendous pressure to answer to a lot of people who want to know "how your job hunt is going." If you say you are still looking and have not gotten any offers, you may feel bad. That's another reason why you may want to get a few offers—even though you are not interested in those particular jobs. On the other hand, if your job hunt seems to be going very quickly, you may not want to waste your time on practice offers.

Make sure you are addressing the company's problems—not your own. A major mistake that I have made myself is focusing on what I wanted rather than on what the company or the manager needed.

Perhaps you are not talking to the right people. Are you interviewing with people two levels higher than you are—those in a position to hire you? If you are spending a lot of time talking to people at your own level, you can learn about the field, but this is unlikely to result in job offers.

If you don't know why, ask them. If appropriate, you may want to call a few of the people with whom you interviewed to find out why you did not get the job. If you are really stuck and feel you are not interviewing well, this can be very valuable feedback for you. You may even be able to turn a negative situation around.

Do Your Best, Then Let It Go

. . . you ought to say, "If it is the Lord's will."
James 4:15

You are trying to find a match between yourself and a company. You are not going to click with everyone, any more than everyone is going to click with you. Don't expect every interview to turn into a job offer. The more interviews you have, the better you will do at each one.

And don't punish yourself later. Do your best, and then do your best again.

Hang in there. Get a lot of interviews. Know your lines. And don't bump into the furniture. You will find the right job. As M. H. Anderson said: "If at first you don't succeed, you are running about average."

So to avoid all that horror, prepare. Apart from anything else, preparation uses up a lot of the nervous energy that otherwise might rise up to betray you. Channel that energy; focus it into areas that you control.

The first step in preparation is to learn your lines until saying them becomes a predictable reflex. And don't mouth them silently; say them aloud until they become totally your property. Hear yourself say them, because the last thing you want is the sound of your own voice taking you by surprise or not striking you as completely convincing.

Michael Caine, *Acting in Film*

The Five O'Clock Club®

Difficult Interview Questions and Possible Answers

Do not allow the interview to get off track. When the interviewer brings up something that takes you in a direction in which you don't want to go, briefly give a response that satisfies the interviewer, and then *get back on track*. Give your answer, and then say, for example, "But I really wanted to tell you about a special project I worked on." It is *your* responsibility to get the conversation back on track.

A sudden, bold, and unexpected question doth many times surprise a man and lay him open.
Francis Bacon, "Of Cunning"

Business is a game, and interviewing is part of the game. You are asked a question to see how well you handle it—and to see how well you play the game. This is not like a discussion with a friend. Don't take questions literally.

For example, if the interviewer asks you why you didn't finish college, should you tell the truth? Should you say, for example:

- I couldn't decide on a major;
- My mother died and I had to help out; or
- I ran out of money.

These answers are not wise because they're negative and they also take you both away from what should be the main discussion: the company's needs and how you can help.

The interviewer is not interested in you and your mother. There is a job to fill. Talking about certain subjects weakens your position—regardless of who brought them up. Keep the interview positive, and try not to discuss subjects that detract from your case. Many times hiring managers say to me, "Why did Joe (the applicant) have to tell me that? I was ready to hire him, but now I'm not so sure. When my boss confronts me about Joe's lack of college, I don't have a good answer."

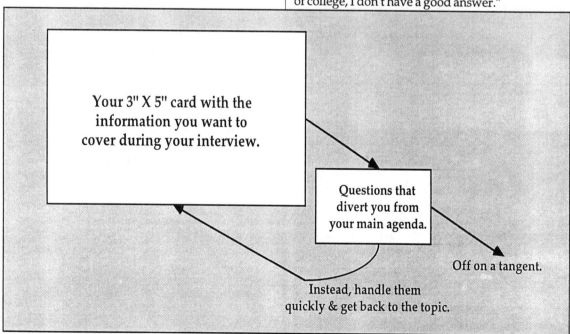

Your 3" X 5" card with the information you want to cover during your interview.

Questions that divert you from your main agenda.

Off on a tangent.

Instead, handle them quickly & get back to the topic.

*Midway in our life's journey, I went astray from the straight road
and woke to find myself alone in a dark wood.*
Dante, *The Inferno*

Some job hunters insist on being "honest." They think, "I'll just tell them the way it is, and if they don't hire me, then so be it." These job hunters are putting their responsibility on the interviewer. We've all had problems. The interviewer doesn't have to hear about them.

A businesslike answer, however, moves the interview along. Let's try the question again— keeping the goal of the interview in mind.

Why didn't you finish college?

"I like to be out there doing things. I finished several semesters, but I wanted to get more done. And that's what my bosses have always said about me: I'm someone who gets things done. They've all been happy with me."

Do not go into long discussions. *Briefly and politely* handle those questions that might take you off course, then smoothly move the conversation back to the company's needs or your abilities—the things on your 3 x 5 card that you had planned to cover. Give your answer, and then say, for example, "but I really wanted to tell you about a special project I worked on." It is your responsibility to get the conversation back on track.

Lettice: *Let me play the interviewer for once: you be the victim.*
Peter Schaeffer, *Lettice & Lovage*

Let's try a few others, but remember that you must find your own answers depending on your situation.

What would you like to be doing five years from now?

"Actually, I'd like to do the best job I can possibly do in the position we're talking about right now. I know that if I do a great job, good things will happen to me later. They always have."

Tell me about yourself.

See Your Two-Minute Pitch.

Tell me about the worst boss you've ever had.

If you say that the worst boss you've ever had simply did not have enough time for his subordinates, they'll wonder why you needed so much of your boss's time. If you say your worst boss yelled and screamed at people, they'll wonder what you did to make your boss so angry.

No matter what your bosses have been like: "I've been really lucky. I've been blessed with good bosses. They've all been different, but I've learned from each of them."

Why are you looking?
Why are you leaving?

You can count on being asked this because it's their job to ask it. Have your answer ready and then move back to the topics on your 3 x 5 card. They're just checking off items on a list to make sure there are no problems. Keep it brief. You are the only one who cares about the gory details.

Some job hunters have very solid reasons for being out of a job. One Five O'Clock Clubber, a PR executive in his mid-fifties, lost the best job of his life when his boss died and the new president brought in her own person. He was out through no fault of his own, and there was no better answer than what really happened to him.

Other than a story like that one, the best strategy is to describe your job loss as something you were proactive about—as if you had some say in the matter—and are also glad about. At the very least, do not describe your job loss as having to do with your own performance. Here are a few examples of positive responses:

"My company is going through a reorganization. I had the option of taking another job internally, but I decided to look elsewhere."

Or

"X company has been great for me, but the career possibilities in the areas that interest me are extremely limited."

Or

"Perhaps you heard that the _____ industry has been going through a major restructuring. I was caught along with three thousand others."

- If you're still employed, or if you're in outplacement and are allowed to look for a job back

There are no hopeless situations. There are only men
who have grown hopeless about them
Clare Booth Luce, *Europe in the Spring*

in your old firm:

"I don't know that I *am* leaving. I'm talking to people around the company. They sure would like me to take another job there, but I feel like I want to look outside as well."

- If you lost your job and received even a little severance, you can say:

"I had the opportunity to grab a package and I took it. I'm so lucky. I was not growing as much as I would have liked and now I can move my career along. That's why I'm glad to be talking to you today. I understand that your department is very involved in the new technologies."

They'll rarely ask how long you will be getting paid, and it's none of their business anyway.

Do what's appropriate for you and for your comfort level. Talk it over with your counselor or with those in your small group. Maybe there's a variation of these answers that's right for you.

- If you had been working long hours:

"I decided I couldn't work 75 hours a week and also look for a job. I couldn't do justice to my staff or to my former employer. I left the company so I could conduct a proper search."

- If you didn't get along with your boss:

Generally speaking, it's not a good idea to say that you left because of personality conflict. People may suspect that *you* are a difficult person. Sometimes those at very senior levels can get away with the "personality clash" excuse, but even then it's better to say, "We have differences on strategic issues."

When you're tempted to talk about conflict with a boss, it's best to say instead:

"I want to move my career in a different direction. My expertise is not the most important thing at my present company, and I want to move to a company where my skills will be put to better use."

What are you looking for?

It takes a lot of thinking to be ready for this question. Nothing turns off interviewers more than candidates who don't know what they want.

So don't speak in generalities, "I'm looking for a job that excites me" or, even worse, "I'm not sure." This amounts to asking the interviewer to come up with ideas for you! You shouldn't be going on job interviews if you're not hungry and *focused.*

Be prepared to name the kinds of positions you think would be appropriate for you. If your Two-Minute Pitch is polished, you will be able to talk persuasively about the kind of things you can do for the company.

How would you handle this?

The interviewer describes a problem situation and asks how you would handle it. You can't think that quickly.

"I'd have to give it some thought. I'm the type who likes to think things through. I've been up against problems like this before, such as when we were behind schedule at X company. I thought about the problem, and quickly decided we should do a, b, c. This reduced our processing time and everyone was happy.

"Everywhere I've worked, I've been able to assess situations and resolve them, and I'd do the same for you. I don't know how to answer your question at the moment, but I know I would handle the problem the way I have handled things in the past. I have a good track record."

What are your greatest weaknesses?

After taking time to mull it over:

"Actually, I can't think of any work-related weakness. My bosses have always thought I was great. I'm the kind not only to do my own job, but also to notice what else needed to be done in other areas and pitch in to help."

Or, name a weakness and show how you have dealt with it, such as:

"Sometimes I get impatient with people because I want the job to get done, but I make sure I find out what's going on and help them with whatever may be stopping them."

What are your strengths?

Don't simply say, "I'm organized, dependable

That is the essence of science: ask an impertinent question,
and you are on the way to a pertinent answer.
Jacob Bronowski

and honest." They won't remember your strengths unless you also give an example to illustrate each one. For example: "I'm very organized. I was asked to straighten out a library of 30,000 boxes of files. Within just three months, everyone in the department could find anything they wanted."

What is your current salary?

See Salary Negotiation.

The most important strategy is to postpone the discussion of salary until you get an offer. And remember, the person who names a number first is in a weak position.

They ask you to fill out your salary on a form.

If you find you are always filling out forms before you get into the interview, it may mean that you are getting most of your interviews through search firms, ads or human resources. Instead, try to get in through networking or through contacting someone directly. Then you won't find yourself filling out so many forms.

How long have you been unemployed?

If you've been unemployed for a long time, and you answer, "twenty-six months," how likely are you to be hired? I have run job-hunt groups of people who have been unemployed two years or more. The first thing we work on is an answer to this question.

From a moral point of view, I must help these people develop a good story so they can get back to work. It would be cruel for me to insist that they tell the truth. Who will hire an applicant who says, "When I was fired, I got depressed for six months and couldn't move, and then my mother got sick and I had to help. By then, I had been unemployed eleven months, and no one would hire me. I'm hoping you will give me a chance."

Very few people are willing to give this person a chance and you can't fault them for that. After all, the "truthful" job hunter is saying, "I've had all these problems, but I'm better now. Will you risk your organization for me?" It's not fair to burden the interviewer. All the interviewer wants to do is fill a job—not save lives.

The solution is to develop a good answer you can live with. Think of what you have actually been doing. Have you been working on your computer? Helping at your church or synagogue? Helping friends with their businesses? Most people can think of something they've been doing—even something little—that they can build a story around.

If you really haven't been doing anything at all, then *go do something*. You are unlikely to interview well if you haven't been out there at all. Get your adrenaline going. Walk dogs, pick strawberries, usher at church. Get active.

Better yet: Learn a new skill. Master new software. Take refresher courses. Volunteer your skills, or get paid something nominally. You might even consider saying you were paid for volunteer work, if you think they would back you up. Then think up a good story:

1. "I've actually been *looking* only a month or so. After I left X company, I spent some time working on a special project for a small company."

Or

2. "I've been looking only a few weeks now. After working for more than twenty years, this was my first time off, and I took advantage of the time to (fix up my house, take care of a sick family member, learn tax accounting, etc.). I was glad to have the opportunity to (help out, learn something new, etc.). But now I'm ready to get back to work and put in another twenty years."

Or

3. Take the work you've done:
"I've been doing public relations work for a small firm. I thought it would be fun to try after so many years with a big corporation, but now I know I like corporate life and I want to get back."

If your answers aren't working — if you're not getting second interviews or job offers —change your answers. Be creative, brainstorm with family and friends, and try new approaches. Positioning is everything; things won't go well until you've positioned yourself correctly.

The secret of science is to ask the right question, and it is the choice of problem more than anything that marks the man of genius in the scientific world.

Henry Tizard

How many other companies are you talking to?

"I've been very pleased with the response to my résumé. I'm looking at several opportunities." Don't tell them the names of the other companies unless you think it's in your best interest.

If you are *not* talking with other companies, you can say that you are just getting started and expect to be talking to a good number shortly. It is *not* a good strategy to pretend that you are on the verge of another offer if you are not. The hiring manager may tell you to *take* the other offer. Instead, get out there are talk to other companies.

We have two different positions. Which would you prefer?

Hedge your bets. "I could see myself doing [this] and I could also see myself doing [that]."

What is your management style?

This is a common question, so don't be blind-sided by it. Be prepared to give examples. Think of stories that demonstrate your management style. Some may be fresh in your mind after having done the Seven Stories. "Four years ago, my staff was cut while workload was increasing ..."

How good are you at . . .

If they ask, "How good are you at computer programming?" it's not good enough to say, "Very good." Instead, elaborate on how good you are: "I'm excellent at what I do, I have always been selected for the toughest assignments, the ones that no one else could do. For example..."

Don't Play Politics

About 15 years ago, I was being interviewed by a large company for a part-time consulting assignment. My prospective boss told me an idea she had that had nothing to do with my job. Her plans didn't make sense to me, but I would not risk discussing them with her until after I was hired.

Then she had me meet with her boss. He told me that he thought the project she was working on was idiotic, and he asked me what I thought. What I thought was, "I'm not going to undermine my prospective boss on a job interview!"

So I said, "She's a smart woman. I couldn't possibly know as an outsider what she knows as an insider. I'm sure she's making the right decisions for the right reasons."

Don't let silly politics stand in the way of your getting a job that you know you can do well.

A horror story

My dearest friend, Sharon, came to her first job in New York City from small-town Monroeton, Pennsylvania. She was "fired" after only nine months in the Big Apple. It was unfair and she was outraged. She decided that she was not going to let New York do this to her and so—as a ploy because the paperwork had not yet been filled out—she told her boss that she was on the verge of finding another job and would leave soon. By saying she needed "just one more week," she stayed for two more months—with pay.

During those two months, she felt a great deal of stress and caused Mike, her boss, considerable embarrassment. People knew she had been fired, but she was still there. But what could he do: Fire her again? She had nothing to lose.

She got an offer for a job that would be an acceptable next step. She would be managing a staff of 7, so it would look good on her résumé. The company itself was not a great fit for her, but she was desperate!

On the Thursday before Sharon was to start, Edgar, her prospective boss, took her out to lunch at a very nice restaurant to celebrate her coming on board. They had just sat down when Edgar leaned way over across the table and said to her, "Sharon, why did your former employer fire you?" And she thought, "I cannot believe this is happening!"

Now remember, Sharon had created a stir in that company and it was quite believable that Edgar had heard about it. Sharon was thinking, "How should I play this?" Edgar said, "I called a few people over there and they all told me the same thing: Sharon was fired."

Sharon's heart was pounding. Her ears were

Any job that has defeated two or three men in succession, even though each performed well in his previous assignments, should be deemed unfit for human beings and must be redesigned.

Peter Drucker

pounding. She thought that if she told Edgar the full truth he would never bring her on board. And so she said, "I don't know why people gossip and spread outrageous stories! I've already given my notice, so you should call my boss and ask him exactly what he thinks of me. Mike loves me."

By then, Mike was so afraid of Sharon that he would have said anything. Sharon's hunch was that he would not say that she had been fired.

Edgar leaned back in his chair and said, "I was just *kidding*. I never called anybody at your old company. But I hadn't done your reference checks and my bosses are bothered about that. My bluff usually works. When I ask people why they were fired, they confess and tell me the truth." Then Edgar paused and said, "Let's eat!"

"Eat!" Sharon thought. "I can't eat. I want to throw up." For the rest of the meal, Sharon could not hear a word he said.

Now remember, Edgar wanted to hire her. Often a hiring manager asks questions because he or she *has* to ask them. I am not advising you to lie on interviews, but do use your judgment.

By the way, Mike himself was fired about four months after Sharon left.

What questions do you have for us?

I go into the interview with an 8-1/2 x 11 pad. At the top of the pad, I put the four or five questions that I want to ask, and I integrate those questions into the conversation. I also take notes during the interview because I want to remember the details for the follow-up letters. If I meet with five people in one day, I cannot possibly remember what each person said. The notes are crucial even if you talk with only one person.

At the end of the meeting, when the interviewer asks, "Do you have any questions for us?" I make a point of looking at my questions (even though I know that I've already asked them all) and say, "No thanks, we've covered them all." But because the questions were written on the pad, I look prepared.

That's what consultants do. They go into a meeting with pen and paper in hand and try to figure out how things work so they can create an assignment for themselves.

What do you need to know? **If they were going to offer you a job that started a week from Monday, what is the gap between what you know now and what you need to know to get started there on Monday?** Ask those questions.

For example:

• "I'd like to talk to the head of manufacturing and also to the head of the operations department so I can get an idea of what they do."

• "I'd like to talk to some of my prospective peers so I can figure out exactly how I would interface with them."

• "I need to give this some thought and then I'd like to meet with you again. I'll have some ideas to discuss with you then." (Then do some research and find out more about this industry.)

• "What are some of the problems that keep you up at night?"

• "What are the most important things that need attention right now?"

And then a consultant will ask:

• "Where are you in the decision-making process?"

• "What other consultants are you talking to?"

• "How do you see me stacking up against them?"

If you ask questions like these—as if you were going to start working there a week from Monday, you will be much more proactive in the interview process. You will be thinking like a consultant.

Level the playing field

Job hunters feel as though they are at a disadvantage. After all, the organization is meeting with lots of candidates and will pick only one. It seems as though the hiring team has all the power. But you can have power too.

You can *put yourself* in a position of power. Get six to ten things in the works. They're talking to other people. Why shouldn't you? Then you can walk away from an abusive company just as easily as a company gets rids of candidates that are not up to the job.

Having six to ten things in the works is also the reason why Five O'Clock Clubbers who have been unemployed a long time still get jobs at market rates. Employers are likely to focus on what you have been doing for the last eighteen months or on what you were making in your last job. Instead, the emphasis shifts to the fact that you're talking to a host of other companies about jobs in the $40,000 to $50,000 range, or whatever.

CASE STUDY: GEORGE
Feeling at a Disadvantage

Some interviewers don't know how to interview! They can be unfocused, or fail to observe simple interviewing etiquette. If a hiring manager allows interruptions—he keeps making calls or answering them—consider saying, "I don't mind waiting outside for a few minutes while you take care of these emergencies. Then we can have a more quiet meeting." Unless that behavior is typical of the industry you're in, consider not putting up with it.

Let me give you an example of the problem a very senior person faced—so you won't think that all of the rudeness is aimed at lower-level people. George met with four or five senior company executives. They liked him and then asked him to meet with a psychiatrist. The psychiatrist reported back to management erroneous impressions about George, such as that he was too detailed a person. In fact, George was an amazing strategist. One of the senior managers said to George, " . . . the psychiatric report was not so good" and they told him about it.

How would such a report make *you* feel? George had a lot to offer, but that conversation made him feel deflated. My attitude was, "Didn't these senior managers themselves have any impressions of George? Did they have to rely so completely on an outsider? And if he did go to work for them, would they be able to make up their own minds or will they have to call in outside experts? Don't they have any guts?"

So when George regained his composure, he wrote them a note to regain the offensive and bolster his self-esteem. He said, "I'm interview-ing with six or seven other companies right now. I'm impressed by your company as well, but I wanted to give you some feedback. I don't think the method you are using for hiring is very sound. The psychiatrist's analysis did not accurately reflect my working style and I think you should be a little cautious about this in the future when you're hiring senior executives."

When you feel you are being mistreated, you *can* respond. You can take the offensive—but not to the point that it takes you off-strategy. Above all, move on. And when you have six to ten things in the works, it's easier to move on. George did not end up working there, nor did he want to. He had plenty of other offers.

Get six to ten things going—not all good ones.

When you have your six to ten things in the works, they're not all going to be brilliant possibilities. A good number will be with organizations you don't ever want to work for.

But getting the offers serves a purpose: It boosts your ego, helps you to better compare one situation with another, and increases your chances of getting offers from the companies that are of most interest to you. You will be able to say, "I've got four offers right now but I don't want to work for the others. I want to work for you." Prospective employers will see you as more marketable. So get some offers – even ones that are not right for you.

Stop Standing in Your Own Way

A Five O'Clock Clubber was having a hard time in his search, and I asked him what he thought the problem was. He said, "Companies don't want to hire me because I'm single." Over the years, I've heard a lot of reasons for getting turned down for jobs, but I'd never heard that one. So I asked him, "What is it about being single that's keeping you from getting a job?" He said, "Look, I've been living with this woman for nine years and I will not marry her." Because it bothered him, he would inadvertently bring up the fact that he was single during the interview process.

Maybe they call it take-home pay because
there is no other place you can afford to go with it.
Franklin P. Jones

If you tell the interviewer, even in subtle ways, that there is something wrong with you, they are unlikely to take a chance. They'll think, "Well it doesn't seem as though there is anything wrong with that, but if you tell me there is, then I trust you." And they're going to stay away from you.

Here's another example, but one that doesn't sound as silly. I was doing a workshop for lower level workers at a major retailer. Richard, the head of the mailroom, had supervised about 30 people—a responsible job. For some reason he was sensitive to the fact that he had been head of the mailroom for "only" two years.

When we practiced the Two-Minute Pitch, he himself brought up what he considered a weakness. He shot himself in the foot at the outset, "Well, I'm head of the mailroom at Bloomingdale's, where I have 30 to 50 people reporting to me and it's going very well *despite the fact that I've been on the job for only two years.*"

When Richard positions himself that way, the hiring manager is going to think there's something wrong with his having been in the job two years. If you feel that something is a handicap for you, think twice about mentioning it—don't bring it up! If you think your age is a problem, you may inadvertently say, "Despite the fact that I'm older" or "Despite the fact I'm only recently out of school." Remember, positioning is everything. Be careful what you say.

Your attitude should be, "Problem? What problem?" Be sensitive to your own sensitivities and get over them.

The Good Interviewer

It probably won't happen to you during your entire job search, but be prepared for the person who conducts a good interview. In a good interview, the hiring manager may start with the beginning of your career, asking, "What did you do in this job?" "Why did you leave that job and go on to the next one?" "What did you like best about that job?" "What about your boss?"

Then he or she asks you about the next job in a methodical, organized way. "What did you en-joy?" "What did you do best in that job?" "Why did you leave it?" "Tell me about the next one."

You're not going to get very many interviewers like that.

How to Handle Discrimination

If the interviewer asks you questions that are illegal (such as questions about pregnancy or your plans to have children), assume they are not being asked maliciously. Instead of answering the question itself, answer the *concern* that may have prompted the question. For example, if someone asks, "Do you have small children at home? Are you married?" You cannot say, "It's illegal to ask that." They'll apologize, but you won't get the job. Who needs a troublemaker?

Instead, try to figure out why they're asking you that question and answer their concern. You could say, for example, "Are you concerned that I might not show up at work? I've never missed a day in 15 years."

Remember the following:

- Be prepared.
- Have your six to ten things in the works so that you're not at a disadvantage.
- The purpose of the first interview is not to get a job offer. The purpose of the first interview is to get the second interview.
- You're trying to give and get information so that you can get that next meeting.
- Half of the interview process is being prepared, but the other half is having that right attitude. They'll sense your self-confidence and you are less likely to buckle under when they ask you idiotic questions—often they don't care about the answers anyway.

Shy persons often act like they were captured
and are being interrogated.
Garrison Keillor

My formula for success?
Rise early, work late, strike oil.
J. Paul Getty

Advanced Interview Techniques

We can become anything. That is why injustice is impossible here. There may be the accident of birth, there is no accident of death. Nothing forces us to remain what we were.
John Berger, *Pig Earth*

Each handicap is like a hurdle in a steeplechase, and when you ride up to it, if you throw your heart over, the horse will go along, too.
Lawrence Bixby, "Comeback from a Brain Operation," *Harper's*, Nov., 1952

A man's accomplishments in life are the cumulative effect of his attention to detail.
John Foster Dulles,
Quoted by Leonard Mosley, *Dulles*

You can never enslave somebody who knows who he is.
Alex Haley

Here's a little number I do before a long take: take a slow deep breath in, then bend over and let your arms dangle, really relaxed. Straighten up slowly, breathing out gently and evenly. This exercise relaxes you, helps concentration and gives you control. . . it gets the oxygen to the brain. You feel and look like a twit, panting away, but you find you get a rush to your head, your eyes begin to sparkle a bit, and you're ready to play an energetic scene, mental or physical. Just be careful not to overdo the panting or you will hyperventilate and pass out.
Michael Caine, *Acting in Film*

If they ask if you own a horse, say yes.
If they ask if you are a horse, say yes.
And you'll learn how to do it that night.
Robert Parrish,
Award-winning film editor-director.
Advice he received from his mother.
Quoted in *The New York Times*

Most people think job hunting consists of lining up interviews and then being brilliant. But there's more to the process than that. And there's much more that you can do to influence the outcome.

Consultative Sale

The interview is only the beginning of the job search. Go into it to learn—not just to sell. When job hunters go into the interview selling themselves rather than giving and getting information, they may be lucky and get the job. On the other hand, if they need to do some follow-up to keep the job prospect alive, they are usually lacking in the information needed to decide what to do next.

When preparing for the interview, remember to act like a consultant. Think about them first, and then think about yourself. Certainly you want to look the part, not ramble, present yourself clearly, understand their needs, and handle the tricky questions. But you can go a lot further.

With Whom Will You Meet?

If you were invited to a business meeting that was going to take place next week, you would naturally want to know who else would be there, and you might want to know something about them, such as:

- their names and job titles;
- the issues important to each of them;
- what they are like;
- their ages; and
- the length of time they have been with the company.

Yet most job hunters go into interviews—which, of course, are business meetings—unprepared, knowing little about the people. As many Five O'Clock Club counselors suggest, it is helpful to your self-esteem to think of interviews as meetings, and even refer to them that way.

Ask the Person Who Arranged the Meetings

To be better prepared, ask whoever set up the meeting—whether it was personnel, the hiring manager, a search firm, or a secretary—to give you the information you need. You can say, "I'm ex-

If you have an important point to make, don't try to be subtle or clever. Use a pile driver.
Hit the point once. Then come back and hit it again. Then hit it a third time—a tremendous whack.
Winston Churchill, on public speaking, quoted by Edward, Duke of Windsor, *A King's Story*

cited about the meeting next week, and want to prepare. I'd like to know something about the people I'll be meeting and the issues that are of concern to them." You may not find out everything you would like to, but even a little bit of information will help.

Think About Their Issues

Then try to go beyond what you have been told. Think about additional issues that are likely to be important to each person. Decide how you will address these issues. A financial person, for example, will most likely be concerned about the bottom line. An operations person, a marketing person, or someone in human resources will probably have different concerns.

You can also think about a person's concerns based on his or her position in the hierarchy. People higher up are generally more concerned about the direction of the department, division or company, while those lower down are usually more concerned about the day-to-day workings of the job. From their own perspective, each person will care about whether or not you can do the job, and perhaps whether or not you will fit in.

In addition, do library research. Find out about how the company and the position you are interviewing for may be impacted by the facts or trends you uncover. Finally, gather information from other individuals who may know about the company, or who may actually work there.

During the Meeting

To better understand the situation, you may need to find out more about their operation, how they are organized, their visions for the department, and the problems they are facing.

Be sure to ask where they are in the hiring process, how many other people they are considering, and how you compare with them. If you don't know something about your competition, you are less likely to win.

Like a Game of Chess

In chess, the idea is to think a number of moves ahead. Based on what you know about the person you are playing with, what you know about yourself, and what you know about the game, as a chess player you would form a hypothesis about what the other player's moves are likely to be. Then you would plan what to do in response to those moves.

So, too, based on the information you have gathered, you can form a hypothesis about the person with whom you will be meeting. Then you can envision various scenarios and your strategy for each in advance. Even if you are incorrect, you will do better in the meeting than if you simply went in there cold.

If you have thought all this through, you can be more observant about other things during the interviews. Afterwards, you can reflect: What was the mood of the meeting? What issues actually were important to this person? What were the pluses—the reason that he or she might want to have me on board? What were the objections—the reason that he or she might not want to have me on board? What would the next steps be to move me along in the process? The work you will do next—the follow-up—is covered in great detail later.

Most Job Hunters Try to Close Too Soon

Job hunters are under a lot of pressure. When they are going in for their first meeting, everyone says: "I hope you get the job." As your career coach, I hope you *don't*. It is unlikely that you will get an offer for a good job after just one meeting. I would wonder what is wrong with the company: Are they the type that hires easily and fires easily?

Instead of trying to land a job immediately, conduct yourself at the first interview so that they will want you back for a second one. Get enough information so that you can follow up intelligently. It is not uncommon in today's market to have twelve to fifteen meetings at one company for one job. You may have fewer, but don't count on it.

Instead, plan to be in this for the long run with this company, and with six to ten other companies.

The trouble with most people is that they think with their hopes or fears
or wishes rather than with their minds.
Will Durant, Recalled by friends at the time of his death, November 7, 1981

Hiring Someone May Not Be Their Most Important Issue

The average job hunter goes into the interview saying, "I sure hope you want somebody like me, and here are my credentials."

This may not be the issue. The issue may be whether or not they should start a new system, for example, and how they should go about it. Until they have figured this out, they won't know who would be right for the job. Address the issue that's bothering them rather than the issue that's bothering you (that is, getting a job).

If they don't know whether or not they want to start a new system, you can say: "I've been sitting here thinking about your new system and how it should be done."

If you can be as objective as possible—taking the stance of coaching them and helping them figure out their problem—you will stand a much better chance of getting the position.

The First Two Minutes

Some say that the hiring decision is made during the first two minutes. While it is true that they will quickly decide against you if you look like a slob or tell an dumb joke, the average job hunter has many more chances than the first two minutes. In fact, by following The Five O'Clock Club approach, you can turn around a situation that normally would have ended in failure.

CASE STUDY: DOROTHY
Overcoming Their Objections

Dorothy, a reserved but highly intelligent and refined woman, was interviewing for a position as a consultant. She prepared thoroughly, dressed in a manner that she thought was appropriate, and conducted the meeting the best way she could.

She asked them if there was any reason that they might be hesitant to bring her on board compared with some of the other people they had seen. The interviewer responded that she was afraid that Dorothy would not come across as strong enough in her meetings with prospective clients: "In this business, you need to wow them."

When Dorothy did her follow-up letter, she stressed how successful she had been in the past with clients. She asked for another meeting.

This time she dressed in a "power" suit—a red one that would have been inappropriate for a first interview, and conducted herself very differently. The interviewer said she wondered why she had ever thought those negative things because they obviously were not true. Dorothy got the job and was very successful.

CASE STUDY: BOB
Prepared for the Meetings

Bob, a marketing executive, had been looking for a job for a while when I met him, and he was very tired. He was now applying for a plum marketing job at a major information-services company, and was going in for his initial meeting.

Before the meeting, he researched to find out what was going on in the company. He formed a hypothesis about why they might have wanted to see him. He prepared his 3 x 5 card to address the issues he thought would be important to them, and wrote out a two-minute pitch specifically for this company.

At this first meeting, he probed to find out the problems the company faced. He also tried to get a feel for the company culture.

When Bob had interviewed at other companies, they loved his ability to think up new product ideas. But he learned that this company already had plenty of new products; they wanted someone who could make their products successful.

Bob did a thorough follow-up after the first round of interviews. He addressed the issues that were important to each person with whom he met, reminded each of the positives they found in him, handled the negatives (the reasons why each person might not want to have him on board). He decided that his next step should be to meet more people.

The Second Round of Interviews

Bob was called back to meet with five more people. Before the meetings, he asked their names and titles, and found out a little about each person, including the issues that might be important to him or her, and the number of years he or she had been

---

with the company.

Bob typed up a sheet with every name and job title and a hypothesis about what each person's concerns might be, how he could address those concerns, and the questions he wanted to ask each person. His sheets included, in brief:

—the head of sales, who Bob thought might be threatened by a new marketing person;

—the head of finance, who would probably be concerned about the profitability of the new products;

—the head of operations, who might be worried about being ignored by sales and marketing;

—the head of human resources, who may be concerned about how well Bob would fit in; and

—his future boss, the head of all marketing. (Bob had prepared three pages of notes on this person!)

Rather than going into each meeting cold, Bob had hypotheses and solutions in mind. Thus he would be in a position to have the best meetings possible. In addition to the questions he designed specifically for each individual, he asked them all:

• What would you like from whomever you hire for the new job?

• What are the things you would be afraid he or she might do in the new marketing position?

• How could the new person make your life easier?

• What are your most important concerns about this job and the new hire?

He also asked questions that had to do specifically with this company, and the job, such as:

• Who are your key competitors for these new products?

• Have you targeted new growth industries?

• I've heard that your company wants to move toward greater predictive offerings. Is this true? Have you been successful?

He also asked questions having to do with organizational issues, such as:

• The job seems to be in a state of flux. What is your impression of it?

• How would the new person work with each of the department heads?

• What would you like to see this person accomplish after the first year? After three to four years?

• What support could the new person look forward to from you?

• Would the new person work only within this one division, or explore appropriate opportunities with other divisions?

In addition, Bob asked other selected people:

• Where are they in the hiring process?

• How many others are they considering?

• How do I stack up against them?

Bob treated everyone he met as an individual to be reckoned with and courted. He handled them all differently. **His goal was to have each person see him as the ideal candidate.** To do this, he probed to understand thoroughly the situation for each of them.

During all this, Bob had to resist his natural tendency to think up new product ideas, since this was not something they wanted.

Don't ask: "Is there anything I can do to convince you that I'm the right person?" The answer is always no. Decide for yourself what you must do to convince them.

Problem Areas

There were a few problem areas:

• Bob's future boss seemed weak and might be threatened by him. Bob had to reassure the boss in his follow-up that he would be a support and not a threat.

• Bob was not happy with the way he had come across to the operations head. When he wrote his follow-up, he said he was not pleased with the way he had addressed some issues, and went into great detail explaining his position.

Bob was able to write a very tailored follow-up to each person only because he had thoroughly prepared—he also took notes during the meetings so he would accurately remember what each person said.

Bob asked to meet with his future boss again to discuss some details, and followed up in writing again after that meeting. Since this was a protracted process, Bob decided the human resources person, who was smart and also open, was the best one to

The meeting of two personalities is like the contact of two chemical substances;
if there is any reaction, both are transformed.
Carl Jung, *Modern Man in Search of a Soul*

keep in touch with for the status of the situation. In addition to all of his follow-up in writing, he wanted to have a feel for how things were going so that he could decide whether additional effort would be needed—for instance, if another candidate were to enter the race.

Round Three

Bob was called back for another round of meetings, this time with the head of management information services, the division head, and the human resources manager. When he went back for this round of interviews, Bob made a point of stopping in to see his future boss, and also the operations head—to keep the contacts alive.

Your goal is to have each person be an advocate of having you on board. If there is anyone who objects to you, make sure you handle it now.

And Then the Wait . . .

Human resources had already asked for six to eight references, and had checked them out. Everything was fine. The head of human resources said, "They want you. In five years, I've never seen such enthusiasm. I'm sure they're about to make you an offer. Are you interested? When do you think you could start?"

Then suddenly everything was put on hold for seven weeks while the company decided to "re-engineer" (reorganize). They assured Bob that everything was okay, and that he would be happy with the results—especially the money.

But Bob panicked. He couldn't stand the stress any more. He had been in search a long time, and his nerves were giving way. He was anxious to force their hand. If they wanted him, they could make him an offer now. What on earth could make them wait seven more weeks?

Don't Force It; Instead, Make Sure You Have Six to Ten Things in the Works

As his career coach, it was all I could do to get Bob to focus on the rest of his search while he stayed in touch with them. Because he had such a

good relationship with the human resources manager, Bob mostly spoke with that person. For the next seven weeks, the manager continued to assure Bob that things were going well, and he should just hang in there.

Bob bravely focused on the rest of his search. He said I couldn't possibly imagine the strain he was under. He told me of his daughter's health problems at home.

I warned him that the strain he was under now would be nothing compared to what he would feel if this job fell through and he had nothing else in the works. Starting a job search from scratch truly would be a nightmare. It's much better not to let one's momentum slip. So Bob got a lot of other things in the works, though he never relaxed.

Finally, the seven weeks was up. The company asked him to wait one more week. Then they made him an offer.

Do not drop your search activities when an offer seems almost certain. If it doesn't materialize, the lost momentum is difficult to recover.
—Advice from a successful job hunter at The Five O'Clock Club

---

Finally . . . the Offer

The offer was for the boss's job! Bob was not the only one who had seen the boss as weak: the rest of management did too. Still, they offered Bob the job only because he played by the rules and did not try to undermine his prospective manager or make him look bad. The pay was phenomenal, and Bob deserved it.

Look at all the planning that Bob put into wooing this one company. Make sure you plan for each person with whom you will meet and keep notes on each (use the Interview Record). Make sure everyone you meet wants to have you on board. Be in sync with their time frame, not your own. And be sure to have six to ten things in the works—just in case. That is what's required in a successful job hunt.

Obviously the way you move will be affected by the character you are playing; but natural movement comes from your "center," from the same place as a natural voice. When you walk from your center, you will project a solid perspective of yourself. Walk with that certainty and ease, and your path becomes a center of gravity. Your force pulls all eyes to you. Slouch or poke your head forward, or pull your shoulders back uncomfortably, and that power seeps away.

Only a relaxed, centered walk creates a sense of strength. A centered walk can be very menacing, too. Even if you don't get film work on the basis of this advice, follow it and you'll never get mugged, either. Mind you, if you look like I do you'll never get mugged anyway because people generally think I have just been mugged.
Michael Caine, *Acting in Film*

What convinces is conviction. Believe in the argument you're advancing. If you don't, you're as good as dead. The other person will sense that something isn't there, and no chain of reasoning, no matter how logical or brilliant, will win your case for you.
Lyndon Baines Johnson

Until you value yourself, you will not value your time. Until you value your time, you will not do anything with it.
Dr. M. Scott Peck

On the next page is a very important worksheet: the Interview Record. Make a lot of copies of this page for your own personal search. Every time you have a meeting— **whether a networking meeting or a job interview**—fill it out. Make note of with whom you met, to whom they referred you, and what happened in the meeting. Attach to the Interview Record a copy of your notes from the meeting, the follow-up letter that you sent, perhaps the letter that led to the meeting.

Two weeks after the meeting, you may not remember what you discussed. If you are having a productive search and you are meeting with 10 to 15 people each week, you will not be able to remember what each person said, let alone how you met that person. To keep track of your meetings, maintain a record of each one.

Some job hunters use a three-ring binder, and arrange all of the Interview Records alphabetically or by industry or in some other logical order, with their letters attached.

Some job hunters methodically cross-reference the names by noting who referred whom.

At the beginning of your search, you may think you will be searching for a short time. But part of a good search is to follow up with your contacts at least every two months. You can have a more intelligent follow-up if you have an Interview Record to refer to.

The Five O'Clock Club®

Interview Record

Name: _____

Position: _____

Company: _____

Address: _____

_____

_____

Phone: Bus: _____

      Home: _____

E-mail:

_____

Referred by:

Link to referral:

People spoken to (May require separate sheets.):

Issues (advice, problems, plans, etc.):

Key points to remember:

Referrals (Write additional names on back.):

Name: _____

Position: _____

Company: _____

Address: _____

_____

_____

Phone: Bus: _____

_____ Home: _____

Date of initial contact:_____

Method used:_____

(If letter, copy and attach to this sheet.)

Planned date of follow-up call to set up
   appointment: _____

(Also record date on job-hunting calendar.)

Actual dates of calls to set up appointment:

                 _____

                 _____

                 _____

                 _____

Appointment:_____

Follow-up note mailed:_____

(Copy attached.)

Follow-up 2:_____

Follow-up 3:_____

Follow-up 4:_____

Follow-up 5:_____

Follow-up 6:_____

(Copies attached.)

Other comments:

- tone of the meeting
- positives about you
- objections to you
- key issues to address
- logical next steps
- influencers
- your feelings about the job

PART FOUR

TURNING JOB INTERVIEWS INTO OFFERS

THE BRAINIEST PART OF THE PROCESS

Follow-Up After a Job Interview:
Consider Your Competition

Bullock shrugged. He'd been thinking about Bill that afternoon, trying to decide how to fit him into Deadwood Brickworks, Inc. It wasn't a question he could be useful. Anybody could be useful when you decided where they fit. That was what business was.
Pete Dexter, *Deadwood*

So far in the interview process, we have considered you and the hiring manager. By acting like a consultant, you can negotiate a job that's right for both you and him or her. But there are other players and other complexities in this drama. First, there are all the other people you meet during the hiring process. They are influencers and, in fact, may influence the hiring decision more than the hiring manager does. These are people the hiring manager trusts and on whose opinions he relies. In addition, there are complexities such as outside influencers, the timing of the hiring decision, and salary considerations. Finally, you have competitors. They may be other people the interviewer is seeing, or your competition can be an ideal candidate in the interviewer's mind.

This chapter contains case studies of how some people considered and dealt with their competition. In the next chapter, we'll give you the guidelines they followed, which helped them decide what they could do to win the job. Remember, the job hunt really starts after the interview. What can you do to turn the interview into an offer? This is the part of the process that requires the most analysis and strategic thinking. Think *objectively* about the needs of the organization and of everyone you met, and think about what you can do to influence *each* person.

If you're in a seller's market, however, you may not need to follow up: You'll be brought back for more meetings before you have a chance to breathe. *If you're in a buyer's market*, you will probably have to do some thoughtful follow-up to get the job.

Because effective follow-up is a lot of work, your first decision should be: Do I want to get an offer for this job? Do I want to "go for it"? If you are ambivalent, and are in a competitive market, you will probably *not* get the job. Someone else will do

what he or she needs to do to get it.

Follow-ups will not guarantee you a specific job, but extensive follow-ups on a number of possibilities increase the number and quality of your offers. If you focus too much on one specific situation and how you can *make* them hire you, that won't work. You need both breadth and depth in your job hunt: You have both when you are in contact on a regular basis with six to ten people who are in a position to hire you or recommend that you be hired. You must have six to ten of these contacts in the works, *each* of which you are trying to move along.

Ideally, you will get to a point where you are moving them along together, slowing certain ones down and speeding others up, so you wind up with three concurrent job offers. Then you can select the one that is best for you. This will usually be the job that positions you best for the long run—the one that fits best into your Forty-Year Vision. It will rarely be sensible to make a decision based on money alone.

Therefore, if one situation is taking all of your energy, stop right now for ten minutes and think of how you can quickly contact other people in your target area (through networking, direct contact, search firms, or ads). It will take the pressure off, and prevent you from trying to close too soon on this one possibility.

CASE STUDY: THE ARTIST
Status Checks Rarely Work

Most people think follow-up means calling for the status of the search. This is not the case:

At Citibank, a project I managed needed an artist. I interviewed twenty and came up with two piles: one of seventeen rejects, and another of the three I would present to my boss and my boss's boss. A few people called to "follow up." Here's one:

Artist: "I'm calling to find out the procedure and the status. Do you mind?"

Me: "Not at all. I interviewed twenty people. I'll select three and present them to my boss and my boss's boss."

Artist: "Thanks a lot. Do you mind if I call back later?"

Me: "No, I don't mind."

The artist called every couple of weeks for three months, asked the same thing, and stayed in the reject pile. To move out, he could have said things like:

- Is there more information I can give you?
- I've been giving a lot of thought to your project and have some new ideas. I'd like to show them to you.
- Where do I stand? How does my work compare with the work others presented?

If all you're doing is finding out where you are in the process, that's rarely enough. *The ball is always in your court.* It is your responsibility to figure out what the next step should be. Job hunters view the whole process as if it were a tennis game where— *thwack*—the ball is in the hiring manager's court. Wrong.

Me to job hunter: "How's it going?"

Job hunter to Kate: *(Thwack!)* "The ball's in their court now. They're going to call me."

When they call, it will probably be to say, "You are not included." If you wait, not many of your interviews will turn into offers.

CASE STUDY: RACHEL
Trust Me

> *A man is not finished when he's defeated;*
> *he's finished when he quits.*
> Richard Milhous Nixon

Rachel had been unemployed for nine months. This was her first Five O'Clock Club meeting. She was disgusted. "I had an interview," she said. "I know what will happen: I'll be a finalist and they'll hire the other person."

Rachel was nice, enthusiastic, and smart: She was always a finalist. Yet the more experienced person was always hired.

Here's the story. Rachel, a lobbyist, was interviewing at a law firm. The firm liked her back-ground, but it needed some public relations help and perhaps an internal newsletter. Rachel did not have experience in either of those areas, though she knew she could do those things. She wrote a typical thank you note playing up her strengths, playing down her weaknesses, but essentially ignoring the firm's objections. She highlighted the lobbying, and said that PR and a newsletter would not be a problem. She could do it. She was asking the firm to "trust her."

Lots of Job Hunters Take the "Trust Me" Approach

The following occurred during a group meeting at The Five O'Clock Club:

Me: "Do you want this job? Are you willing to go through a brick wall to get it?"

Rachel: "Yes. I am. I really want this job."

Me: "Let's think about overcoming their objections. If you can write a PR plan after you get hired, why not do it now? Why ask them to trust you?"

Two people in the group had old PR plans, which they lent her. Remember: The proposals or ideas you write will probably be wrong. That's okay. You're showing the company you can think the problem through and actually come up with solutions.

Rachel's lack of experience with newsletters was also an objection. We suggested Rachel call law firms in other cities and get their newsletters.

After doing research, Rachel sent a very different note. In this one she said she had been giving it more thought, and was very excited about working for the firm. She had put together a PR plan, *which she would like to review with them,* and had gotten copies of newsletters from other law firms, which gave her ideas of what she could do in a newsletter for them. Of course, she got the job.

Uncovering Their Objections

Rachel got the job because she overcame the objections of the hiring committee. Start thinking about how you can overcome objections. This will change the way you interview, and you will become more attuned to picking up valid objections rather than quashing them. Then you can even solicit negatives. For example, you can ask:

- Who else is being considered?
- What do they have to offer?
- How do I stand in comparison with them?
- What kind of person would be considered an ideal candidate?
- What would you like to say about a new hire one year from now?

Get good at interviewing so you can solicit valid objections to hiring you.

Act Like a Consultant

Since most jobs are created for people, find out what the manager needs. Hiring managers often decide to structure the job differently depending on who they hire. Why not influence the hiring manager to structure the job for you?

Probe—and don't expect anything to happen in the first meeting. If you were a consultant trying to sell a $30,000 or $130,000 project (your salary), you wouldn't expect someone to immediately say, "Fine. Start working." Yet job hunters often expect to get an offer during the first meeting.

Forget about job hunting. This is regular business. You're selling an expensive package. Do what a consultant or a salesperson does: Ask about the company's problems and its situation; think how you could get back to the interviewer later. Get enough information so you can follow up and give the interviewer enough information so he'll want to see you again. Move the process along: Suggest you meet with more people there. Do research. Have someone influence the interviewer on your behalf. Then get back to him again. That's what a consultant does. Remember to move the process along; outshine and outlast your competition.

CASE STUDY: KEN
Identifying the Issues/Timing

Ken was the first person interviewed for a senior vice president of marketing position. When Ken asked, the interviewer said he would see five

or six more people. As you will see shortly, being first is the weakest position. Get rid of your competition quickly, or find ways to maintain the interviewer's interest and meet with him or her again.

Ken identified the company's most important issue—it was not wondering what Ken would do as the head of marketing, but something more basic: It was debating the *role* marketing should play in the new organization.

Determining the real issues is critical in deciding your follow-up plan. And since the timing was against him, Ken acted fast. He wrote a handsome four-page proposal about the role marketing should play, and he sent it overnight.

When Ken was called for a second round of interviews, he found there were no other candidates. Ken had gotten rid of his competition. Ken not only identified the issues, he was in sync in terms of timing. The company was planning to decide quickly, so he acted quickly, too.

CASE STUDY: LEON
How Did He Get the Job?

Leon came to The Five O'Clock Club after fifteen months of interviews. After three Club meetings, he got two job offers simply because he followed the group's advice and wrote proposals. When he told the group his good news, someone asked him how he got the two jobs. He said that one offer was from a search firm, and one was from networking. Leon had been pursuing jobs through networking and search firms for fifteen months, but it wasn't until he decided to do real follow-up on these that he was offered a job.

CASE STUDY: JOHN
Consider Your Likely Competitors and Go For It

Most job hunters think *anxiously* about the competition out there. Instead, be *objective* about your likely competitors.

John thought he had been job hunting for a year. He answered ads, met with search firms, and even went on interviews, but he wasn't job hunting: *In a tight market, the job hunt starts* after *the interview.*

At our first meeting, John recounted his activity.

One ad he'd answered was for a job at the Kennedy Foundation, and he'd met three people there two weeks earlier. He was waiting for their call. Before John went on, I stopped him.

"John," I said, "do you want that job?"

"Well," he replied, "I'll see what happens next. If they call me, I'll consider it."

"The way things stand, John, you are *not* going to get that job. If they call, they'll say they found a better match. Are you willing to go through a brick wall to get that job? If you are, I can help you—and it's a *lot* of work. But if you essentially want to sit on the bench answering ads, there's not much a coach can do."

John said he was willing to go after the job. A job hunter's total commitment is absolutely necessary, or he will not be willing to do—or even notice—what needs to be done to win the job.

Who Are John's Likely Competitors?

The Kennedy Foundation wanted a controller. John had been a controller in a major corporation for twenty years. What kind of controller would the Kennedy Foundation most likely want?

Develop a prototype of your likely competitors. You have to guess about your competition. But once you form a hypothesis about who your competitors are, you can figure out a plan to outshine and outlast them. It's better to have some hypothetical competitor in mind than nobody. Remember, your competition might not be real people, but an ideal in the mind of the hiring manager. Get rid of that competitor, too, or the hiring manager will continue looking for that ideal person.

John thought his likely competitors were people who had been controllers in not-for-profit organizations. I suggested that he spend a day at The Foundation Center (a library), and research the controllership function at other foundations. I told him to make sure he could handle the work and knew the jargon.

John came back with good news: "I know how to do that kind of accounting. It's actually what I've done all along."

How Does John *Now* Stand in Relation to His Likely Competitors?

Don't forget that it (your product or service)
is not differentiated until the customer
understands the difference.
Tom Peters, *Thriving on Chaos*

John now has twenty years of corporate controllership experience and a day in the library. His likely competitors have real hands-on experience. At this stage, John is *not* even with them. He has to do more if he wants the job.

John and I searched his background for areas that might interest the Kennedy Foundation—experience his likely competitors would not have, such as securities accounting.

Look at all the work and thought John has put in so far—without a request from the hiring manager. The ball is *always* in your court.

John had met with three people at the Kennedy Foundation. Among the three was a financial person and someone from personnel. His first draft of the letter to the financial person was negative: "Despite the fact that I have no not-for-profit experience, I believe my credentials . . . "

Wrong. Come up with something that *beats out* your competition. You must be in a position to say, in so many words, "Unlike others who have spent a lot of time doing this work, I bring something extra to the party."

Also remember that you are interviewing with individuals—not organizations. You are *not* interviewing with the Kennedy Foundation or IBM. Each person you meet has his or her own opinions about the issues that are important, the things that person likes about you, and the reasons he or she might not want you there. Address these points with *each* person.

The Other Decision-Makers/Influencers

The people you want to reach . . . should be
viewed as distinct target audiences that
require different approaches and strategies.
Jeffrey P. Davidson, marketing consultant
Management World, September/October 1987

Many job hunters assume the hiring manager is the only person who matters. Big mistake. Others are not only influencers; in some cases, they may actually be the decision-makers.

I'm a good example. I make terrible hiring decisions: Everyone I interview seems fine to me. So I have others meet with the candidates. Their opinions weigh more than mine. Any applicant who ignores them is ignoring the decision-makers—or at least the serious influencers.

Take seriously every person you meet. Don't be rude to the receptionist. She may say to the boss, "If you hire him, I'm quitting." That receptionist is definitely an influencer.

Identifying the Issues

*You must call each thing by its proper name
or that which must get done will not.*
A. Harvey Block

When John first met with the personnel person at the Kennedy Foundation, she asked him questions such as, "So, what do you do on weekends?" and "Where do your kids go to school?" Assuming these were not idle questions, what issue was she getting at?

We decided the issue was *fit*. When John wrote his first follow-up letter to her, he said he was excited about the position and had spent a day doing research—and he addressed the issue of fit. He did this by emphasizing his qualities of loyalty and commitment. Also, he correctly sensed that they would be impressed with where he went to college and his relationship with his family.

Three months, eleven grueling interviews, and seven in-depth reference checks later, John's credentials were presented to the board of directors for approval. To make sure his important arguments were brought before the board, John prepared one more follow-up letter (see the next page). By the way, John had three more interviews after the board meeting. He got the job—and he's still there.

Many job hunters ask John how he got the job. They are asking the wrong question. They mean, "How did you get the interview?" John is forced to reply, "I got it through an ad." I hope you can see that John got the *job* through his analysis and follow-up. It was just the *interview* that he got through an ad.

What Happens As Time Passes

*He had made a fortune in business and owed it to being
able to see the truth in any situation.*
Ethan Canin, *Emperor of the Air*

Most jobs are *created* for people: Most interviewers don't know clearly what they will want the new person to do. Yet job hunters expect the hiring manager to tell them exactly what the job will be like, and get annoyed when the manager can't tell them.

Generally the job description depends on who will be in the job. Therefore, help the hiring manager figure out what the new person should do. If you don't help him, another job hunter will. This is called "negotiating the job." You are trying to remove all of the company's objections to hiring you, as well as all of *your* objections to working for them. Try to make it work for both of you. But time is your enemy. Imagine what happens in the hiring process as time passes:

You have an interview. When I, your counselor, ask how it went, you tell me how great it was: The two of you hit it off, and you are sure you will be called back. You see this interview as something frozen in time, and you wait for the magical phone call.

But after you left, the manager met with someone else, who brought up new issues. Now his criteria for what he wants have changed somewhat, and consequently, his impression of you has also changed. He was honest when he said he liked you, but things look different to him now. Perhaps you have what he needs to meet his new criteria, or perhaps you could convince him that his new direction is wrong, but you don't know what is now on his mind.

You call to find out "how things are going." He says he is still interviewing and will call you later

July 18, 20xx

Mr. Harvey Kaplan
The Kennedy Foundation
1234 13th Street, NW
Washington, D.C. 12345

Dear Harvey:

Now that you are in the final stage of your search, I wanted to take the opportunity to summarize my feelings about the position and address what I see as some of the major issues affecting your decision.

Long-term commitment

My almost twenty-year career at Gotham unequivocally attests to my loyalty and commitment to my employer and my job. It is only because this opportunity is so exceptional that, for the very first time, I am seriously considering leaving Gotham. You can be assured that this sense of loyalty will remain with me at the Foundation.

Profit-making background

I feel strongly that my experience in the for-profit sector represents value added to the Foundation. I base this upon the following:

- My experience in securities accounting, clearance and custody, where virtually 100% of your assets and revenues reside, is critical to your organization.
- My review of the Marwick Report on its review of the Comptroller's Office very interestingly included recommendations identical to the initial conclusions I drew from some of the specifics we discussed Thursday.
- The cultural changes you are introducing represent concepts ingrained in me. My experience in the for-profit sector would nicely complement, support and help expedite your initiatives to become more businesslike in your operations.
- My independent research on foundation accounting, primarily at The Foundation Center, illustrated the striking similarity in the Statements on Financial Accounting Standards and the Statements on Financial Accounting Concepts between the two sectors.
- My in-depth study of the Foundation's Annual Report assured me that the differences in accounting and financial reporting between the two sectors are insignificant. My conversation with Mark Klein, Senior Manager at Ernst & Young, confirmed my conclusion.

I have a very positive feel for the Foundation, its philanthropic work, its infrastructure and its personnel practices, both in general terms and as it would affect me directly.

Harvey, I believe that the Foundation and I are ideally suited for each other. My broad managerial and technical expertise is needed for the immediate tasks at hand but will also be of value in your other areas of responsibility. My experience in operating in a decentralized environment has honed my decision-making skills and my ability to interface with others at all levels.

I am looking forward to your favorable decision.

Very truly yours,

John H. Norton

when he has decided. Actually, then it will probably be too late for you. His thinking is constantly evolving as he meets with people. You were already out of the running. *Your call did nothing to influence his thinking*: You did not address his new concerns. You asked for a status report of where he was in the hiring process, and that's what you got. You did nothing to get back into the loop of people he might consider, or find out the new issues that are now on his mind.

> *Oh I could show my prowess,*
> *be a lion not a mou-esse,*
> *if I only had the nerve.*
> The Cowardly Lion in the movie *The Wizard of Oz*
> (from the book by L. Frank Baum)
> by E. Y. Harburg and Harold Arlen

The manager meets more people, and further defines the position. Interviewing helps him decide what he wants. You are getting further and further away from his new requirements.

You are not aware of this. You remember the great meeting you two had. You remind me that he said he really liked you. You insist on freezing that moment in time. You don't want to do anything to rock the boat or appear desperate. You hope it works out. "The ball is in his court," you say. "I gave it my best. There's nothing I can do but wait." So you decide to give it more time . . . time to go wrong.

> Annie: . . . *you want to give it time—*
> Henry: *Yes—*
> Annie: . . . *time to go wrong, change, spoil. Then you'll know it wasn't the real thing.*
> Tom Stoppard, *The Real Thing*

You have to imagine what is going on as time passes. Perhaps the hiring manager is simply very busy and is not working on this at all. Or perhaps things are moving along without you. Statistics prove that the person who is interviewed last has the best chance of being hired. That's because the last person benefits from all the thinking the manager has done. The manager is able to discuss all of the issues of concern with this final applicant.

What You Can Do During the Interview

If you go into an interview with the goal of getting a job, you are putting too much pressure on yourself to come to closure. When you walk away without an offer, you feel discouraged. When you walk away without even knowing what the job is, you feel confused and lost.

> *Boone smiled and nodded. The muscles in his jaw hurt. "What I meant was did you ever shoot anybody but your own self. Not that that don't count."*
> Pete Dexter, *Deadwood*

Instead of criticizing managers who do not know what they want, try to understand them: "I can understand that there are a number of ways you can structure this position. Let's talk about your problems and your needs. Perhaps I can help."

Your goal in the interview is not to get an offer, but to build a relationship with the manager. This means you are on the manager's side—assessing the situation, and figuring out how to move the process along so you can continue to help define the job.

Pay Attention to Your Competition

Most job hunters think only about themselves and the hiring manager. They don't think about the others being considered for the position. But you are different. You are acutely aware at all times that you have competition. Your goal is to get rid of them.

As you move the process along, you can see your competitors dropping away because you are doing a better job of addressing the hiring manager's needs, coming up with solutions to his problems, and showing more interest and more competence than they are.

You are in a problem-solving mode. Here's the way you think: "My goal isn't to get a job immediately, but to build a relationship. How can I build a relationship so that someday when this person decides what he or she wants, it'll be me?" You have hung in there. You have eliminated your competition. You have helped define the job in a way that suits both you and the hiring manager. You have the option of saying, "Do I want this job or don't I?"

The Five O'Clock Club®

Follow-Up Checklist: Turning Job Interviews into Offers

D o you want a job? Follow-up is the only technique that influences the person who interviewed you. You may *think* you can get a job through a search firm, answering an ad, networking, or directly contacting a company. But what you are getting is *interviews* in your target area. You are not job hunting yet. You prove your mettle by seeing how—over the long run—you can turn each interview into a job. *Now* you're job hunting. And that's where follow-up comes in.

Remember, you generally don't want a job offer at that first meeting. An easy hire decision may mean an easy fire decision later. Instead, establish a long-term relationship. It is not unusual to be brought in for anywhere from three to nine or more interviews.

Biblical waiting,
the kind of waiting Abram and Sarai did,
and which you and I must learn to do,
is a very active kind of waiting.
It's a faith-journey; the waiting of a pilgrimage.
We can only wait for God to give us what we cannot do
ourselves; but, paradoxically, we must move toward it
in faith as we wait, asking, seeking and knocking . . . .
Ben Patterson, *Waiting*

Waiting is not just the thing we have to
do until we get what we hoped for.
Waiting is part of the process of
becoming what we hope for.
Ben Patterson, *Waiting*

We are what we repeatedly do. Excellence, then,
is not an act, but a habit.
Aristotle

In the last chapter, you read a few examples of job hunters turning job interviews into offers. They had to think hard about what to do next. They objectively and methodically analyzed *all* the interviews they had and developed strategies for addressing every issue for *each* person with whom they met. They thought about who their likely competitors were, and what the hiring managers probably preferred. Who are your likely competitors? How do you stack up against them? Prove you're better than they are, or you won't get the job.

> **Follow-up**
> **will dramatically increase**
> **the number of job offers you get.**
> **It is one of the most powerful tools you**
> **have to influence the situation.**

Why Bother with Follow-Up?
Follow-up can be used:
- to influence both the decision-makers and the influencers.
- to move things along.
- to show interest and competence.
- to knock out your competition.
- to reassure the hiring manager.
- to turn a losing situation into a winning one.
- to make it difficult for them to reject you.
- to set the right tone/buy yourself time after you are hired.

In a tight market, follow-up helps. But still *strive to have six to ten contacts in the works at all times.* The job you are interviewing for may vanish: The manager may decide not to hire at all, or hire a finance instead of a marketing person. There may be a hiring freeze, or a major reorganization. Follow-up techniques will generally not help in these situations. If you are in a competitive market, put extra effort into those job possibilities that are still alive.

Nothing is more dangerous than an idea
when it is the only one you have.
Emile Chartier

And if you have lots of other contacts in the works, you will be less likely to allow yourself to be abused by hiring managers trying to take advantage of "desperate" job hunters. You can assess ridiculous requests and be more willing to walk away.

The Interview Record is a checklist of items to consider in assessing your interviews and planning your follow-up. Try to remember everything that happened at each of your meetings. Many job hunters take notes during the interviews so they will do a better follow-up. After all, wouldn't a consultant take notes during a meeting? How else can you remember all the important issues that come up? At the very least, take notes immediately after the meeting. Some job hunters keep track of every person with whom they met by using the Interview Record. Make plenty of copies of the form for your job search. Keep them in a folder or a three-ring binder, in alphabetical order within target area.

Assess the Interview(s)

Anyone who fears effort, anyone who backs off from frustration and possibly even pain will never get anywhere.
Erich Fromm

Anyone who listens well takes notes.
Dante

Effective follow-up depends on knowing what happened in the interview. In fact, you will begin to interview very differently now. You now know you are there to gather enough information so you can follow up, and to give enough information back so the interviewer will be willing to meet with you again. As your counselor, I'd want the following background information:

- How did it go? What did they say? What did you say?
- How many people did you see?
- How much time did you spend with each?
- What role does each of them play?
- Who is important?
- Who is the hiring manager?

- Who is the decision-maker?
- Who most *influences* the decision?
- Who else did you meet (secretaries, receptionists, bosses from other areas)? How influential might they be? (Do not dismiss them too readily. They may be more influential than you think. A trusted secretary, for example, has a lot of influence. She had better want you there.)
- How quickly do they want to decide? A year? Months? Next week?
- What do you have to offer that your competition doesn't?
- What problems did the interviewer have? Do you have any solutions to those problems?
- How badly do you want this job? (If you want it a lot, you will be more likely to do what you need to do to get it. Or perhaps someone wants it more than you. *That* person will do the things he or she needs to do to get the job.)

The key to being a strategic player is to be in play, working on a significant level.
Thomas Krens, Director,
The Guggenheim Museum,
The New York Times, May 29, 1988

Follow Up with *Each* Person

There is a tide in the affairs of men,
Which, taken at the flood, leads on to fortune;
Omitted, all the voyage of their life
Is bound in shallows and in miseries.
William Shakespeare
Julius Caesar, IV, iii

For *each* person with whom you interviewed, analyze and craft a follow-up note which takes into account:

- **the tone of the conversation**. Was it friendly? Formal? Family-like? Follow up with a similar tone.

- **the positives about you.** Why would this person want you there? If you interviewed with

Whoever loves discipline loves knowledge,
but he who hates correction is stupid.
Proverbs 12:1

peers, why would they want you on the team? In the interview, it is *your* job to make sure each person you meet can see the benefit of having you on board.

- **the objections to you**—for *each* person you met, whether or not these objections were expressed. For example, you may know that the company typically hires someone with a background that is different from yours, or you may not have certain experience it is looking for, or your past salary may be too high, or it may see you as overqualified. A future peer may see you as a threat (let that peer know you are not) or think you will not fit in. You may be seen as too old or too young or too something else. If you think the company is worried about having you on board for some reason, address that reason. For example, if someone sees you as too old, think of the benefits that come with age. Then you might say, "I hope you are interested in hiring someone with maturity and a broad base of experience."

Even in a highly controlled meeting, there is a lot . . .
going on. The real process of making decisions,
of gathering support, of developing opinions, happens
before the meeting—or after.
Terrence E. Deal and Allan A. Kennedy,
Corporate Cultures

Many job hunters want to ignore or gloss over the objections; instead, pay attention to why *each* person may not want you there. Joel DeLuca, Ph.D., author of *Political Savvy*, noted that if you are observant, you should come out of a meeting with a good sense of how hard a sell this is going to be, as well as some idea of the political lay of the land.

If [a man] is brusque in his manner,
others will not cooperate. If he is agitated in his words,
they will awaken no echo in others. If he asks for
something without having first established a proper
relationship, it will not be given to him.
I Ching

- **the key issues**. Was the interviewer concerned about interdepartmental relationships? Work overload? The political situation with a key

vendor? How you will support people in other areas? How you can make his or her job easier? What makes you different from your competition? Identify those issues that are key to the interviewer(s).

- **your feelings about the job**. If this is the one place you really want to work, say so. If you would enjoy working with your prospective manager and peers, say so. **At the executive level, most decisions are based on fit.** In addition to competence, people want someone they'd *like* to work with and someone who *wants* to work with them. Write with enthusiasm. Let your personality come through.

- **the next steps**. Regardless of *who* should take the next steps, what exactly are the next logical steps? What will move the process along?

The average sale is made after the prospect
has said "no" six times.
Jeffrey P. Davidson, marketing consultant
The Washington Post, May 20, 1985

For example, the next step could be:
- another meeting to discuss something in greater detail.
- meeting(s) with other people.
- another meeting after the other candidates have been interviewed.
- an in-depth review of documents.
- discussing a few of your ideas with them.
- drafting a proposal about how you would handle a certain area.

Let him who wants to move and convince
others be first moved and convinced himself.
Thomas Carlyle

State the "next steps" in your follow-up note. For example, "I'd like to get together with you to discuss my ideas on . . ." or "If I don't hear from George in a week or so, I'll give you a call."

If you were the first person interviewed, try to be interviewed again. "As you interview others, you may more clearly define what you want. I would appreciate the opportunity to address the new issues that may arise."

Influence the Influencers

Progress always involves risk.
You can't steal second base and keep your foot on first.
Frederick B. Wilcox

Success seems to be largely a matter of
hanging on after others have let go.
William Feather

Most job hunters pay attention to the hiring manager and ignore everyone else. However, most hiring managers want the input of others. You may be rejected if a future peer or subordinate says that you seem difficult to work with, or the receptionist complains that you were rude to her. Remember that everyone is an influencer. *Follow up with everyone you met formally.* Cultivate as many advocates as you can. Have people inside rooting for you. It's better if your future peers, for example, say that you would be great to have on the team. You can influence the influencers with a letter or phone call.

Who might *influence* the hiring decision? **If they are future co-workers, follow the analysis in "Follow Up With *Each* Person" above.** Tell outside influencers the position in which you are interested and why, and how they can help you.

Joe, a well-known top-level executive, felt one of his interviews went very well, but he was afraid the interviewer would tap into the corporate pipeline and hear untrue negative rumors about him. Joe has two choices: He can hope the interviewer doesn't hear the rumors, or he can fight for the job he deserves.

Joe has to try to control the pipeline—the key influencers in this situation. First, Joe called some influential people who thought well of him and who the hiring manager would respect. He stated why he wanted this job, and asked them to put in a good word for him. Second, Joe thought of the people the hiring manager was most likely to run into or call for information. Joe called them next and did his best to influence them to support him. Joe successfully fended off bad reports and landed the job he wanted.

Be in Sync with Their Timing

Even if you're on the right track,
you'll get run over if you just sit there.
Will Rogers

Move the process along to the next step, but at *the interviewer's* pace, not yours. The timing depends on the personality of the interviewer and his or her sense of urgency.

If the situation is urgent, write your letter overnight, and hand-deliver it in the morning. If the manager is laid back, an urgent delivery is inappropriate.

Use your judgment. If things are going along at a good clip, and you are being brought in every other day, you may want to let it ride *if* you think you have no competition.

Also be aware that if things are *not* moving along quickly, it may have nothing to do with you. It may well be that the interviewer is not doing *anything* about filling the position—he or she may be busy with other business. If you were the hiring manager, you would find that you can't work on the hire every minute, because you have your regular job to do, and emergencies come up as well.

If you have no idea what is going on, it would help if you've formed a good relationship with the hiring manager's secretary. Then you could call and say, "Hi, Jane. This is Joe. I was wondering if you could help me with something. I haven't heard from Ellis [her boss] for two weeks and I had expected to hear something by now. I was going to drop him a note, but I didn't want to bother him if he's really busy. I was wondering if he's still interviewing other people or if he's just been tied up, or what." Who knows what she'll say? But if she says he had a death in the family and has been out of town, that gives you some idea of what is happening. He is not sitting around talking about you all day long. He is doing other things, and the hiring process often moves more slowly than you think.

Understanding is a wellspring of life
to him that hath it.
Proverbs 16:22

Sometimes I go off on a tangent, but I follow my intuitions and if it doesn't work, it doesn't matter. There's no such thing as failure; you just learn from it and go on.
David Hockney (from the audiocassette: David Hockney: A Retrospective, Metropolitan Museum of Art, July 1988

How Can You Tell If a Follow-Up Letter Is a Good One?

There is no such thing as "soft sell" or "hard sell."
There is only "smart sell" and "stupid sell."
Charles Bower, President, BBD&O
Editor & Publisher, December 7, 1957

A good letter is *tailored* to the situation. It would be impossible to send it to someone other than the addressee. *It sells you, separates you from your competition, addresses all issues and objections, and states a next step.* Finally, its tone *replicates* the tone of the interview (or creates a good tone if the interview wasn't so good). For example, John's various follow-up notes to those he met at the Kennedy Foundation addressed each manager's issues.

Your letters to some people will be very detailed and meticulous. These may take you half a day to write. For others, you will write a simple letter saying that you thought they would be great to work with, and addressing the issues they brought up.

Most job hunters err, however, when they assume someone who is lower-level has no influence. Be careful about whom you dismiss. During the interview, try to pick up on the relationships between people. In brief, remember to influence the influencers. Write notes to prospective peers you have met. They have some say in the hiring decision—maybe a lot of say. If they don't want you, you might not get hired. For each person you met, think of why he or she would want you there. What do you bring to the party? Make sure you are not a threat. Overcome his or her objections. Address any issues raised. Use the tone set in the interview.

A job hunter, Philip, put a lot of thought into his follow-up with *a prospective peer*, Jonathan. Philip considered Jonathan an important influencer, and had noted the following from their meeting:

- Philip sensed that Jonathan was worried about losing his standing as the second-in-command to George, the hiring manager, when the new person came in.

- He was also concerned that the new person might not be a team player or a hard worker, or might not be willing to help out with his special projects, which involved computer simulations.

- He was concerned about losing the camaraderie in the department, and hoped the new person would have a good sense of humor to offset the stress of working under deadline.

- He was obviously trying to conduct a very professional interview, and asked Philip a number of times what he thought of the questions.

- He was relieved when Philip said he would enjoy developing materials for the department, although it was not central to the job. This is a project none of the other competitors would be able to handle.

- He wondered about the department's reputation outside the company.

The conversation had been light and friendly. Philip considered Jonathan to be the key influencer, and thought George, the hiring manager, would be making the decision with Jonathan. Philip wrote to each of his prospective peers and also to George. This is the letter he wrote to Jonathan:

Dear Jonathan:

I was glad finally to have a chance to meet you. George had spoken of you so proudly, I knew you had earned everything you've gotten at Bluekill and have worked very hard. I, too, am a hard worker, and I know we would complement each other.

I liked your professional approach to the interview, and found your questions and direction quite interesting. I hope I "did okay." I believe I could work out a schedule to accommodate your many projects—and one thing you can count on is that I'm good at developing computer simulations. In my last position, I was considered the best, and would enjoy doing the same for you. I work very hard at it, and it pays off.

My impression is that George depends on you a lot, and perhaps I could help out also. I think I could develop materials that could be used both inside and with customers, and I will be glad to hear your ideas on the matter. I've developed a great deal of material in the past that I will be happy to show you.

All things considered, I think I would make a good addition to the group, and I believe you and I would enjoy working together. As I said to you when we met, I've worked in a few companies, and I do my best to make every place I work as enjoyable as it can be. Your sense of humor surely helps, and I'm sure mine will also.

Cordially,
Philip Johnson

Time passed. Philip met again with George and with other peers. But he was concerned about whether Jonathan would still be in favor of him in light of the number of additional applicants Jonathan had met by then. Philip decided to contact Jonathan again, this time more informally. In reviewing his notes, he fixed on what Jonathan had said about the reputation of the department. Philip then arranged a networking meeting with an important person in the industry so he would have something to contact Jonathan about. The information would also help him make up his mind in case he received a job offer. Then he wrote on informal stationery:

Dear Jonathan,

In our meeting, you wondered about the reputation of your department. I'm sure you will be happy to hear, as I was, that your department is thought of as the best in the industry. I met with Cheryl Jenkins yesterday and she raved about each person in your group—including you. You should be proud of her commendation, and I admit that I was proud as well because I sincerely hope I wind up working with you.

I mentioned to you that I would be happy to show you the computer simulation materials I have developed in the past. I have finally put them together, and will call you to see if you still want to look at them. It shouldn't take more than fifteen minutes of your time.

Hope all is well.

Best regards,
Philip

Sometimes an important influencer is the best way to sway the hiring manager. Philip got the job, but he got much more: He started the job with a very good relationship with each of the people with whom he would be working. When you analyze what is important to each person, you not only increase your chances of getting the job, you increase your chances of having the new job go smoothly.

> **Discuss your follow-up problems with your private Five O'Clock Club coach or at Five O'Clock Club meetings. Make the effort required to develop strategies for your follow-up moves. It's worth the trouble.**
>
> **As one Five O'Clock Clubber advised, "Make sure the follow-up letter you write is absolutely the best the company will see—or don't write it." Be sure to read the follow-up case studies in this book.**

The
Five
O'Clock
Club®

Job Interview Follow-Up:
Sample Letters

Influence belongs to men of action, and for purposes of action nothing is more useful than narrowness of thought combined with energy of will.
Henri Frédéric Amiel, *Journal intime*

Motivation will almost always beat mere talent.
Norman R. Augustine, *Augustine's Laws*

Method is much, technique is much, but inspiration is even more.
Benjamin Nathan Cardoza,
U.S. Supreme Court Justice, *Law and Literature*

The fearful Unbelief is unbelief in yourself.
Thomas Carlyle, *Sartor Resartus*

We are perplexed but not in despair.
New Testament, II Corinthians 4:8

It is better to wear out than to rust out.
Richard Cumberland, 1632 - 1718
Bishop of Peterborough, Attributed

To him that will, ways are not wanting.
George Herbert, *Jacula Prudentum*

It is fatal to enter any war without the will to win it.
Douglas MacArthur, Speech to the Republican National Convention, July 7, 1952

> **Job follow-ups are not merely "thank you" notes. Your primary goal is not to *thank* the interviewer, but to *influence* him or her.**

How can you tell whether a follow-up letter is a good one?

A good letter is <u>tailored</u> to the situation. It would be impossible to send it to someone other than the addressee. It <u>sells the writer, separates the writer from the competition, addresses all issues and objections, and states a next step</u>. Finally, its <u>tone replicates the tone of the interview</u> (or creates a good tone if the interview wasn't so good).

For example . . .
Look at the follow-up letter on the next page.

Paragraph 1:
- talks about the next steps.
- separates me from the competition: They're talking about counseling, but I'm trying to offer something additional—the development of program materials.

Paragraph 2:
- handles an objection: Would I enjoy working with this kind of client?

Paragraphs 3 & 4:
- another objection: Would I be too independent in the job, (or would I listen to my boss)?

Paragraph 5:
- another objection: Why hire a strong, older person when someone with less experience would do?

Paragraph 6:
- recalls the camaraderie of the interview.

Note: Most objections are unstated. You have to notice them for yourself based on the questions at the interview or your assessment of who your competition is likely to be. Also be aware of tone, facial expression, and body language.

M. Catherine Wendleton

163 York Avenue - 12B
New York, New York 10000
(212) 555-2231 (day)
(212) 555-1674 (message)

July 18, 20xx

Ms. Joy Muench
Director of Outplacement
RightBank
100 Madison Avenue
New York, NY 10000

Dear Joy:

Now I've met everyone in your group, and I'll be glad to get together with you again. I can see how carefully you have parcelled out your assignments to each person. I can also see where I would fit in—something we can discuss in more detail when we get together. I certainly am expert in developing program materials, and will be happy to show you things I have done in that area.

In general, I enjoy the type of client you get at RightBank because a good deal of my approach is business-oriented and based on business systems and logic. That is essentially the way I operate with people from other banks as well as from the Big 8 accounting firms. These people tend to be self-motivated and direct, and I like that. They tend to not want to be psychoanalzed too much, and that's fine with me. I'm all for getting on with it.

On the other hand, I believe I can learn a lot from you, and am looking forward to the opportunity to do so. I am even planning to join the Jung Foundation, and visited there for the first time today.

I know you are in a delicate position dealing with the RightBank corporate problems, and I do understand the difficulties of your job. For most of my career, I have worked for Senior Management. All of my bosses have been able to count on me to see what needs to be done, to do it, and to work smoothly with the rest of the organization. I have a lot of ideas, but I also follow through on them, and know how to get the willing cooperation of others.

I hope you are looking to hire a strong person—one you can depend on to carry out your vision as well as add to it—a person with maturity and strong corporate experience as well as one who is a solid counselor and good at running a small business—which is what you are trying to do. I look forward to helping you and will do more than my share to support you.

I hope you have a wonderful vacation, and I can't tell you how jealous I am. I've never had two weeks together in my life.

I'll see you when you get back. Don't think about all of this.

Cheers,

Follow-Up After a Job Interview

Influence the Influencers.
These are <u>notes to prospective peers</u> for the job on the preceeding page.
They have some say in the hiring decision. Maybe a *lot* of say. Make sure your follow-up letters influence them. If they don't want you, you might not get hired. Write to *each* person with whom you interviewed. For each, think of <u>why they would want you there</u>. What's in it for them? What do you bring to the party? Make sure you are not a threat to them. Overcome their objections. Address any issues raised.
Use the tone set in the interview.

M. Catherine Wendleton

Dear Carolyn:

I was glad to finally have a chance to meet you. Sandy had spoken of you so proudly, she made me proud too. I can see that you've earned everything you've gotten at RightBank and have worked very hard. I too am a hard worker, and I know we would complement each other.

I liked your professional approach to the interview, and your questions and direction were quite interesting to me as a professional. I hope I "did OK." I believe I could work out a schedule to accommodate your needs in the group training area—and one thing you can count on is that I'm <u>good</u> at it. I believe I was the favorite counselor at JC Penney—which was essentially all group work. I put a lot of effort into it, and I got rave reviews.

My impression is that Sandy depends on you a lot, and perhaps I could help out also. I could develop materials that could be used in the group as well as in the individual program, and I will be glad to hear your ideas on the matter. I've developed a great deal of material in the past that I will be happy to show you.

All things considered, I think I would make a happy addition to the group, and I believe you and I would enjoy working together. As I said to you when we met, I've been around, and I certainly do my best to make every place I work as enjoyable as it can be. Your sense of humor surely helps, and I'm sure mine will also.

Cordially,
Kate Wendleton

M. Catherine Wendleton

July 18, 20xx

Dear Peter:

It certainly was a pleasure meeting you. You add a lot of humor and a lot of ability to the place. All things considered, I think I would make a happy addition to the group, and I believe you and I would enjoy working together. I believe you are a person I would turn to to broaden my expertise in the area of evaluation. I would also help you out with the reception area, as I can see that is one of your major duties. (Just kidding.)

Sandy said she would like me to concentrate on the area of materials development—something I have some experience in and would enjoy doing.

I hope you and I will have the opportunity to work together.

Cordially,
Kate

M. Catherine Wendleton

Dear Alan:

I'm glad to have met you. Your smile seems to soften things in the office, and I'm sure we would enjoy working together. I believe I could learn from each person in the group, and I also think I bring a lot to the party. My special assignment from Sandy would be in developing program materials—something that is right up my alley.

All things considered, I think I would make a happy addition to the group. As I said to you when we met, I certainly do my best to make every place I work as enjoyable as possible. Your attitude surely helps in that area, and I'm sure mine will also.

Cordially,
Kate Wendleton

Psalm 23

The Lord is my shepherd, I shall not want.

He makes me lie down in green pastures;
He leads me beside quiet waters.
He restores my soul;
He guides me in the paths of righteousness
For His name's sake.

Even though I walk through the valley of the
shadow of death, I fear no evil; for Thou art with me;
Thy rod and Thy staff, they comfort me.

Thou dost prepare a table before me
in the presence of my enemies;
Thou hast anointed my head with oil;
My cup overflows.

Surely goodness and lovingkindness will follow me
all the days of my life,
And I will dwell in the house of the Lord forever.

The most overlooked part of job follow-up is the statement of next steps. It is *your* responsibility to make sure the process is moved along to the next step.

For example, if they say they'll call you in a week, you can say: If I don't hear from you in a week or so, I'll give you a call."

Don't be surprised if they don't call: Everyone is very busy, and you are probably not at the top of their list. Gently move them along—within *their* time frame—in your follow-up note.

> Although this note is short, it still contains a strategy for moving this process along to the next step.

Penelope Webb

To: Wally Dobbs

I enjoyed our conversation last week. Your need to modernize and integrate existing systems, and to make them flexible enough to accommodate future opportunities such as the repeal of Glass-Steagall, certainly sounds like an intriguing challenge.

I appreciate your suggestion that I meet with some of the people in your group, and would like very much to talk with you further. I'll call you in a few days to set something up.

Best regards,
Penny

The
Five
O'Clock
Club®

Follow-Up After a
Job Interview

Renée Rosenberg

Street Address
City, State, Zip
(555) 555-2231

July 18, 20xx

Mr. Roy Cohen
General Counsel and Senior Vice President
Valentino
100 Madison Avenue
New York, NY 10000

> Applying to be Assistant General Counsel.
> The hiring manager
> considers the "family environment" crucial.

Dear Roy:

The opportunity to meet and speak with you last week was a real pleasure. It is clear to me that Valentino offers the close, family environment and real team feeling that I so much enjoyed at Campeau. Since we were great friends there, we were very supportive of each other as colleagues and the experience was one of the most rewarding I have had. I know that I would feel equally at home at Valentino, as the chemistry seems right for me.

It also seems that my 20 years' experience with Fortune 20 companies in the fashion/retail industry, both as a merchant and as a legal executive, could not be more ideally suited for heading up your new leather division.

In addition, after talking with you, I can't imagine a legal background that's a better fit:
   • Extensive marketing law experience (and Valentino is a "marketing-driven" company);

> During the interview,
> she convinced him to
> hire a legal generalist.
> But just in case he
> wants a specialist,
> she's covered.

   • Litigation (both actual practice and complex management);
   • Environmental compliance (set up a $40 million program);
   • Commercial contracts (UCC Article 2);
   • Antitrust compliance;
   • Responsibility for a worldwide trademark program
     (with 200 domestic and 70 foreign registrations in 35 countries);
   • Licensing arrangements; and,
   • Legislative matters (we do need to do something about grey market matters).

> Can you handle
> these young,
> unmanageable
> clients? Yes, I can.
> And I also work
> well with the top
> brass.

Finally, I enjoy working with the type of client you have: young, innovative, creative people who have an enthusiasm and eagerness to get the job done quickly. I appreciate their creativity because I am a creative person myself. Since I have a business background (which most attorneys do not have), I also empathize with their desire to get on with things—but in their eagerness important issues may be overlooked. I'm able to bring to bear on those issues (business as well as legal), yet encourage their initiative and still protect the company from any unwarranted liability or exposure.

Of course, I'm also experienced in working with Senior Management. At Campeau I advised them on a daily basis and understand the type of advice appropriate at that level.

I'm very excited about being part of the team you are building. I just know that it would prove to be a mutually rewarding experience. I look forward to getting together with you again. As you meet other candidates, other issues may arise, and I would appreciate the opportunity to address them. In the meantime I will keep you apprised of any new developments in my search.

Cordially,

The
Five
O'Clock
Club®

Follow-Up After a
Job Interview

*In the realm of ideas, everything
depends on enthusiasm;
in the real world,
all rests on perseverance.*
Goethe

---

*All right, I hated the job. You're
right: I admit it. I'm glad to be
done with it—all right!*
Peter Schaeffer, *Lettice & Lovage*

---

*The mode by which the inevitable
is reached is effort.*
Felix Frankfurter

A Few Hints

1. This note and the one on the following page were written after a job interview. This one is to personnel, while the other is to the hiring manager.

The strategy is to keep personnel informed (and perhaps have them as an advocate), but to **"do the deal" with the hiring manager**.

2. It's rare that a job offer is made after the first interview. In fact, you don't want an offer that early in the process. Therefore, think of what would be required next to move the process along so it *could* turn into a job offer.

What logically do you think should happen next? For example, should you meet with another department or division head to get more information? Should you come up with a few ideas and meet again with this manager? Think it through. Take a look at the other letters in this section to see how other job hunters handled the follow up. **It's your responsibility to think of what is needed next and to make it happen.**

Nancy Friedberg

March 24, 20xx

Dear Kim:

I enjoyed the chance to meet with you and discuss American Express. I also found John to be a very dynamic and stimulating individual.

The position we discussed requires a combination of creative, strategic thinking and hard-nosed, practical, get-it-done skills. I think it would be a very good fit for my abilities and experience, and would be the most stimulating and exciting thing that I have ever done.

Thus I would like to meet with John again. I suggested to him that we discuss one region's business in depth, to better understand the key business issues and opportunities, and give him a clearer sense of how I would approach them.

I look forward to hearing from you.

Sincerely,

Nancy

Nancy Friedberg

March 24, 20xx

Dear Bob:

I greatly enjoyed the chance to meet with you and learn about the structure and needs of your business.

It became increasingly clear to me that the position we discussed would be a good fit for my skills and interests. You are confronted with a complex mosaic of regional businesses, with very different profit dynamics, competitive situations and broker/customer relationships. Major variations in regional economic trends and industry structures make this situation even more complex.

Thus you clearly need someone who can quickly develop an understanding of each regional business, and of the needs and goals of the profit centers, and then <u>visualize</u> opportunities that this creates. These could take the form of improved marketing or product development programs against current businesses, or innovative plans for the new industries and market segments that will emerge as the regional economies develop.

I think that this is consistent with my strongest skills. I am a quick study and a good strategic thinker who can digest a lot of complex information and build a coherent, actionable structure from it. I am also very good at sensing marketing opportunities and creating unique ways to capitalize on them. My broad-based marketing background provides a wide range of ideas and experience to draw from. At the same time, line management assignments in the branches have tempered my "visionary" thinking with a hard-nosed practical approach and an appreciation for the day-to-day realities of running a business.

For these reasons, I think the assignment we discussed would be more exciting and intellectually stimulating than anything I have ever done. Thus I would like very much to talk more about it.

As a next step, it might be valuable to discuss one region in some depth, reviewing American Express's current business, broker and customer relations, competitive factors and economic trends in the market. This would allow me to give you a clearer sense of how I would actually identify opportunities and develop programs against them, and would give me a more detailed understanding of the key opportunities and problems faced by your business.

I think this discussion could be of value to both of us, and I look forward to meeting with you again.

Sincerely,

Nancy

James Borland

Street Address
City, State
(212) 555-2231

May 10, 20xx

Mr. David Yegerlehner
Senior Vice President
United Way of Tristate
Street Address
City, State, Zip

Dear David:

First of all, thank you for giving me the opportunity to speak with you last week. It was really a pleasure for me to meet you, and I appreciated learning about the goals and needs of the Unted Way of Tristate from your perspective and experience.

Because of our discussion I am even more eager to pursue finding a place for myself in the planning, management, and support of human-care services. I am encouraged that there might be such an opportunity for me within the United Way of Tristate.

I spent some time reading the materials you gave me and am especially impressed with the Strategic Plan. I believe that I have skills, experience, and motivations that would be instrumental in the successful implementation of the Plan, for example:

- strong quantitative skills: conducting research, financial, and technical information analyses.
- experience in developing and assessing marketing plans and strategies for diverse target markets.
- problem-solving ability that is challenged by new and continually varied situations.
- excellent oral and written communication skills, with experience in delivering presentations to top-level corporate executives.
- enthusiasm for the mission of United Way.

I welcome and appreciate the effort you are making to explore the possibilities for me within your organization. I would like to stay in touch with you during this time, and would be pleased to meet again for additional discussions.

Thank you for your support. I'm looking forward to hearing from you when you have more information about your situation and its potential for me.

Sincerely,

James Borland

Robert Riscica
Glen Ridge Cove
San Francisco, CA 66666

April 15, 200x

Ms. Sara Lohaus
Technology Planning Division
Bank of America
One Pickalilly Square-40th Floor
San Francisco, CA 66620

> **This is a logical format to follow. Each issue identified in the interview process becomes a paragraph heading.**

Dear Sara,

Your department is an impressive one. I remain very interested in the position we discussed, and think that the following elements of my skills and relevant experience would serve me well in accomplishing your objectives:

Project Management
My responsibilities as <u>Project Director</u> at General Dynamics included collecting data from a project team comprised of accounting and technology professionals and <u>writing comprehensive functional specifications</u> for a new front-end interface to the General Ledger System. I also prepared and gave periodic progress presentations to a steering committee comprised of senior bank executives.

Computer Systems/Technology Exposure
Throughout my career, I have had close involvement with technology professionals, most significantly:
- at <u>Bank of America,</u> particularly in my most recent position as Project Manager where I was involved in the conversion of the community banks to B of A's "Utility" systems;
- at <u>General Dynamics,</u> as mentioned above and as an <u>Accounting Systems Liaison</u> where I was responsible for ensuring adherence to bankwide accounting standards in the development of new application systems;
- at <u>Wells Fargo,</u> where I was directly involved in the detailed evaluation of new General Ledger software vs. Wells' older, in-house developed package;
- at <u>Walt Disney Co.</u>, where I reviewed and approved new application systems for inclusion of effective audit controls.

Finance
My experience as Regional Financial Controller for B of A's West Region corporate business units and that as a Business Manager within the former National Corporate Division required a thorough understanding of global finance products and services.

In business, willingness is just as important as ability.
Paul C. Hoffman

Training
In my most recent position at Bank of America (Project Manager), I provided extensive training via "Hands-on" workshops in the use of automated Proof Collection/Clearance to employees in retail business units nationally. I also prepared training materials and developed test procedures for use in connection with training exercises.

PC Skills/Lotus Notes
I have extensive PC skills and experience at developing PC based applications for general use:
- As Controller for B of A in San Francisco, I developed a <u>PFS database application</u> which tracked premises receivable and billed all tenants for rent and other costs.
- As Business Manager for Corporate Finance Analysis, I developed comprehensive <u>Paradox databases</u> to control Personnel/Staffing as well as Accounts Payable.

I have a high level of technical proficiency in Lotus Notes based on my intensive self-training efforts over the last few months and, as I mentioned, have a Notes Server and two workstations setup on the computer network which I maintain in my home.

As we discussed, should you select another candidate for the position, I would greatly appreciate consideration for a temporary position involved with Lotus Notes. The benefit of such an arrangement, besides the obvious one of extending my severance period, is that it would provide me the opportunity to contribute to B of A's Notes environment and thereby establish myself as a viable candidate for future Notes-related positions within the bank.

Again, thank you for your interest. I look forward to hearing from you.

Sincerely,

Robert Riscica

Peggy Lumpkin
444 Pound Ridge Road
Dallas, Texas 44444

April 4, 200x

Charles Conlin
Kendall Guaranty Trust Company
666 Brick Wall West
Dallas, Texas 44444-0060

> Here's another approach to organizing your follow-up around the important issues. Of course, Peggy wrote a customized follow-up to every person with whom she met.

Dear Chip,

It was an exciting and eventful day. Thank you for giving me the opportunity. I learned even more about Kendall and training's mission there.

In my view, three issues about me came up during the day's meeting. I wanted to tell you about them.

- There was some concern about my lack of experience with Fortune 500 clients. But I think my experience with a wide range of underwriting and advisory work is more to the point. I know firsthand what it takes to develop a corporate finance opportunity, compete for a mandate and take an issuer to market. I can bring that practical perspective to my work in training, even if I've had relatively few Fortune 500 clients in my recent banking career.

- My job changes understandably drew comments. I realize Kendall is a company where long service is the norm. As you know, I've put a lot of time, thought and effort into this career change, and I'm committed to it and to Kendall as well. You have the kind of challenging standards and defining principles that I found compelling in the Navy and have missed in my work life ever since.

- There may have been some concern about whether I bring to the job a larger vision of training's strategic role. I know from the Navy how crucial corporate values can be to success and how training at all levels can be used to reinforce values. In business, I've been very interested in how General Electric is using values to improve its competitiveness and performance. Aside from that, I've been more focused on corporate finance practice than strategic issues in training.

I hope you had a good time in New Orleans and Natchez. If you have any questions or other concerns I can address, please don't hesitate to call.

Sincerely,

Peggy Lumpkin

JEANNETTE MOBLEY
10 Park Terrace East
Chicago, IL 00007

December 1, 200x

Ms. Ruth Robbins
Vice President - Manager Asset Securitization
Bank of Germany
1211 Bird-in-Cage Way
Chicago, IL 00007

Dear Ruth:

I admired greatly your thoroughness and enthusiasm, and I came away with a good understanding of Bank of Germany's strategies for growing the business in North America. I believe that given Bank of Germany's size and reach worldwide, you could become a major bank in the U.S., and I would like to help you to do that. I have given it a great deal of thought and I have decided that I'd love to work for you and for Bank of Germany.

I believe I could add value to Bank of Germany's asset securitization business in the following ways:

Ability to immediately close deals and also address critical tax accounting issues

Because of my in-depth knowledge of the market, I am able to immediately contribute to closing existing transactions and make necessary marketing calls jointly and separately to build a profile of active deals for 1995 1st quarter closure. I have structured and closed asset securitization deals in the past and I am willing to do the detailed, unexciting, plodding work that it takes to execute the transactions.

Moreover, I am intimately aware of the complicated tax issues facing Bank of Germany as a U.S. branch of a foreign bank.

Superb contacts

Having worked with Fortune 500 companies and foreign banks for over 16 years in project finance, tax leasing, debt and equity placement, lending and structuring corporate finance solutions for multinationals, I am confident that Bank of Germany could become a niche player in several product lines including lead manager for asset secured deals for a select number of corporations. In the past 6 months I have had numerous discussions with several companies and institutional investors, and I have already done the target marketing. These companies place high value on competence, debt rating and execution skills. They would relish working with us and Bank of Germany.

It may be that the race is not always to the swift,
nor the battle to the strong, but that's the way to bet.
Damon Runyon

Broad-based background and cross-sell opportunities

The tax law has changed in the U.S., and it is being modified in Germany. These changes will create tax arbitrage opportunities for German subsidiaries operating in the U.S., since they will be able to avoid loss of interest deductibility.

Given the current legislative environment in both countries, cross-sell opportunities exist for tax leasing, project and trade finance, as well as product enhancements involving derivatives. I believe that my experience in these product areas will be very useful in creating new opportunities for Bank of Germany.

Teamwork

As a small branch of a foreign bank, Bank of Germany seems to have a corporate culture that encourages teamwork and rewards cooperation and results. I have managed groups of people in the U.S. and abroad. I have also worked in the U.S. and overseas, and I am confident that I would fit quite comfortably in your organization.

I would like to continue our discussions, and I look forward to meeting the other members of your organization. I will call you the week of December 11th to follow up for another meeting.

Sincerely,

Jeannette Mobley

The Five O'Clock Club®

Following Up When There Is No Immediate Job

*Contrary to the cliché, genuinely nice guys
most often finish first, or very near it.*
Malcolm Forbes

During each meeting, you have taken up the time of someone who sincerely tried to help you. Writing a note is the only polite thing to do. Since the person has gone to some effort for you, go to some effort in return. A phone call to thank a person can be an intrusion, and shows little effort on your part.

In addition to being polite, there are good business reasons for writing notes and otherwise keeping in touch with people who have helped you. For one thing, few people keep in touch, so you will stand out. Second, it gives you a chance to sell yourself again and to overcome any misunderstandings that may have occurred. Third, this is a promotional campaign, and any good promoter knows that a message reinforced soon after a first message results in added recall.

If you meet someone through a networking interview, for example, he or she will almost certainly forget about you the minute you leave, and just go back to business. Sorry, but you were an interruption.

If you write to people almost immediately after your meeting, this will dramatically increase the chance that they will remember you. If you wait two weeks before writing, they may remember meeting someone, but not remember you specifically. If you wait longer than two weeks, they probably won't remember meeting anyone—let · alone that it was you.

So promptly follow the interview with a note. It is important to remind those to whom you write who you are and when they talked to you. Give some highlight of the meeting. Contact them again within a month or two. It is just like an advertising campaign. Advertisers will often place their ads at least every four weeks in the same publication. If they advertised less often than that, few people would remember the ad.

What Michael Did

This is a classic—and it worked on me. I wanted to hire one junior accountant for a very important project, and had the search narrowed down to two people. I asked my boss for his input. We made up a list of what we were looking for and we each rated the candidates on twenty criteria. The final scores came in very close, but I hired Judy instead of Michael.

In response to my rejection, Michael wrote me a note telling me how much he still wanted to work for our company, and how he hoped I would keep him in mind if something else should come up. He turned the rejection into a positive contact. Notes are so unusual, and this one was so personable, that I showed it to my boss.

A few months later, Michael wrote again saying that he had taken a position with another firm. He was still very much interested in us, and he hoped to work for us someday. He promised to keep in touch, which he did. Each time he wrote, I showed the note to my boss. Each time, we were sorry we couldn't hire him.

After about seven months, I needed another helping hand. Whom do you think I called? Do you think I interviewed other people? Do you think I had to sell Michael to my boss? Michael came to work for us, and we never regretted it. Persistence pays off.

What to Say in Your Follow-Up Note

Depending on the content of your note, you may type or write it. Generally use standard business-size stationery, but sometimes Monarch or other note-size stationery, ivory or white, will do. A *job* interview follow-up should almost always be typed on standard business-size ivory or white stationery.

After an information-gathering interview, play back some of the advice you received, any you intend to follow, and so on. Simply be sincere. What did you appreciate about the time the person spent with you? Did you get good advice that you intend to follow? Say so. Were you inspired? Encouraged? Awakened? Say so.

If you think there were sparks between you and the person with whom you met, be sure to say that you will keep in touch. Then do it. Follow-up letters don't have to be long, but they do have to be personal. Make sure the letters you write could not be sent to someone else on your list.

Sample Follow-Up to a Networking Meeting

Max McCreery

To: Ruth Shapiro

Thanks again for contacting Brendan for me, and for providing all those excellent contact names.

There's such a wealth of good ideas in that list that it will take me awhile to follow up on all of them, but I'm getting hard at it and will let you know what develops.

Again, thanks for your extraordinary effort. (By the way, should you ever want to "review your career options," I would be delighted to share a few names, or more than a few, with you.)

Stay tuned!

Max

To keep in touch, simply let interviewers/network contacts know how you are doing. Tell them whom you are seeing and what your plans are. Some people, seeing your sincerity, will keep sending you leads or other information.

It's never too late to follow up. For example: "I met you a year ago and am still impressed by . . . Since then I have . . . and would be interested in getting together with you again to discuss these new developments." Make new contacts. Recontact old ones by writing a "status report" every two months telling how well you are doing in your search. **Keeping up with old networking contacts is as important as making new ones.**

Some job hunters use this as an opportunity to write a proposal. During the meeting, you may have learned something about the company's problems. Writing a proposal to solve them may create a job for you. Patricia had a networking meeting with a small company where she learned that it wanted to expand the business from $5 million to $50 million. She came up with lots of ideas about how that could be done—with her help, of course—and called to set up a meeting to review her ideas. She went over the proposal with them, and they created a position for her.

However, you are not trying to turn every networking meeting into a job possibility. You *are* trying to form lifelong relationships with people. Experts say that most successful employees form solid relationships with lots of people and keep in touch regularly throughout their careers. These people will keep you up-to-date in a changing economy, tell you about changes or openings in your field, and generally be your long-term ally. And you will do the same for them.

---

*Has a man gained anything who has received
a hundred favors and rendered none?
He is great who confers the most benefits.*
Ralph Waldo Emerson, "Essay on Compensation"

The
Five
O'Clock
Club®

PART FIVE

THE FIVE O'CLOCK CLUB APPROACH TO SALARY NEGOTIATION

A FOUR-STEP STRATEGY

The Five O'Clock Club®

Four-Step Salary Negotiation Strategy

I've got all the money I'll ever need if I die by four o'clock.
Henny Youngman

There arises from the hearts of busy [people] a love of variety, a yearning for relaxation of thought as well as of body, and a craving for a generous and spontaneous fraternity.
J. Hampton Moore
History of The Five O'Clock Club, written in the 1890s

Now you know you not only have to impress the hiring manager, but also other influencers so they will want to have you on board. In addition, you have to think about your likely competitors, and how you can convince everyone you meet that you are the best choice. During the interview, a job hunter may also think about salary.

When job hunters ask about salary negotiation, they usually want to know how to answer the questions What are you making now? and What are you looking for? We'll cover these issues in detail a little later, but it is more important to first look at salary negotiation from a strategic point of view. From the very first meeting, you can set the stage for compensation discussions later.

Most job hunters think about salary—unconsciously and anxiously—during their first meeting. They think, I'm making $50,000 now (or $150,000), but I know this person won't pay more than $35,000 (or $135,000). Most job hunters try to get rid of the anxiety. They don't want to waste their time if this person isn't going to pay them fairly. So when the hiring manager mentions money, the job hunter is relieved to talk about it.

Hiring manager: How much are you making now?
Job hunter: I'm making $50,000.
Hiring manager: That's a little rich for us. We were thinking about $35,000.
Job hunter: I couldn't possibly take $35,000.

End of discussion. Another wasted interview. But there is a better way. Intend to turn every job interview into an appropriate offer. Overcome the company's objections to hiring you, and overcome your own objections to working there. If the salary or something else bothers you about the job, think about how you can change it.

Think more consciously and more strategically. Intend to negotiate. Most job hunters don't negotiate at all.

- They don't negotiate the job. They listen passively to what the job is, and try to fit

themselves into it—or reject it.
- They certainly don't negotiate the salary. They listen to the offer, and then decide whether they want to take it.

Don't accept or reject a job until it is offered to you.

Job hunters decide whether or not they want the job without negotiating to make it more appropriate—and without even getting an offer! Career counselors have a maxim: Don't accept or reject a job until it is offered to you.

We'll see how you can be more proactive rather than passive. The following guidelines will allow you to take more control and more responsibility for what happens to you. Following these steps will not guarantee you the compensation you want, but you will certainly do much better than if you do not follow them. Remember the four steps you will learn here—and pay attention to where you are in those steps.

If you can remember these four steps with regard to a particular company, you will do better in your salary negotiation —*and in your entire search as well.*

Step 1: Negotiate the Job

By now, you have already negotiated the job. You have created a job that suits both you and the hiring manager. Make sure it is at an appropriate level for you. If the job is too low-level, don't ask about the salary—*upgrade the job*. Add responsibilities until the job is worth your while. Make sure the hiring manager agrees that this new job is what he or she wants. Don't negotiate the salary yet.

Step 2: Outshine and Outlast Your Competition

By now, you have already killed off your competition. You have kept in the running by offering to do more than your competitors. You have paid more attention to the progress made in your meetings, and you have moved the process along. You have satisfied every need, and responded to every objection. For some jobs, it can take five interviews before the subject of salary is discussed. All the while, your competitors have been dropping out. It is best to postpone the discussion of salary until they are all gone.

Step 3: Get the Offer

Once a manager has decided that you are the right person, you are in a better position to negotiate a package that is appropriate for you. Until you actually get the offer, postpone the discussion of salary.

Step 4: Negotiate Your Compensation Package

Most job hunters hear the offer and then either accept or reject it. This is not negotiating. If you have never negotiated a package for yourself, you need to practice. Why not try to get some offers that don't even interest you, just so you can practice negotiating the salary? Here are some hints to get you started:

- Know the company's, and the industry's pay scales.
- Know what you want in a negotiation session, and know what you are willing to do without. Negotiate one point at a time. Negotiate base pay first and then the points the employer would easily agree to. Save for last the issues of conflict. Be prepared to back off, or not even bring up, issues that are not important to you.
- You are both on the same side. Each of you should want a deal that works now and works later—not one that will make either of you resentful.
- Care—but not too much. If you desperately want the job—at any cost—you will not do a good job of negotiating. You must convince yourself, at least for the time you are interviewing, that you have alternatives.
- Try to get them to state the first bid. If they say: "How much do you want?" You say: "How much are you offering?" If pressed about your

> *The moment you feel foolish, you look foolish. Concentrate, block it out,*
> *and relax. Of course, that's not always easy.*
> Michael Caine, *Acting in Film*

---

prior salary, either say instead what you are looking for, or be sure to include bonus and perks. Some include an expected bonus or increase in salary.

• If the manager makes you an unacceptable offer, *talk about the job.* Look disappointed and say how enthusiastic you are about the position, the company, and the possibility of doing great things for this manager. Say everything is great, and you can't wait to start—but your only reservation is the compensation. Ask what can be done about this.

Be reasonable. As the saying goes: Bulls win, and bears win, but pigs never win.

It Works at All Levels

Once I did a salary negotiation seminar for low-level corporate people. One person had been a paper-burster for twenty-five years: He tore the sheets of paper as they came off the computer. But because he had been at the company for twenty-five years, his salary was at the top of the range of paper-bursters. He had the same kind of salary problem a lot of us have.

The four steps worked for him, too. He told the hiring managers, "Not only can I burst the paper, But I can fix the machines. This will save you on machine downtime and machine repair costs. And I can train people, which will also save you money."

He was:

1. Negotiating the job

And:

2. Outshining and outlasting his competition

And after he:

3. Gets the offer

He'll have no trouble:

4. Negotiating the salary.

Know where you are in the four steps. If you have not yet done steps one, two and three, try to postpone step four.

CASE STUDY: BESSIE

It Can Even Work Against Me

Once when I was a CFO for a small firm, I wanted to hire an accounting manager who would supervise a staff of four.

I told an excellent search firm exactly what I wanted and the salary range I was looking for: "someone in the $50,000 range."

I received lots of résumés—all of which the search firm had marked at the top: "Asking for $50,000." I interviewed a lot of people, but Bessie stood out from the crowd. I had Bessie meet with a peer of mine and also with the company president. Everyone loved her.

Finally, I told Bessie that we were pleased to offer her the $50,000 she wanted. Bessie said, "I would love to work here, but I would not be happy with $50,000. I didn't put that there."

I was stunned, but I was also stuck. We had made an investment in Bessie. Everyone had met her and loved her, and she wisely stayed mum about the money until she received the offer. A more anxious job hunter might have said early on, "I see that it says $50,000 at the top of my résumé, but I just want you to know that I am already making more than that." That would have been admirable honesty but the person would have been out of the running.

Bessie wound up with $55,000, which is what she was worth—and we wound up with an excellent employee. Bessie had followed the four steps exactly.

---

1. Negotiate the job.

2. Outshine and outlast your competition.

3. Get the offer.

4. Negotiate your package.

CASE STUDY: KATE, 1980

All Four Steps in Action

I was earning, let's say, around $60,000 in 1980. A search firm called me about a job that paid $40,000. Remember, search firms are a means for getting *interviews*—not for getting jobs. Don't negotiate salary with the search firm. Simply decide whether you want the *interview.*

I asked the recruiter what the job was. "It's with

an advertising agency," she said. "They're looking for a woman to supervise the secretarial staff."

I had an MBA, was making $60,000, and specialized in turning around troubled firms. The average recruiter cannot negotiate job content but *can* give information. When she described the situation, it seemed to me that the company was in trouble and was using the wrong solutions to solve their problems. I told her I would like to meet with the president. She said, "You *would*?"

I like situations in which I know who my competition is: people who want to supervise secretaries for $40,000. I asked the president:

- How is your company organized?
- What are your biggest accounts?
- What is the profit margin on each?
- Do you have a cost-accounting system?
- May I see your computer system?
- Did you know that certain reports would give you better profit control?

His eyes lit up. I was headed in the right direction—and was killing off my competition while I created a job more appropriate for myself. I kept talking to him about his business and what we could do to turn it around. I was trying to move it along, move it along, move it along—and kill off my competition.

After the offer, we got into the formal discussion of salary. At this point, I wanted:

- the title "VP of Operations,"
- to chair the executive committee so we could turn the company around,
- easy access to the CPA firm. They would be my partners in this.

The actual salary was not a problem. But you can see that it would have been if I had discussed it too early, when the president was thinking about a much lower-level job. After we defined a new job and he definitely wanted me, we were in a better position to discuss a salary that was right for the new position.

"Salary negotiation" involves more than salary. It can involve negotiating for anything you need to do the job well, in addition to your compensation package.

Moving From Negotiating the Job to Negotiating the Package

Once they make you an offer, it's human nature for them to want to close.
You have to keep it open.

Negotiating the job/moving it along

Negotiating the package/keeping it open

Your competition getting killed off.

B They want to close quickly.

A They make you an offer.

Do the Deal Yourself

If possible, negotiate directly with the hiring manager—yourself. You can see from the last example that I did all of my negotiation with the president of the firm and not through the recruiter. The recruiter was not in a position to do the kind of negotiation that I was able to do on my own. Yet the recruiter still received a fee based on the larger amount that I was offered.

By the time you receive an offer, the hiring manager has already decided that he or she wants you, and is the only one who can see your true worth. He or she has an emotional stake in the outcome, and is therefore usually an easier person with whom to negotiate. In addition, the negotiation is not simply about compensation, but about the work you will do in return for that compensation. All of these issues are difficult to negotiate through a middleman.

If you are scared, you may actually prefer to negotiate your compensation through a search firm or through human resources. But it sometimes happens that the message you were trying to send through the middleman winds up very different from what you intended.

The recruiter feels that he or she has a stake in the outcome because, after all, it could mean the loss of a fee if you mess up. But the recruiter does not understand that you know a lot about negotiating. On the other hand, there are recruiters who do an excellent job in handling the negotiation. Simply make sure you are aware of everything they are doing so you can interject yourself back into the process if need be.

How to Interject Yourself Back into the Process

This is tricky. Sometimes you find yourself dealing with a middleman when you really want to speak directly to the hiring manager. Simply tell the middleman that you have come up with a few more issues related to the job that you would like to discuss with the hiring manger. Once you have gained access to the manager, discuss those job-related issues, develop a rapport, and then bring up the compensation issues you would like to discuss.

Certain issues, such as benefits, are usually discussed with personnel—so don't burden the hiring manager with those. Meet directly with personnel to review the benefits package.

If you are in a complex situation, you may want to work with your career coach on this. It's very helpful to have the point of view of a trusted advisor.

Be sure the person with whom you are negotiating is at the right level. If you find yourself constantly bumping up against the salary level of the people with whom you are negotiating, the problem is not your salary negotiation technique. The problem is that you are talking to people who are at the wrong level.

CASE STUDY: GEORGIA
Using All Four Steps

I had been coaching Georgia throughout her job search. She had interviewed to head a small profit center at a hospital. She would be involved with eleven radiologists who gave cancer tests in a mobile unit, and two administrators. She also had competition.

Georgia had met with six doctors. One particularly unpleasant one asked for a proposal on how she would handle the job. This was Wednesday—the day before Thanksgiving. He wanted it back the Monday after Thanksgiving!

Georgia and I worked at my dining room table over Thanksgiving. "You can be sure no one else is putting in this much effort," I told her.

Georgia hand-delivered not one proposal, but *six*, and on time. She did not want her fate in the hands of one nasty doctor. Her cover notes were different, but essentially said, "Dr. So-and-So asked for this proposal. I felt duty-bound to give you a copy as well, since the things we discussed are reflected here."

Within an hour of the delivery, Georgia got a call from her future boss (not the nasty doctor). She told me that he was elated: "We want to offer you the job. If you don't take it, we're stuck. We don't want any of the other people who interviewed, and we'll be forced to start our search over." This was music to my ears, because in effect he was telling her that she *no longer had competitors.*

Now we were in a different phase of the search. It's human nature that the person making the offer simply wants to come to closure. However, you need time to discuss things.

I said to Georgia, "You've spent plenty of time defining the job. You need an equal amount of time to define the compensation."

She went back to the doctors and repeated my words verbatim: "We've spent plenty of time defining . . ."

They immediately backed off. "You're right. We'll spend whatever time it takes to resolve these issues."

They didn't want to lose Georgia. She had paid her dues, and now she was in a strong position to negotiate. They made her a written offer. Then we worked up a counteroffer.

- She wanted a certain base pay.
- She would need entertainment expenses to sell this program.
- The bonus was important to her.

Calculating the Bonus

We wanted a bonus based on the volume the high-tech $250,000 trucks could handle. We decided that each truck would probably need one day of maintenance a month, and that each radiologist would be able to do *x* number of tests.

With the bonus based on truck volume, we figured what Georgia's maximum salary would be. To allow for year two, we asked the hospital to buy another truck if the volume reached a certain amount.

When Georgia delivered the counteroffer, the doctors couldn't believe it; they now had a truck operating at almost no volume, and Georgia was talking about buying another truck! It showed that she planned on making this a successful venture.

Georgia got the compensation she wanted, and something else . . .

Georgia Got to Keep Her Job

Because she followed up with every person with whom she met, and because she wrote such a detailed proposal, they were committed to her. Georgia had bought six months of safety in the job: She could do no wrong. The very first day, Georgia realized she'd had a misunderstanding during the interview process and needed to change something about the way the job was done. It was no problem. A job hunter who is thorough in the search process has laid the foundation for keeping her job. Unlike other new hires, the jury is *not* out on her. Georgia had proved herself. The doctors knew that no one knew more about this business than she did. She knew even more than *they* did!

That's why you want to follow up with *everyone*—including future peers and subordinates—during your search. You may be working with them later. And if any of them has an objection to hiring you, try to settle it during the search, rather than handling it after you are hired. Build strong relationships during the interview phase.

Know where you are in the process. Take the steps in sequence. You will not get the offer until after you have negotiated the job and also killed off your competition.

If a job pays $20,000 less than you want, that's fine for now. Postpone the salary discussion. Remember that you are there not for this specific job, but for a position that has not yet been completely defined—and in which you have some say.

A skilled negotiator has a different approach—and much more power—than someone who does not know these techniques. A skilled negotiator chases companies, not jobs. A certain position may not be right, but the job hunter wants to make a good impression anyway because there may be other places in the organization that are right for him or her.

Have you already received an offer? If they are *thinking* about making you an offer, that's not the same as actually *making* you an offer. It's not time to negotiate your compensation until you actually receive an offer.

**Where is your competition, by the way?
You cannot assess your negotiating
leverage until you know how the hiring
team sees you compared with your competition. You may have already received the
offer, but could the company easily consider someone else? If so, you are not in a
strong negotiating position. If the hiring
team wants nobody but you, you are in a
stronger negotiating position.**

CASE STUDY: STANLEY
Using All Four Steps

Stanley, an executive who had been in the
fashion industry his entire life, heard about a job
opening that was being handled by a search firm.
He met with the recruiter who could not put him
in for the job because Stanley's salary was a great
deal more than what the company was willing to
pay.

This is not the search firm's fault. They represent the company. They were hired by the company to fill a certain job at a certain salary level.
They cannot go back to the company and say, "I
know you wanted me to find someone at
$100,000. I have found someone who is at
$200,000, but I think you should see him."

After it was clear that the search firm would
not put Stanley in for the job, he approached the
firm directly.

He first wrote to the chairman (this is a targeted mailing) and followed up with a phone
call. The chairman refused to see him. Then he
wrote to the president, followed up with a phone
call, and got a meeting.

The president said, "Not only is your base too
high by $50,000, your total package would be so
high that it would be out of the question." Stanley
said, "I assure you that salary will not be a problem." (You will see this technique in the next
chapter.) "I have always done well every place I
have ever worked, and I am sure the same would
happen here. May I keep in touch with you?" (He
intended to "follow up" as every good Five

O'Clock Clubber does.)

Stanley kept in touch by meeting with others
in his industry and coming up with ideas for the
president. They met a number of times. Stanley
started to look better and better compared with
the other candidates. This was understandable,
since they were all much lower-level than he was.

Eventually, Stanley got the job—at the salary
that was appropriate for him. After Stanley had
met with the president—and the chairman—a
number of times, they tried to figure out some
way to get Stanley on board.

As it happened, the chairman was planning to
retire in two years, and the president was going
to become chairman. Stanley was brought in to
be the heir apparent to the president.

For more on this topic, read "What To Do
When You Know There's a Job Opening."

In summary, think about where you are in the
four steps. It will help you concentrate on what you
should be doing. If you still have competitors, for
example, it is too early to negotiate salary. And
practice. Salary negotiation takes a lot of skill, but
by doing it right you are more likely to wind up
getting paid what you are worth.

---

*They're only puttin' in a nickel,
but they want a dollar song.*
Song title

---

*To do this job right is an all-encompassing
proposition. I felt I wasn't doing as good a job with the
kids as I wanted, and I wasn't doing as well with the
business as I wanted. I needed to have a better balance
between work and my family,
and have some time left over for me.*
Jeffrey A. Stiefler, resigning as
president of American Express Co.
Quoted by G. Bruce Knecht,
Wall Street Journal, November 22, 1995

> **Are you presently at market rates?**
> **Below market?**
> **Above market?**
> **Knowing where you stand will help you**
> **answer the questions:**
> **"What are you making now?"**
> **and**
> **"What are you looking for?"**

By now, you know where you are in the four steps. In fact, for each company with whom you are meeting, you know exactly where you are in the process. If you are conscious of where you are, you will do much better than if you simply do what seems reasonable without regard to where you are in the process.

In addition, the more experienced you become in negotiating your compensation, the more you can assess what is appropriate for a given situation and deviate from the rules. However, until you are an experienced negotiator, it is best to play by the rules.

What Are You Making Now?
What Are You Looking For?

Now we'll look at the questions you've been waiting for. But we'll look at them strategically—so you can *plan* an appropriate answer depending on your situation. First, you need to develop some background information before you can plan your strategy for answering the questions. The strategy will also give you hints for postponing the discussion of salary until you have an offer.

Background Information: Figure out what you really make.

Start with your base salary, but also include your bonus and any perks, such as a company car, a savings plan, deferred compensation, company lunches, company contribution to insurance plans, and so on. That's what you really make—but that may not be what you will tell the prospective employer.

Background Information: Figure out what you are worth in the market.

Talk to search firms, ask people at association meetings, look at ads in the paper, and—most of all—network. At networking meetings, ask, "What kind of salary could someone like me expect at your company?" A few networking meetings will give you a good idea of the market rates for someone like you.

However, you must remember that you are worth different amount in different markets. You may be worth a certain amount in one industry, field or geographic area, and a different amount in other industries, fields or geographic areas.

What's more, you may be worth more to one company than you would be to another.

Research what you are worth in each of your target markets. And when you are interviewing at a specific company, find out as much as you can about the way they pay.

Background Information: Compare what you are making (total compensation) with what the market is paying.

You need to know if you are presently at market rates, below market, or above market. *This is the key* to how you will answer a hiring manager or search firm that asks you, "What are you making?" or, "What are you looking for?"

How to Answer:
If You Are Within the Market Range

Most companies want to know what you are making and, if you are within the market range, they will pay you 10 to 15 percent above what you are currently making. Therefore, if you are making $40,000 and you know the market is paying $43,000 to $45,000, then you could say, "Right now I'm at $40,000, but I'm looking to move a little away from that." The only time you can safely state your current compensation is when you are at market rates.

How to Answer:
If You Are Above Market Rates

A counselor asked me to have a meeting with his client Sam, who was having problems finding a job because of his high salary. I did an interview role play with Sam. At one point I said, "So, Sam, what are you making now?" Sam replied, "Two hundred thousand dollars plus-plus-plus." I said, "I know you're a very competent person, but we simply cannot afford someone at your high level."

Sam's salary was not hurting him, but his way of talking about it was. Even if your salary isn't $200,000-plus-plus-plus, you can easily put off the hiring manager if she thinks your salary will be a problem. You have to give her a chance to find out about you, and you have to think about how you can create a job that is appropriate for your salary. You must tell her, "Salary will not be a problem"— *especially if you know it is a problem.* You have to think to yourself that it won't be a problem when she gets to know you better and understands what you will do for her. Otherwise, you will not get anywhere.

Your position has to be that "salary won't be a problem." It is your job to reassure the hiring manager that you are both on the same team and can work this out. When they get to know you better—and what you have to offer—salary *won't* be a problem.

If you are making more than the market rate, do your best to create a job that warrants the salary you want and defer the discussion of salary until you have the offer. When you're asked, "What are you making now?" use a response from the list below to reassure the hiring manager that you are both on the same team and can work this out. These responses are listed in sequence from easiest to most difficult. Try the easy response first. If the hiring manager persists you may have to move on to one of the other responses. You are simply trying to postpone the discussion of salary until she knows you better and you have an offer.

The manager asks, "What are you making now?" You respond:

- "I'd prefer to postpone talking about the salary until I'm more clear about the job I'll be doing. When we come to some agreement on the job, I know that salary won't be a problem."
- "Salary won't be a problem. But I'm not exactly sure what the job is, so maybe we can talk more about that. I'm very flexible, and I'm sure that when we come to some agreement on the job, we can work out the salary."
- "Salary won't be a problem. I know that you

do not want to bring someone in at a salary that makes you resentful, and I'm sure you do not want me to be resentful either. I know that we'll come to a happy agreement."

• "I'm making very good money right now, and I deserve it. But I'd hate to tell you what it is because I'm afraid it will put you off. I know that salary will not be a problem. I'm a fair person and I'm sure you are, too I know we'll come to an agreement."

• "I'm being paid very well, and I'm worth it. But I'm very interested in your company and I'm willing to make an investment in this if you are. As far as I'm concerned, salary won't be a problem."

Marie successfully postponed the discussion of salary for two years. When she came to The Five O'Clock Club, she had been unemployed for a long while. It took six months before she was on the verge of a job offer at a major fashion house, the company of her dreams. On the day she was to receive the offer, the company went "into play." That is, another company was trying to take this one over, so all hiring was put on hold. Marie was more desperate than ever. Within a month or two, she received an offer from a major entertainment company, went to work there, and continued to keep in touch with the fashion house.

Over the next year and a half, she had meetings with the president and most of the senior executives at the fashion house. Each one asked her about her salary, and to each one she replied with one of the statements listed above. She eventually got a tremendous offer—after having postponed the discussion of salary for two years. By the way, Marie's boss at the entertainment company told her that he hired her because she was so persistent in her follow-up. He thought she acted a little desperate, which she was after having been unemployed for so long, but he gave her the job because it seemed to mean so much to her. And, of course, she later got the job at the fashion house because she followed up with them for *two years!* If this desperate job hunter could postpone the discussion of salary, so can you. But you need to practice with someone. It does not come naturally.

How to Answer:
If You are Making Below Market Rates

Again, you have a few options. For example, if a manager asks what you are making, you could answer instead with what you are looking for:

Manager: "What are you making right now?"
You: "I understand the market is paying in the $65,000 to $75,000 range."
Manager: "That's outrageous. We can't pay that."
You: "What range are you thinking of for this position?"

Note: You haven't revealed either what you are making or what you want—but you've still tested the hiring manager's expectations. The person who states a number first is at a negotiation disadvantage.

Or you could say, "My current salary is $32,000. I know the marketplace today is closer to $45,000. I have been willing to trade off the salary in order to build my skills [or whatever]. But now I am in a position where I don't need to trade off money, and I'm ready to take a position at market rates."

If You Are Pushed to Name Your Salary

Don't simply state your salary—develop a line of patter to soften it. Simply stating a number can be very confrontational, as with the $200,000-plus-plus-plus job hunter. If you have exhausted all the responses, and the hiring manager throws you up against the wall and shouts, "I want to know what you are making!" you can still soften your answer by saying, for example:

• "I'm earning very good money right now—in the $90,000 to $120,000 range, depending on bonus. And I'm certainly worth it. But I'm very interested in your company, and I know we can work something out."

• "My salary is very low—only $20,000, and I know that's dramatically below market rates. But I was willing to do that as an investment in my future. Now, however, I expect to make market rates."

You should name your salary only as a last resort. Managers want to know your last salary as a way of determining your worth to them, but it is certainly not the most reasonable way to decide what you are worth. For example, you would want to be paid more if the job requires seventy hours a week and lots of travel, versus one that requires only thirty-five hours a week. How do you know how much you want unless you know what the job entails? You are being sensible to talk about the job first and the salary later.

Some managers cannot deal that way, so you have to be prepared in case you are forced to discuss salary prematurely. And even if you do name your salary, there are different ways you can couch it. For example:

- "My current salary is $32,500."
- "I make in the high 60s."
- "My base is around $25,000 and my bonus [commissions] is usually around $15,000, which brings my total package to $40,000."
- "I make in the range of $100,000 to $200,000, depending on my bonus." (This, of course, tells them very little.)

Remember to soften your mention of your salary with a line of patter or your response will sound too confrontational and too much like a demand: "I make . . . but salary won't be a problem because . . ."

More Complex Compensation Situations

Most people are in the position of negotiating salary, perhaps a bonus or commission, and perhaps a training program, association membership, or the timing of the first salary review.

Others have a more complex situation. For example, a senior executive may say (at the appropriate time), "You'd like to know how much I'm now making? Let me write it out for you." (Or perhaps he or she would go into the meeting with the information already filled out.) The following table contains the current year's compensation, the next year's compensation (if it is relevant) to account for bonuses, pay increases, and so on. The third column would contain a skeleton of what you are looking for, or would be left blank and used as a worksheet. Be sure to write footnotes as commentary on those lines requiring it. For example, you may want to document that if you leave before April you will lose your year-end bonus. Therefore,

you could not start work until after April, or the hiring company would have to make up for your loss:

	19xx	20xx	Looking For
Base salary	$89,000	$95,000	$95,000
Bonus	26,000	35,000	
Deferred Comp.	20,000	30,000	
Car Allowance	8,000	8,000	
Stock Options	40,000	40,000	
Addtl Medical	4,000	4,000	
TOTAL COMP.	187,000	212,000	250,000

You may leave the third column completely blank and fill it in as you are speaking. For example, you could say, "This is an exciting opportunity you are presenting, and I want to be part of it. To make it easier for you, I could imagine staying at my present base compensation level for next year, $95,000. To make the move worth my while, I could imagine a total package of $250,000, for example, and we could figure out the numbers in between."

In stating your "requirements" in a collaborative way, there is plenty of room for flexibility as well as for their comments and input. You do not run the risk of having the offer fall apart before you have actually gotten one. As you will see later, you want to hear their best offer, and *then* you can accept it or reject it.

CASE STUDY: BETSY
Simplifying the Request

Betsy went to Europe on a consulting assignment, and was later offered a full-time position. She had a list of 20 or so expenses that she thought the company should cover: moving expenses, household purchases, trips home, phone calls home, gym, and so on. When we added up the entire package it exceeded $200,000, but it would have been too clumsy and too unprofessional to itemize all the things on her list.

Instead, we came up with a very neat package that included having the company pay completely for her apartments in both Prague and Duseldorf, where housing was very expensive. Those items alone more than made up for the extra expense of phone calls and other miscellany. The resulting

Armies of worried men in suits stormed off the Lexington Avenue subway line and marched down the crooked pavements. For rich people, they didn't look very happy.
Michael Lewis, *Liars Poker*

package was well in excess of what she had originally wanted, and gave her the comfort of knowing that unexpected expenses would not cause her great loss.

You are trying to postpone the discussion of salary until after you have an offer, but in real life that is not always possible. Therefore, postpone it if you can. And if you can't, be sure you *know* how you want to answer the questions:
- **"What are you making now?" and**
  - **"What are you looking for?"**

No Absolute One Way

Salary negotiation is the most nervewracking part of the job hunting process. At the beginning of your job hunt you are at loose ends—not knowing where you are going, and feeling like you will never get there. But salary negotiation is the part people fear the most. It is a surprise monster at the end of your search.

You're in a great negotiating position if you can walk away from the deal. Therefore, make sure you have six to ten things in the works. If this deal is the only thing you have going, see how quickly you can get something else going.

Search Firms

Search firms must know the *range* of salary you are making or the amount you are looking for. They do not need an exact amount.

Ads

In answering ads, you will rarely give your salary requirements. The trend at the moment is for many ads to read, "Please state salary requirements." Most job hunters do not, and the hiring company does *not* exclude them. Stating your salary or requirements not only puts you at a negotiating disadvantage, it also allows you to be eliminated from consideration because you are too high or too low.

On the other hand, some ads state, "You will absolutely not be considered unless you state your salary requirements." Then, you should state them.

What Is Negotiable?

Everything's negotiable. That doesn't mean you'll *get* it, but it is negotiable. First, think of what is important to you. Make a personal list of what you must have versus what you want. Decide where you can be flexible, but also know the issues that are deal breakers for you.

Think of your musts versus your wants. If you get everything you "must" have, then perhaps you won't even mention items on your "want" list. Go in knowing your bottom-line requirements, what you would be willing to trade off, and what benefits/perks could compensate you if you hit a salary snag. Have your own goals in the negotiation clearly in mind.

Salary is not the only form of compensation that might be negotiated. Other items might include:

- the timing of the first review
- closing costs on a new home or a relocation package
- use of a company car
- association or club memberships
- reimbursements for education
- bonus

Which is the most meaningful or valuable to you?

Forms of Compensation

Basic Compensation:
- the timing of the first review
- base salary
- deferred compensation
- incentive compensation (short and long term)
  - performance bonus
  - sales commission
  - sales incentive plans
  - stock options
- sign-on bonus
- matching investment programs
- profit sharing

The pay is good and I can walk to work.
John F. Kennedy, on becoming president,
quoted by Ralph G. Martin, *A Hero for Our Time*

Vacations:
- extra vacation: vacation length is becoming tied to level or length of work experience rather than time spent with one company.

Perquisites:
- expense accounts
- company car or gas allowance
- memberships
  - country club
  - luncheon club
  - athletic club
  - professional associations
- executive dining room privileges
- extra insurance
- first-class hotels or air travel
- personal use of frequent-flyer awards
- paid travel for spouse
- executive office
- private secretary
- employee discounts
- financial-planning assistance
- C.P.A. and tax assistance
- tuition assistance
- continuing professional education
- conventions
- furlough trips for overseas assignments

Relocation Expenses:
- moving expenses
- mortgage-rate differential/housing allowance
- mortgage prepayment penalty
- real estate brokerage fees
- closing costs, bridge loan
- home-buying trips
- lodging while between homes
- company purchase of your home
- mortgage funds/short-term loans
- discounted loans/mortgages
- temporary dual housing
- trips home during dual housing
- outplacement assistance for spouse

Related to Severance:
- severance pay and outplacement
- consulting fees after termination
- insurance benefits after termination

GLOSSARY

Deferred compensation: Ability to make deposits to a deferred salary plan from your pay on a before-tax basis so that amount of income is subject to taxation in the year you make the deposit.

Employment contract: A formal written agreement between yourself and the employer guaranteeing certain benefits such as severance pay should you lose the job through no fault of your own. At high levels sometimes known as a "golden parachute."

Letter of intent: A written confirmation of a job offer summarizing the items agreed upon (salary, benefits, perks, etc.). Not a formal contract but hard for a company to rescind. If you write it, it's called a reverse letter of intent.

Matching investment programs: Savings incentive plan in which company matches employee basic award or personal contribution toward investment.

Performance bonus: An amount of money to be paid you contingent on your performance on the job. May be a specific amount or a percentage. Can be tied to individual, group, or corporate performance.

"Perks" or perquisites: Extra benefits that come with the position such as executive dining room privileges, company car, etc. May be negotiable or standard company policy.

Profit sharing: Cash award based on corporate earnings. Unusual outside of banks.

Sales commissions: Compensation directly related to sales at a predetermined percentage.

Sales incentive plans: Additional compensation based on sales volume.

Signing bonus: A one-time amount of money paid as an inducement for you to join the company. Also known as a signing or "up-front" bonus.

Stock options: A grant to purchase stock at a fixed price.

How to Gain Negotiating Leverage

**The most important negotiating leverage you
have is being in demand elsewhere.
Develop other options. Be able to walk away
from the deal. You can create this situation
without much difficulty.**

Most job hunters say to themselves, "I'm
so far along with this one possibility, I'll
just ride it out and see what happens. If
I don't get an offer from them, then I'll think of
what else I should do."

Bad move. Have at least a tentative answer to
the question of what you would do if this doesn't
work. Having an alternative:

• helps you to be more relaxed in your
discussions.

• increases your chances of having this
possibility work out.

• puts you in a better position to negotiate
this position wisely.

• helps you to tolerate the months that may
go by before it comes to closure.

• gives you something with which to compare this offer so you can make a more objective
decision.

As one Five O'Clock Clubber said during her
"graduation speech" after accepting a new position, "When you are going after only one job, you
think that, if it falls through, you will lose a few
weeks in your search. Instead of losing a few
weeks, you lose a few months. First, you have to
recover from the disappointment. Then you have
to gear yourself up and decide where to look
next. Then you have to get your entire search
going again. Take it from me, it's better to never
lose that momentum at all."

CASE STUDY: GREGORY
Skipping a Step
When I met Gregory, he had three job possibilities in the works, and wanted to bring them to
closure. After all, he said, he had a family to
support.

It seemed to me that Gregory's prospects

were not a good match for him. After much
discussion, Gregory agreed to contact additional
prospective employers: This would not slow
down his current negotiations, and may even
make things move faster.

To develop more appropriate targets, Gregory had to complete the assessment process
(The Seven Stories and other exercises in our
book *Targeting the Job You Want*), which he had
skipped. Perhaps Gregory could find work that
he would enjoy doing and also meet his family
responsibilities.

Gregory received six job offers. The three new
companies offered him appropriate positions
before the first three companies made him any
offers at all.

Do not skip the assessment part of your
search. The results help you to target correctly
from the start, give you something against which
to compare your offers, and help you to be more
objective about which job you should take next.

CASE STUDY: CAROLINA
Self-Discipline to Do The Right Thing
Carolina had only one job prospect, and was
anxious about whether she would get an offer.
Her most important meeting with the company
was scheduled for the following week, and she
wanted to land that job. "Believe it or not," I told
her, "you will do better in your upcoming round
of interviews if we could first develop a strategy
for getting more possibilities in the works."

That day, after Carolina prepared for the
interview, she went to the library, researched 150
other companies in her target area, wrote a great
cover letter and sent it with a résumé to all of
them.

By the time her important meeting came
around, Carolina was so relaxed that she had
almost forgotten about it. When the small things
inevitably went wrong, she could say to herself,
"At least I've got 150 letters in the mail working
for me."

Three weeks later, Carolina got the offer she
wanted. In addition, she received calls because of

*No one can possibly achieve any real and lasting success
or "get rich" in business by being a conformist.*
J. Paul Getty, *International Herald Tribune*

her mail campaign. She accepted the job with the company with whom she had been meeting, but continued to speak with the other companies just to be sure she had made the right choice. For a few weeks after starting the new job, she still kept in touch with the other companies—until she was completely sure that she had made the correct decision.

CASE STUDY: SERGIO
Acting Like a Consultant

In search only two weeks, Sergio had no trouble getting interviews. However, he was having an important first interview the day after our Five O'Clock Club meeting. He was hyped up, stressed out, and breathlessly told the group, "This job pays a lot of money. I want to go in tomorrow and get them to hire me. I think they want someone who is more technical than I am, so I have to sell myself really hard. I've prepared a handout to give them at the end of the meeting. Take a look at it and see if she is likely to give me the job."

At first, the group was mildly confused. No one looked at the handout. They knew that was not the problem. Then people in the group commented:

"Do you really want this job, Sergio?"

"What other companies are you talking to? It's so easy for you to get interviews."

"You've got to slow down."

"If this job pays as much as you say it does, they're not going to make you an offer at the first meeting."

I built on the group's good comments: "Sergio, become this woman's friend. To help her, you need more information. Find out why she wants a person with strong technical experience. Find out more about her vision for the department. Help her decide what is really best for her—even if it seems, from time to time, as though you are putting yourself out of the running. Tell her that you will think about her situation, and get back to her later. Then do some research. What you want from this first meeting

is another meeting."

Sergio immediately calmed down. The group could hear it in his voice. In his panicky state, Sergio could not have done well in that interview. He was very grateful for the group's guidance.

Sergio met a few times with that company, kept his search going, and received four excellent offers from other companies. The one he had been so eager about faded from his interest.

If You Are Presently Working

Employed people have the same leverage as those who have other possibilities in the works. If a hiring manager says to you, "Why are you leaving?" You can say, "I don't know that I am. I may stay right here." You don't know that for sure *what* you are going to do. To be in a strong negotiating position—and an appealing candidate—you need options.

Pretending to Have Other Offers

Why not say that you have other possibilities when, in fact, you have nothing else? Pretending you have other offers rarely works. The danger is not that you may be caught in a lie. The danger is that the company may say, "You should take the other offer," and three months later you still have no other alternatives, and you have also closed off this possibility. It's so easy to get other job possibilities in the works, focus on doing that.

*Human . . . life is a succession of choices, which every
conscious human being has to make every moment.
At times these choices are of decisive importance;
and the very quality of these choices will often reveal
that person's character and decide his fate.
But that fate is by no means prescribed:
for he may go beyond his inclinations,
inherited as well as acquired ones.
The decision and the responsibility is his:
for he is a free moral agent,
responsible for his actions.*
John Lukacs, *A History of the Cold War*

The
Five
O'Clock
Club®

Communications Skills
for Negotiating

Most Job Hunters
Try to Close Too Soon

If you were a consultant trying to land a contract, you would not expect to land that contract after just one meeting. You would not leave the meeting and say, "I think they liked me," expecting to get the contract based on that alone. You would know that the purpose of that meeting was to get information so you could better understand their issues and needs and who the players are, go back and think things through, and figure out how you could help the company. Then you would figure out what else you would need to know. Perhaps you would have to do some outside research, meet with additional people inside or outside the company, find out what other consulting firms they are considering so you would know how you stack up, or call a friend who could put in a good word for you.

Yet many job hunters come out of their very first meeting hoping they will get the job; they actually expect to get that job based on just that one meeting. There's a lot more work to be done. Be sure to read the chapter "Follow Up After a Job Interview: Consider Your Competition." Otherwise, you may try to close too soon.

There can be no greater reward than
goodness to your fellow man.
Charles Dickens
A Christmas Carol

It's time to negotiate. You have an offer. You and the hiring manager are no longer, figuratively speaking, on opposite sides of the table; you are now side-by-side. In this part of the process, it's up to *you* to set the tone of the conversation.

Obstacles and disagreements may arise, but your intentions are in agreement: You want to work together, pending the outcome of the negotiations.

Ideally, you will both use a collaborative, problem-solving approach—perhaps with some compliments thrown in because you value each other. You will each resolve the details calmly, and try to understand the ideas and the situations faced by the other person. The goal of any negotiation is to reach an agreement.

It may take some time to hear the various aspects of the offer, respond to them, and discuss a compromise that will be acceptable to both of you. After all is said and done, you may decide to accept or reject the offer, once you hear all of the details.

However, you bear the larger part of the burden in the compensation discussion. After the hiring manager has spent so much time interviewing prospects and has made a decision about whom to hire, he or she wants to come to closure. It is your job to keep the conversation open until all of the items you want to discuss have been discussed. It is your responsibility to manage the conversation, keep it flowing, and thank the hiring manager for discussing these details when all he or she wants to do is get someone into the job and get on with it.

Express Enthusiasm

Some job hunters think that showing enthusiasm for the job will negatively impact their negotiating position. Quite the contrary. I have seen many an offer retracted because the job hunter did not seem enthusiastic about the position during the negotiating stage. I cannot imagine a consultant or freelancer feigning disinterest, thinking it would help to negotiate a

A man is great not because he hasn't failed;
a man is great because failure hasn't stopped him.
Confucius

higher rate. Instead, be sure to show enthusiasm for the position throughout the negotiation process. You can always turn the offer down later—after you have heard the entire package.

A Few Hints

Here are a few things to remember:

- Aim for a win-win situation.
- Go in knowing what you want, and what you would settle for.
- Keep the business discussion going.
- Do not be rigid or demanding.
- When the hiring manager says that he or she is faced with a problem, such as other employees who would make less than you, acknowledge the problem, and try to show why it is not relevant in your case. Perhaps, for example, the job you will be doing is somewhat different from what the others are doing.
- Do not get ruffled, upset, confrontational, or sarcastic.
- Maintain a tone of speech that is business-like, positive, and calm.

If the hiring manager will not budge on the offer, you may still decide to ask for the offer in writing so you can think about it—and to make sure you have at least one offer in your pocket. You would also still say that you want to work there. You are "Playing the End Game" (see that chapter).

Preparing Your Response to the Offer

To keep things simple, let's assume you are negotiating salary alone, although your compensation discussion may have many more elements. Some experts say that you should listen to the offer, and say that you'll get back to the manager in a few days. In real life, that often does not work.

For example, if you are currently making $80,000, and you are offered $40,000, you can't say, "Thank you for the offer. I'll think it over and get back to you in a few days." Whatever you say in a few days will seem idiotic. With an offer so out-of-line, it seems that you could have had *some* response, such as: "I just want to be sure we're talking about the same job. As I understand it,

you would like me to [describe the job]." This lets the manager know that you are disappointed with the offer.

Low Offers

One time I received an extremely low offer. I was making $80,000. The manager offered me $40,000—obviously trying to see what he could get away with.

I said: "I was thinking more like $160,000."
He said: "$160,000?!?!"
I said: "I was just kidding. I thought you were too."

And then he became more realistic. You should probably not try this, but I don't like to get too serious when I know someone is playing with me.

I actually wound up with a very good offer and went to work for that company. The position fit perfectly with my Forty-Year Vision. I stayed there three years while I continued to build The Five O'Clock Club.

If the offer is $60,000 and you want $80,000, perhaps you could express a little disappointment, such as: "Well, I'm thrilled to receive an offer. I really want to work here and I especially want to work for you. That salary is a bit low compared to what I had been thinking. Let's keep talking about it."

If you have the manager put the offer in writing, then you can hustle around to the other companies with whom you have been meeting, and see how much better you can do (see "Playing the End Game"). At the very least, it will give you time to think. Then you could say to them, for example, "I've been giving it a lot of thought . . ." (or "My wife and I have been talking about this . . ." or "I've talked this over with my accountant and we can't figure out how I could manage on the amount you've offered me. I was wondering how far you could move away from this amount. What are the possibilities of [name something for the manager to consider]?"

High Offers

Let's say, for example, that you would like an

offer of $90,000, and you think that is an appropriate amount.

What if you are offered $120,000? (Remember, you don't want to be greedy. Can you live up to that amount?) If you decide it is a fair figure, then you can say, "I'm very pleased with your offer, and I'm not one to quibble, so let's call it a deal."

If you are offered $110,000, $100,000 or even $90,000, your response may well be exactly the same.

Once, when I had decided to take a straight career-counseling position—after having worked for many years as a CFO—I went through the entire negotiation process, but postponed discussing salary for four months while I met a dozen or so people. I went in for the offer meeting, and the manager asked me what I had been making before. She was astonished to find out that we had not already discussed salary. After some consultation with her boss, she said that she was happy to offer me what I had been paid previously. It was a salary that was way out-of-line (too high) for the responsibilities we were talking about. After all, I was not going to have a staff or any of the other responsibilities I had previously had. I wanted this job so I could have virtually *no* responsibilities and simply concentrate on growing The Five O'Clock Club.

I told her that the amount she offered was very generous, but seemed too high for what I expected I would be doing there. I named a number that was fair—but much lower. She said, "Okay. How about if we split the difference?" And I was still paid handsomely.

It doesn't pay to be greedy. If I had come in at a salary level that was too high, I might have lost my job the first time they needed to cut expenses, or my boss might have given me assignments to justify my high salary, such as a lot of overseas travel, coaching foreign executives. I wanted to coach executives only in the city where I lived because I had to run The Five O'Clock Club at night. You are always aiming for a fair compensation.

The Middle Ground

In the middle ground, that is, an offer that is just below or just above your goal, you may want to think it over, develop your lines, and then get back to the manager.

It is usually best to do all compensation negotiations in person so you can get a feel for the manager's response. Work with him or her to come up with something that is acceptable to both of you.

Other Negotiation Communications Hints

Ask open-ended questions such as, "Can you think of anything else we can do to bring our positions closer together?"

Offer ideas or information. One Five O'Clock Clubber was thrilled to get an offer to work for a certain major company, but their hands were tied. She wanted $90,000. They wanted to give it to her, but could only manage $80,000. Then she realized that two association memberships would have cost her $500 each. Would they pay for them? And what if she went to two conferences a year? Those conferences usually cost around $3,000 each, including room and transportation and conference fees.

The company was very happy with this suggestion. It was much easier for them to give her the conferences and memberships than it would have been to give her extra pay. (Managers have to be conscious of keeping the salaries equitable among employees, but may have more flexibility in other budget categories.)

Build on what you have already agreed upon. "Your suggestion that you pay for my trips back home once a month helps a lot. I was wondering if you would also pay if my husband were to visit me some of those times instead of my going home."

> When you are negotiating,
> use a collaborative tone.
> You are both on the same
> side of the table now.

The more a man lays stress on possessions, and the less sensitivity he has for what is essential, the less satisfying is his life.
Carl Jung

Negotiating Items that are "Nonnegotiable"

Peter received a written offer from a major corporation. He liked it, all except the job title: He'd been offered the title of vice president, but he wanted senior vice president. The company policy was that no one could be hired from outside with a title higher than vice president.

I said to Peter, "Are you willing to walk away from the job if you don't get the title you want?" I needed to know that so I could help him plan his strategy. Peter said he would walk away from it. Then I needed to know why. Peter said he had had the title of vice president fifteen years ago, and it was too much of a blow to his ego to go back to that title. Furthermore, he felt he would not be able to do a good job if he had the lower-level title, because everyone would know his title and therefore would not respond to his requests. He felt he would fail in the job if he had the title of vice president.

The rule here may surprise you. If you are at an impasse because the hiring manager wants to give you one thing and you want another, you have only one recourse: *Talk about the job!* If Peter had directly addressed the title issue, they probably would not have come to an agreement. He would have quoted company policy. In fact when job hunters are negotiating, hiring managers sometimes get the impression that the job hunter does not care about the job, but only about the salary and the benefits. Therefore, be different. Talk about the job to reassure him that that is what is most important to you. Below is a shortened, paraphrased version of the letter Peter sent to the hiring manager. Please note the italicized part, which is an important strategy for you to use:

Dear Mr. Williams:

I was thrilled to receive your offer to head up the Rickety Division, and am eager to work with you to move it in a new direction. I know we will hit all of the targets you and I spoke about.

I was pleased with the compensation package you offered, and am also glad about the car situation. However, I *find it difficult to accept the offer* with the title of vice president. I had that title fifteen years ago, so I feel I'd be going backward in my career. But I am also concerned that the lower title will affect my credibility and effectiveness.

I am sure we can come to some agreement. I am very eager to dig in and am looking forward to hearing from you.

Peter did not reject the offer; he said he really wanted to work there, but would find it difficult to accept. It took three weeks for the company to get back to him and give Peter the title he wanted. But that was not necessarily the only result that would have been positive. For example, the company could have said, "Come in and get started, Peter. We can give you the title after three months." Or it could have said, "Peter, I'm sorry, our hands are tied on this one. But I assure you that you will not experience the problems you are dreading. Our employees will know you are division head, and that will matter to them more than the vice president title. Beth Segal came in as vice president only two years ago, and look at her now."

Peter kept the process open until he heard their best offer. That allowed him to either accept that offer if they gave him the higher title, or to change his mind and take the job with the lower title and the reassurances from the company that it would be okay.

If you are at an impasse because the hiring manager wants to give you one thing and you want another, you have only one recourse: *Talk about the job!*

That's what you want to do also. Hear the entire offer before you decide. *Do not accept or reject any job until it is offered to you.* Before their first interview with a company, some job hunters say, "I really want this job" or "I don't want this job." They don't even know what the job is, and they have already made up their minds. This is the wrong attitude. Go into each interview intending to make it into the best job for you and for the company. This means you will probably have to negotiate—both the job and the compensation.

You must establish your dreams
and quietly move in the direction of attaining them.
Dr. Hugh Gloster, past president, Morehouse College

How to Talk About the Items You Want

Here's the rule to follow when you want to ask for something:

- Talk about the job (if you haven't been doing so already).
- Describe the situation as you see it.
- Venture a solution.

You can imagine what it feels like when you are making an offer to someone who talks incessantly about all the things he or she wants. In the back of your mind, you say to yourself, "I don't believe this person cares about the job at all. All they care about is the benefits." Sometimes job hunters even find that the offer is retracted for this reason. So make sure you mention how excited you are about the job.

Talk first about the job.
Then explain why you want something.

Let's say that you want a company car. Don't say, "I want a car." Instead, say, for example, "I appreciate your offer, and cannot wait to get started. I know we will really turn that place around. I am looking forward to starting on the twenty-third, and am pleased with the package you have offered. However, I was wondering what we might do about a car. I was thinking that I would have to do a lot of traveling between these three cities, and wonder what we might do about that. I have no car at present, and I think that renting a car might be a big expense. Is there any possibility that we could lease a car? It would be much cheaper."

Compensation negotiation is a problem-solving session. Don't be rigid. Hear them out and see what they come up with, but also come up with suggestions yourself.

How to Negotiate Severance

After you have negotiated everything else, you may bring up the issue of severance. Here is one scenario:

You have settled on everything, including the start date. The deal is in the bag—but perhaps not in writing.

Set the stage by telling them how happy you are

to be joining their firm. Then further set the stage by expressing your concern that you may be at risk through no fault of your own. For example:

You: "I am thrilled to be joining your firm. I know this is a good match, and I believe in what you are trying to accomplish."

Hiring manager: "We're glad you will be joining us."

You: "My only hesitation is that I am leaving a firm where I felt very secure. I'm afraid that there is the chance that your company may be taken over, or that you may wind up leaving the firm, and I wonder what would happen to me. I was wondering if there was any way you could give me some comfort about that."

Hiring manager: "Well, that's always the chance you take in today's market."

You: "Yes, you're right. But I was wondering if I could receive, for example, six months' notice if my job [or assignment] were to go away for any reason."

Notice that you are asking for payment if your are dismissed for *any* reason, but when you set the stage, you named situations that have nothing to do with you. This way, you will not appear worried about whether or not you can do a good job.

Asking for six months' notice is the same as asking for six months' severance. When your offer letter gets written up, it will usually be written up as severance. That will give you the cushion you could need for your next search.

These days, six months is common. One executive had to move across the country to take a job. He got three years' severance during the first two years, and then two years' severance if something happened during years two to four, and eighteen months' severance after that. That severance would alleviate the trauma of losing his job shortly after a major move.

Overcome Their Objections—
And Also Your Own

Throughout this chapter, we have focused on

the company, what their objections might be, and how you can overcome those objections. You also need to be aware of your own objections and handle those during the negotiations. Many job hunters think that the negotiation is strictly about salary, but it is also about whatever else worries you, and whatever else you may need to have to do well in your job. You may want to discuss some of those things before you come on board, and other things after you are in the saddle.

What if, for example, the company expects you to travel 60 percent of the time? You could negotiate for 40 percent travel. People have negotiated to work out of their homes two days a week, have a budget for a special project, and so on. Think these things over, and be sure they are included.

Win-Win

You want a win-win situation—one with which you can both live. After you have received a job offer, the situation is no longer adversarial. You and the company are both on the same side of the table, trying to make this deal work.

Actually, it is up to you to control this part of the process. You have the most at stake. The fact is, once a hiring manager has made an offer, he or she usually wants to close quickly. His or her job is done. Now your job begins.

Therefore, you must make sure you bring up everything you want in a way that is collaborative. Set a tone that reassures the hiring manager that you are thrilled to have the job, cannot wait to get started but have just a few details to work out. You can say, for example, "I really appreciate your spending this time. Some of these things may not mean much to you, but they mean a lot to me."

Look at the Entire Package

Look at the entire compensation package. Do your homework so that you know the typical compensation for a similar position in the industry, and make allowances—especially in the area of benefits—as you move from one industry to another. The benefits may differ, but they should be on a par. Find out which items are automatic

benefits and which are negotiable; every company's plan is different.

Be reasonable. In the past, it has almost been a given that job seekers would move only for a salary increase of 20 percent or more. In these economic times, lateral moves are much more common. Know your market worth.

Do not be swayed by the possibility of making $2,000 or $10,000 more. Select the job or assignment that positions you best for the long term. That is the most important criterion.

Job Seekers Are Too Eager to Take Pay Cuts

An estimated 40 percent of all job seekers may start new jobs for less money than they should be getting because they do not know how to handle salary negotiations.

When people call to attend The Five O'Clock Club, we need to know their salary range and field so we can assign them to the right counselor. No matter what their salary is, they often say, "Right now I'm making x dollars, but I'm willing to take a pay cut." I usually say back to them, "Isn't is a little early to negotiate?" They haven't even started their searches, and they are willing to settle for less.

Many job hunters think that a willingness to take a pay cut will make them more marketable, but this may not be true. For one thing, there are plenty of job hunters at that lower salary, and so there will be plenty of competition at that level too. What's more, employers may be reluctant to hire someone who they think may leave when a more appropriate offer comes along.

Instead, learn to play the game, and find out what you are worth on the market. Use that as your gauge. If you were overpaid before, then you may have to take a pay cut. But if you were underpaid, you are likely to get what you are worth.

Are You Negotiating to Be a Permanent Employee?
Or a Temporary Consultant?
The Answer May Surprise You.

Jim landed a great job with a large financial services company. They were starting a new technology effort and wanted him to be a key player. The base pay of $100,000 a year was more than he had made before, and he would learn things that fit in ideally with his long-range career goals as developed in his Forty-Year Vision. It would mean a major company-paid relocation for him and his family. But the prospects were enticing, so he accepted it. Two months after he had joined the company and his family had relocated, the project was canceled. He was out of a job, far from home—with only two weeks' severance.

Marcia landed a four-year consulting assignment working for a major management consulting firm at the rate of $70,000 a year. She would be paid through an intermediary (a temporary services firm) from which she would also get benefits such as health insurance and paid time off. In addition, if the project ended early, she would get four months' pay.

Given the two examples above, which seems more secure: to land a full-time "permanent" position on payroll with only a few weeks' severance if you should lose your job, or to take on a "temporary" assignment with a four-month guarantee? Which company has made a greater commitment to its workers? Which workers are more at risk; which have more security? Let's take a look at some other cases to learn more.

Case Study: Ellen
A New Way of Thinking About Herself

After an active search and more than fifteen meetings with one prospective employer, Ellen received an offer from them for a high-level position in the banking industry. She had developed excellent relationships with everyone she met, and her follow-up notes were right on target. She even talked with the vice chairman of this large company.

The first compensation package offered her was mediocre, so she put a lot of thought into planning the conversation she would have to get the package increased. When she presented her

ideas, the hiring manager actually told her that he would have been disappointed if she had not come back asking for more. They agreed to her request for an increase in the base, the bonus, and various perks. But they balked at her request for a fair severance package. As a new employee, she would get a mere two weeks' severance, despite coming in at a package of almost $200,000.

She discussed with them how banking was slated to continue going through downsizings. What would happen to her if the company or her division were acquired (not an unlikely scenario)? What kind of reassurance could they give her about that? None, they told her.

Ellen would have no cushion or support from the company if she lost her job. The annual salary and bonus they offered sounded great but would be almost irrelevant if she did not get to stay there awhile. For how long would she be at a salary of $200,000?

For their part, the company was taking virtually no risk at all. If she lost her job, they would be out $5,000 (two weeks' severance on her base pay). She had interviewed with a lot of people there, which represented a certain investment on the bank's part. In the old days, when a company made that kind of investment, it usually indicated that they intended to keep you. Once you had found a job, you had found a home. But the old rules are gone. If a company does not grant you a reasonable severance package, they are taking hardly any risk in having you come on board. It's almost as if they are saying, "What the heck! We did our best in selecting you. If it works, that's great. If it doesn't, it won't hurt us."

Even if you are placed on payroll, a lack of severance represents a lack of commitment on their part. Payroll is merely the way they are choosing to pay you and has no relevance to how long they will keep you. If Ellen didn't work out or if the company's circumstances changed, it would be easy to let her go.

Ellen was aware of this large imbalance, and was discouraged. She had planned to cut off her discussions with other companies (which were in the early stages anyway) to commit herself to this one. She had been thinking like a true-blue, loyal employee—putting all of her eggs in one basket. As her career coach, I discussed this with her. She felt better when she realized why there was no reason to do that. Her new employer was making a very small commitment to her. Why should she make a big commitment to them?

She decided to continue talking to the other companies, and hoped they would "hurry up with their decisions." "What's the hurry?" I asked her. "If you accept this job, you can't afford to view it as permanent. Rather, tell yourself and others that you've landed a very nice assignment, and that you don't know exactly how long it will last. It does fit in with your Forty-Year Vision, and it actually makes you more marketable. When these other firms ask what you are doing these days, you can tell them about this wonderful 'assignment' which may or may not go on for a long while." This thinking made her feel more in control.

I continued: "Perhaps you will start working with this bank, and four months later something will jell with one of the other companies. Then you can decide whether to stay or leave. You do not have a job in the old-fashioned sense. The company that hired you is acting more as if this is a short-term assignment than a permanent job, and that's how you must also see it. You're simply playing by the rules that they have set up."

Ellen decided to speak with even more companies before she started the job. She reasoned that soon she would be working long hours, and it would be easier to keep up contacts she had established than to start from scratch to make new contacts later. Ellen now sees herself as a consultant who happens to be on payroll.

How's the New Person Working Out?

When you are new in a job, the jury is still out on you. "How's Ellen doing?" someone may ask. "We'll have to see," another person may reply. "It's too soon to tell." When a company makes so little investment in whether or not you stay, they are less likely to keep you if something goes awry. The company should be allowed to get rid of you when they want to, but they should have to pay for this privilege. If they have to part with a substantial amount, they will think twice about letting you go.

If you have no severance, you have no breathing room—no time to feel safe and get your bearings. If Ellen had gotten a six-month severance agreement, she would have had the comfort of a six-month window to settle in and devote herself to the job and the comfort of feeling that the company was truly committed to her. The company, in turn, would have been motivated to try harder to make things work out.

In fact, this is becoming more the norm. In the last few years, many companies have realized that the traditional policy of giving two weeks' severance for one year of work is completely out of date for mid-level people.

Today, everyone knows that employees are unlikely to last ten or twenty years and accumulate better severance arrangements, as they would have in the past. Therefore, companies are tending to grant severance packages based on the level of the person they are hiring. At present, a six-month severance arrangement is becoming more common for those earning over, say, $80,000 a year. After all, a person earning a large amount is likely to have a longer search than someone earning a small amount.

Case Study: Stephen
Could He Get a Real Commitment?

Stephen was making a huge career change—from telecommunications development to the energy industry. He and his family were also making a major geographical change: from New Jersey to the Midwest. The company offered him $90,000 base plus bonus. It was a great company, and he got along well with everyone. The move fit in perfectly with his Forty-Year Vision because he had wanted to work in the energy industry on development projects. This was a dream come true. Or was it a nightmare waiting to happen?

Before the negotiations were over, Stephen asked for severance the way we suggest doing it at The Five O'Clock Club. The company asked, "What kind of severance would it take to make you comfortable so you could concentrate on your job and not worry about having moved your family here?" He answered with a smile: "The longer the severance, the better I'll feel."

The company offered Stephen an astounding two years' severance if he lost his job for any reason during the first two years; one year's severance if he lost his job during the following two years, and the normal company policy after that.

Now Stephen can concentrate on his job. The company is taking some risk on his move, and is making a commitment that is at least equal to his own.

Protect Yourself by Hedging Your Bets

Stacy moved from her native Philadelphia to Boston to take a job as a senior litigator with a not-for-profit. Three months later, the organization faced serious budgetary problems that were unknown to the board at the time she was hired. They had to cut back, so Stacy's job was eliminated. Here she was in a new city, with no job and only four weeks' severance.

But Stacy had planned ahead and protected herself. Though the company had paid for the move, they had not agreed to a severance package that was adequate. So she sublet her apartment in Philadelphia and rented one in Boston, rather than purchasing another residence. The company was making little commitment, so why should she take unnecessary risks?

Stacy devoted herself to the job. But she had been warned by plenty of fellow Five O'Clock Clubbers to keep up her contacts while in the new job. She had wisely heeded their advice. Thus when her position was eliminated, she was shaken but not totally unprepared. At the time of termination, she even negotiated an additional month's severance—arguing that the company had upset her life. She could not move back to her own home for the next few months because she could not kick out her tenant. Her search was back to full steam in no time at all, and she was

able to move back to her old apartment within a matter of months when the sublet lease was up.

Stanley received an offer to work for a company in Pittsburgh. The pay was less than he had made in Chicago, but the cost of living was lower. He had a wife and three kids. Though the company would pay to relocate the whole family, they refused to offer him more than two weeks' severance. Stanley accepted the position anyway because he needed to work. He told the company how excited his family was about moving to Pittsburgh. However, he said that they needed to stay in Chicago until the end of the school year. Then Stanley continued to interview with other companies he had met during his search. He has seven months (until the end of the school year) to find a job that would be better for himself and his family, or to decide that it would be worth it to take the Pittsburgh job, despite the risk. In either case, he has bought himself time—time that the company would not give him.

We Are All Consultants and Temporaries —No Matter How We Are Paid

Jim, Ellen, Stacy, Stanley—each have what amounts to a temporary job. So do you and I. We can consider that we are all on consulting assignments. It's just a question of terminology. And in today's market, this is a healthier attitude to have. It doesn't matter whether we are on payroll or are paid as consultants, through the company or through an intermediary firm. In effect, we are all "temporaries" when we do not have a reasonable severance agreement that forces a company to pause before getting rid of us.

Hiring companies may decide the rules of the game, but workers still have the ability to respond appropriately. We can take better care of ourselves by planning our career paths, and by treating companies the same way they treat us: We'll stay there as long as it suits our plans, and move on when it makes sense.

At The Five O'Clock Club, job hunters report to the group when they have landed a full-time job or consulting assignment. They give advice to

History records the successes of men with objectives and a sense of direction.
Oblivion is the position of small men overwhelmed by obstacles.
William H. Danforth

those who are still looking to make a move. Sometimes those "graduates" who made the mistake of not keeping their options open end their talks by saying: "I will never again be caught off-guard. I resolve to keep up my contacts by having a networking meeting every week or two so I know what's happening in the outside world." They are right to do this: It is a fact that those who have a base of contacts in their targeted fields have a much shorter job search than those who have to start from scratch.

Be like these Five O'Clock Clubbers who learned their lesson. Hedge your bets. Maintain your contacts with other companies. Stay active in your industry or professional associations. Read the trade journals. Continue to improve your skills. Develop a new attitude to be in sync with the realities of the world of work in the 21st century.

The Length of Unemployment Has No Effect on a Person's Future Pay

The Five O'Clock Club is a research-based organization. Therefore, we study such things as the length of a person's unemployment in relation to the pay at which they are hired. Most of those Five O'Clock Clubbers who had been unemployed a year and a half to two years were able to get jobs at their old pay or more.

Most of these participants had had trouble landing a new job because of the techniques they had been using—not because of a lack of competence or because of their pay rates. When they started using the right search techniques, they quickly got jobs at the level they were worth in the market. For most people, this was at—or greater than—their old salaries.

Many noticed that their searches took a turn for the better after only two or three sessions at The Five O'Clock Club. Here, they were encouraged to:

• Develop a positive attitude and refresh themselves after a period of discouragement.

• Consider this a new search, and be willing to use our methodology in their search from this day forward.

• Make sure they were positioned properly for the areas they were targeting.

• Recontact those with whom they had already met *who were in an appropriate target area.*

• **Get six to ten things in the works.** Then the issue became "Who else are you talking to?" rather than "How long have you been looking?" (See "Playing the End Game.")

• Most of the searchers found appropriate positions with appropriate salaries within ten sessions.

CASE STUDY: JANE
Abused in Her Present Position

Jane had earned good money in the financial-services industry. She lost her job, and took something with a major retailer out of desperation. She earned only one-third of her former salary.

By the time we met her at The Five O'Clock Club, she had been working there for over two years, and spending eighty hours a week with no end in sight and no hope.

After only six weeks at The Five O'Clock Club, she landed a terrific position in an industry related to the financial-services industry at more than she had previously been making. Her present compensation never came up. It was not an issue.

Job-Hunting Hint

It's a good idea to have a calendar that you use only for job hunting. That way, you will clearly see how much effort you have (or have not) put in, as well as the amount of follow-up you plan to do.

Note the following:
• all interviews (networking, job, and search firm)
• mailings
• networking notes written
• follow-up notes written
• follow-up calls made, and
• the dates when you plan to make future calls.
You can also list ads answered.

A Monthly Job-Hunting Calendar is included in this book.

Negotiating a Consulting or Freelance Assignment

CYRUS (trying to be friendly): *I'll tell you what. You want to work, I'll give you a job. Nothing permanent, mind you, but that upstairs room over there—the one above the office—is a hell of a mess. It looks like they've been throwing junk in there for twenty years, and it's time it got cleaned up.*

RASHID (Playing it cool): *What's your offer?*

CYRUS: *Five bucks an hour. That's the going rate, isn't it? . . . If you can't finish today, you can do the rest tomorrow.*

RASHID (Getting to his feet): *Is there a benefits package, or are you hiring me on a freelance basis?*

CYRUS: *Benefits?*

RASHID: *You know, health insurance, dental plan, paid vacation. It's not fun being exploited. Workers have to stand up for their rights.*

CYRUS: *I'm afraid we'll be working on a strictly freelance basis.*

RASHID (Long pause. Pretending to think it over): *I'll take it.*

Paul Auster, Smoke

---

*Here comes the future, rolling towards us like a
meteorite, a satellite, a giant iron snowball,
a two-ton truck in the wrong lane, careening
downhill with broken brakes, and whose fault is it?
No time to think about that.
Blink and it's here.*
Margaret Atwood,
Good Bones and Simple Murders

---

*Hey, no matter what—it's better than
working at the post office.*
Jerry Sterner, *Other People's Money*

Being a Consultant or Freelancer

All positions are temporary. You may receive a W-2 form at year-end, or you may receive a 1099—but no work you do is permanent. However you are paid, make sure you are paid fairly. And make sure you are gaining experience that will help you get your next assignment—inside or outside your present company. Have a backup plan. What would you do if your current assignment or situation ends?

If you happen to be looking for full-time work on payroll, you still may be offered consulting assignments. So you should learn how to negotiate them.

Today, more and more companies are bringing in workers on a contract, consulting, or freelance basis. Such workers usually get no benefits (health insurance, paid time off, training, memberships, company-paid contribution to Social Security, etc.). Other contract or temp workers are hired through an intermediary company that may or may not put the workers on payroll, and pay for their benefits.

Even very senior managers find themselves serving as full-time consultants. Some companies are actually doing this illegally. If you are working full-time for a company which decides your hours and the content of your work, you are not a consultant but an employee. This means that the company must put you on payroll and pay the extra costs associated with that.

At one very large company where I was consulting, there was a relatively low-level person who worked on computers, kept the same hours as everyone else on staff, but who was paid a flat $15 an hour as a "consultant"—no benefits, no insurance, no paid time off. Large companies are sometimes even more likely than smaller companies to get away with this because they have so many employees. A manager may hire "consultants" because the company has a "freeze on head-counts"—he or she is not allowed to put more people on payroll because that would count as a "head." Yet the manager is allowed to hire consultants, temps, and freelancers.

The amount of money you receive will always be in direct proportion to the demand for what you do, your ability to do it, and the difficulty of replacing you.
Napoleon Hill, paraphrased by Dennis Kimbro,
Think and Grow Rich: A Black Choice

The worker is stuck. The company has all of the power. If the worker wants to work, he or she is not going to complain about unfair treatment.

To counteract this trend, workers are sometimes opting to have "a job and a dream"—a job that pays them regular wages, and other work done on the side to build a future that may be more secure than working for one company. Some workers are able to grow what was once a sideline into a stable source of income. That work may include consulting or selling part-time, trying to build a business, and so on.

Regardless of how you are paid, develop your skills and your marketability to the point where you are less likely to be taken advantage of.

The Search for Consulting or Freelance Work

The search for consulting or freelance assignments is exactly the same as the search for full-time work "on payroll." Target the areas in which you are interested—following the system we use at The Five O'Clock Club. At your meeting with your prospective employer—or perhaps even in your cover letter—you can mention that you would be open to either full- or part-time work. Sometimes a consulting assignment turns into an on-payroll assignment. Sometimes the reverse is true.

Those who have successfully made the transition to consulting or freelance work often say they would never go back to working for someone full-time. Some feel and indeed may be much more secure having a number of sources of income rather than just one.

The downside to consulting is that you must both market and deliver your services. Some consultants get so involved in delivery that they don't allow time to market. They suffer having intense periods of work, with periods of no work in between. Consultants don't get unemployment benefits during those down times. Some consultants may tend to take no time off: If you don't work, you don't get paid.

Therefore, you must set your consulting rates high enough to allow for time off. You also need time for marketing. A rule of thumb is to allow half of your time for marketing and administration, and half for the actual delivery of your services. "Marketing" includes everything you do to make yourself known, such as writing articles and then reprinting them as handouts to build your credibility, delivering speeches, building a database of possible targets and mailing to them regularly, and calling on companies.

Decide if you want to start a consulting business, or if you would simply like to take a few consulting assignments while you are searching for full-time employment. This will influence what you decide to do in marketing yourself. At some point—but not now—you may need a brochure, business cards, and even an office. If you are truly trying to build a consulting business, think through how big you would like your practice to be, how many others you would eventually like to work with you, and everything else you need to develop a rudimentary business plan.

In any case, you must be positioned properly (see Two-Minute Pitch). Decide what your target market is, what you have that would be of interest to this market, the services you want to offer, and how you can position yourself to seem worthwhile. Whether you are looking for on-payroll or consulting work, you must learn how to differentiate yourself from your likely competitors. Then you must call on prospects.

Follow the Stages of the Search and pay attention to the stage you are in (Stage 1, 2, or 3). Be sure to have six to ten things in the works at all times. Next, figure out how to price your services.

Pricing Your Services

There are two numbers you need to start with to determine your consulting fee. One is what you are now making—or have been making most recently, or what others are making—in the field you are targeting.

We are assuming your consulting will be in the field where your are now considered an expert. If you want to consult in a new field (perhaps as a way to learn that field), instead of your present base plus bonus, use the rate of those at your level in the new field.

The second number to consider is what the market will bear.

Calculating Your "Cost Rate"

Take your present base plus bonus. Let's say it's $50,000 a year. Add a factor for benefits, such as health insurance. Let's say 20 percent (this includes health insurance, company-paid Social Security, and so on, but does not include paid time off).

So that's $50,000 X 1.20 = $60,000

Divide that number by the number of hours the average person is available to work in a year. We'll use 2,000 hours, just to keep the calculation simple.

(You may want to use 1,600 hours, which allows for 10 holidays and 4 weeks of vacation and sick time.)

$60,000 / 2,000 = $30 per hour.

Your cost is $30 per hour—which is very different from what you will bill your customer. If you were to be able to bill 2,000 hours a year at $30 per hour, you would stay even with what you are now making.

A Model for Estimating Your Billing Rate

Base Salary & Bonus	Adj. Base = Base x 1.20 for benefits	COST (Adj. Base/ 2000)	Low Billing Rate[1] (cost x 1.2)	Aver. Billing Rate[2] (cost x 2)	High Billing Rate[3] (cost x 3)	Aver. per diem rate (aver. billing x 7)	MARKET RATES	My Tentative Rate
$20,000	$24,000	$12/hr	$14.40/hr	$24/hr	$36/hr	$168/day		
$30,000	$36,000	$18/hr	$21.60	$36	$54	$252		
$40,000	$48,000	$24/hr	$28.80	$48	$72	$336		
$50,000	$60,000	$30/hr	$36.00	$60	$90	$420		
$75,000	$90,000	$45/hr	$54.00	$90	$135	$630		
$100,000	$120,000	$60/hr	$72	$120	$180	$840		
$125,000	$150,000	$75/hr	$90	$150	$225	$1,050		
$150,000	$180,000	$90/hr	$108	$180	$270	$1,260		
$200,000	$240,000	$120/hr	$144	$240	$360	$1,680		
$250,000	$300,000	$150/hr	$180	$300	$450	$2,100		
$300,000	$360,000	$180/hr	$216	$360	$540	$2,520		
$500,000	$600,000	$300/hr	$360	$600	$900	$4,200		

[1]. Low Billing Rate. Use this rate if you are just starting out, or if you are on a long-term consulting assignment with a guaranteed significant number of hours per week.

[2]. Average Billing Rate. Use this rate if you are in a specialized field and in demand. You may also use this rate if you are a serious independent consultant and want to sell your consulting services long-term. You will need to make up for the time you spend marketing and so on.

[3]. High Billing Rate. If you have or are setting up a consulting firm, the rule of thumb is to bill out at three times labor cost to cover the cost of overhead, which includes support staff who are not billable, rent, marketing, and so on.

*You work Saturdays? Well, you must make good money. Well, so you hate it, I'm
sorry, I can't help that. What are your aspirations, in that case?*
Craig Lucas, *Prelude to a Kiss*

However, not only are you unlikely to bill 2,000 hours a year, you still have to buy your own health insurance, put money aside for your vacations, pay your own Social Security, arrange for your own training, subscriptions, memberships, and so on.

Calculating Your Low Billing Rate

To account for some of that expense, increase your cost rate by 20 percent—just so you will come out a little higher than your adjusted cost rate. This allows for benefits and also for paid time off. (See chart: Low Billing Rate)

$30 x 1.20 = $36 per hour (Low Billing Rate)

You would try to bill at your Low Billing Rate if you are just starting out, or if you are on a long-term consulting assignment with a guaranteed significant number of hours per week.

A rule of thumb for short-term consulting fees is twice your cost.

Calculating Your Average Billing Rate

If you need to have more than one customer, you probably won't be able to bill 2,000 hours a year because you will have to spend time marketing your services. Earlier you saw that a rule of thumb is to spend half your time marketing. So to keep even with what you made before, you would have to bill twice your cost rate.

That's $30 X 2 = $60 per hour.
(See chart: Average Billing Rate)

You would try to charge the Average Billing Rate for your salary level if you are in a specialized field and in demand. You would also try this rate if you are a serious independent consultant and want to sell your consulting services long-term. You will need to make up for the time you spend marketing.

Calculating Your High Billing Rate

If you are well-established as a consulting firm with lots of overhead, such as office space and administrative support, two-times cost will

probably not be enough to cover your overhead. The standard factor for this situation is three times cost. In addition, if you are seriously starting a consulting firm (rather than being an independent consultant representing only yourself), you would most likely charge the three-times rate for every billable member of your staff, or for each person you bring in to work on a project.

Finally, if you are well-known in your field, you may also insist on three times your cost rate—or, lucky you, whatever the market will bear.

$30 X 3 = $90 per hour.
(See chart: High Billing Rate)

Charge this rate if you are well-known in your field, or to cover your overhead if you have or are setting up a consulting firm. Overhead includes support staff who are not billable, rent, marketing, and so on.

Your "Market Worth" Is Whatever the Market Will Bear

When I'm hiring someone as a consultant, I ask them their hourly rate, multiply it in my head by 2,000, and decide if the person would be worth that much on-staff. For example, if someone wants to charge me $25 per hour, I estimate whether that person would be worth $50,000 on staff including benefits. That way, I can quickly assess whether the person is worth it to me.

If there are plenty of people who can do the same job for less, I can simply find someone else. If, however, this person is a known expert, my friends tell me that he or she is reliable, or if there is some other reason for me to think that this person is special, I may be willing to pay more than the typical going rate.

When you think about the rates you will charge as a consultant, remember that someone will be deciding whether or not you are worth it. So decide whether you are someone who can be easily replaced, or are unique and in demand. "What the market will bear" will be the most important determinant of what you can charge.

What you charge will probably change over time. At first, you simply want to get a few jobs and a few clients. Later, as you become better-known in your field, the amount and the way you charge will change.

You must test the waters. Talk to others in your field and find out what they are charging, network in to see prospective hiring managers and see what they would pay. When all else fails, start negotiating with the hiring manager and observe his or her reaction. Follow exactly the rules in the "Four-Step Salary Negotiation Strategy."

After you are well-established—and have a name in the market, there is a lot of flexibility. I have counseled clients who have ended up working two days a week for one company, and two days a week for another company—getting a flat $100,000 a year from each company! These clients had paid their dues in their respective fields, and deserved what they got. They each worked only four days a week, and if they lost an assignment at one company, they still had the other one to keep them going while they looked for a replacement. Not a bad way to earn a living.

Corporate Rates

Although the three-times rate is standard for organizations with overhead, companies use different numbers of hours as the base. That is, instead of using 2,000, they may use 1,600 or even as low as 1,300 to 1,400 hours. This increases the hourly rate. Or they may hike up the direct labor rates by including not only base plus bonus, but also all benefits, payroll taxes, estimated raises, car allowances, and so on.

Then they come up with a rate card, which may contain inflated rates. When it comes time to negotiate, they may come down quite a bit from their rate card.

For example, one company's "Rates to Use in Pricing Projects" are as follows:

Use a billing rate of $225/hr. or $1,800/day for:
- Employees with salaries in the $65,000 to $80,000 range.
- Outside consultants who cost us more than $500 per day.

Use a billing rate of $190/hr. or $1,500/day for:

- Employees with salaries in the $50,000 to $64,000 range.
- Anyone not on staff who costs us $300 to $500 per day.

Use a billing rate of $150/hr. or $1,200/day for:
- Professional staff with salaries less than $50,000.
- Anyone not on staff who costs us $150 to $275 per day.

Use a billing rate of $50/hr. or $400/day for:
- Administrative support staff.
- All temps assigned to this project.

You too may want to create a rate card for your consulting firm. But be sure to be realistic about your worth in the market.

Setting Your Rates

When you are starting out, you will probably use just one system for charging your clients, such as an hourly rate.

When you are experienced, you may still wind up charging every client the same rate, or each client a different rate. For example, you may have one or two clients who form a stable core for you, and you may have gotten far enough in your career that you are able to be on a monthly retainer with them. You may charge other clients an hourly fee. You may charge one client per project, one a low hourly fee, and another a high hourly fee. You may charge a large corporation a higher rate than a small company, a for-profit organization more than you charge a not-for-profit (although not necessarily).

Your rates may differ by geographic area. You may charge a certain rate in the big urban areas, and a lower rate in the countryside; or one rate for one part of the country, and another rate for a different part.

If you are offering your services to individuals, you may use a sliding scale depending on the person's ability to pay, the way that many therapists do.

Finally, you may charge different rates for different kinds of work. When I am hiring a

We are what we repeatedly do.
Excellence, then, is not an act, but a habit.
Aristotle

public relations person, to name one example, I may hire someone who is already working full-time for someone else and wants to earn extra money on the side. That person may charge me a certain hourly fee for the brainy work, such as developing strategy, writing press releases, and so on, and a lower hourly rate for the "mindless" work, such as stuffing envelopes.

Find out the standard fee arrangements for the industries or fields that you are targeting. The variety is endless.

Fee Structures

Therapists and attorneys charge per hour. Workshop leaders usually charge per diem. Determine how people in your field charge, and do the same—at least when you are starting out.

The two basic structures are per time (such as per hour, per diem, etc.) and per project. There are almost infinite variations on charging structures going, from a per-head rate for running a seminar, to a percent of gross billing (as in the old days of advertising). There are certain fields in which a success fee rules (that is, if the project works, you make lots of money; if it doesn't, you don't). And then there are lots of combination fee structures, such as a success fee for completion with a guaranteed nominal base amount. If you are working with a start-up company, and already have a full range of consulting assignments, you may be paid in stock. Other common arrangements are retainer, commission, percent of sales, bonus, or a combination of the above. Find out the standard fee structures for the industries or fields you are targeting. The variety is endless.

For now, we will cover the "per time" and "per project" structures. The thought processes behind these form the core of most other billing methods.

When considering the fee structure you want to use for a certain situation, remember that some structures are low-risk with a predictable reward. Others are high-risk (that is, you may wind up losing money or making no money), but high-reward (big bucks if things work out). All fee structures can be analyzed using this criterion.

Project pricing vs. time-based pricing

The benefit of pricing per project, rather than charging a time-based rate, is that you could make much more money that way. You could also lose money if you price incorrectly or if you do not control your costs while delivering the service.

With time-based pricing, on the other hand, you can be sure of getting paid for every hour you work. As long as you get paid, there is no risk on your part. However, you cannot make a great deal of money.

If you simply want to pick up some consulting work while you search for a full-time job, you may want to stick to time-based pricing so you are not at risk. If you want to have a consulting business, you may want to become very good at project pricing (although actually many consulting businesses charge solely by time-based pricing).

Out-of-Pocket or Pass-Along Expenses

Depending on the kind of work you are doing, certain expenses may be passed along directly to your client. Out-of-pocket expenses include items such as telephone, postage, and overnight mail expenses. Travel could also be considered an out-of-pocket expense—depending on the situation. Even entertainment sometimes falls into this category. If I hire a public relations consultant, I expect that person to keep track of out-of-pocket expenses and bill me monthly.

This is standard operating practice. However, check with others in your field or industry to be sure that this practice applies.

Pass-along expenses could include the cost of hiring an outside photographer, for example. Established consulting firms often "mark up" the cost of these pass-along expenses, say by 15 percent, to make a profit on them. In many cases, this is acceptable.

Pass-along expenses are not to be confused with the cost of outside consultants you may use as if they were part of your staff. These outside consultants would be billed the same as if they were on your staff, but you would have to think through the multiplier to use: perhaps two or three times the rate they charge you. Of course, you have to do what seems reasonable.

Time-Based Pricing

If you are in a field that normally charges an hourly rate, as is the case with a therapist or attorney, you need to find out what you are worth in the field, and then develop yourself to the point where you have no trouble saying with confidence, "My rate is $50 per hour."

But if you are doing project work for which you want to be paid hourly, that is another matter. As the hiring manager, I will be afraid of how much time you will spend on the project. If you tell me that your rate is $30 per hour, I will still want an estimate of how much a particular job will cost me. I cannot afford to pay you $30 an hour to do graphic design work, for example, if there is no limit. You may decide to fiddle with a design for 40 hours "just to make it perfect" when all I wanted was something that was "good enough." You may stay up all night working at home on your slow computer. Why should I pay you $30 an hour for that work, when you could have gotten it done in half that time if you had worked on my faster computer? You may have decided to make four different sketches for me, but if you were working out of my office instead of yours, I might have told you exactly what I wanted and saved all that extra time.

Therefore, if I am paying you per hour for a project, I want to know the limit on this project. Perhaps you will do 15 hours of work at your regular rate, and then come back to me to see if everything is on track before you rack up 50 hours for which you expect me to pay.

If you are willing to do the job on-site, there is less risk that you will go off in a direction I don't want. The on-site work is safer for both of us.

You will get paid for every hour you work, and I will know what you are doing for the time you are billing me.

If you are working for an hourly rate, you will charge less for per-diem work, and even less for a monthly rate. Of course, you must spell out the number of hours you will work for a per-diem rate. If you charge $200 per day and don't specify the number of hours in a day, your employer may expect 10- or 12-hour days. If you charge per month, you must specify that it is an 8.0-hour day (or 7.5-hour day), 20-day month (there are 4.3 weeks in an average month; 21.5 work days in an average month—not allowing for holidays or other time off). If you don't specify the number of days you will work per month, your employer will expect you to be there every day for the agreed-upon monthly rate. You will never have a day off.

If you are charging an hourly rate for on-site presentations, or for other work for which you have preparation time, make sure your hourly rate includes your preparation time.

If you are required to be on-site, bear in mind that most consultants charge a 4-hour minimum to make the unbillable travel worthwhile. However, if you are doing a lot of work for a certain client, you may come in for an important meeting and charge only for the time the meeting takes, even if it is only two hours. That's called establishing good will.

If you are straight hourly, you do not charge, of course, when you and your prospective client are discussing a possible assignment, or when you both are reviewing the work you did.

How long will the assignment last?

Another consideration is the length of the assignment. If you should normally get $86 per hour, but the company wants to pay you per diem, you would not normally charge the company $86 x 8.0 hours = $688. If it's likely to be an 8-hour day, you would then charge them, say, $600 per diem ($86 x 7.0 hours). And if the company wants to pay you monthly, you probably would not charge them $600 x 21.5 = $12,900

Man is born with his hands clenched, but his hands are open in death,
because on entering the world he desires to grasp everything, but on leaving,
he takes nothing away.
The Talmud

(because the average month has 21.5 work days). Instead, you would say that your fee is normally about $15,000 ($688 x 21.5), but you will charge them only $10,000 per month for a 20-day month with, for example, a six-month minimum with 60-days, (or 30-days), notice to terminate. That's still $60,000 for six months, with time to search if the contract is not extended.

Your rates are reduced for longer amounts of time because you will have to do less marketing than if you sold your services by the hour.

Billable vs. Unbillable time

Sometimes every hour you spend is billable, and sometimes it isn't. This can be tricky, and you should think about it with regard to the situation you are in. For many of your assignments, you may bill a straight hourly, per diem, or other kind of rate. But if you wind up at a company on a regular basis, you may attend weekly staff meetings, travel on company business, and so on. May you charge for this time at your normal rate? It depends. If you are at a large company, and being paid on a monthly basis, there is no discussion. They are paying you monthly, so that includes everything.

If, however, you are being paid hourly, you may or may not be paid for extraordinary travel time. Large companies may sometimes pay you for travel at half your normal rate—depending on the circumstances, while smaller companies may pay you nothing for travel. This is something you may want to negotiate if you think it could get out of hand.

If you are attending staff or other meetings—where you aren't really "working"—may you charge for that time? Again, it depends. If you are on an hourly basis, you may be able to charge half-time for regular (such as weekly) staff meetings. If the staff meeting is an unusual event, you may be able to charge at your regular rate. If you are attending a training seminar just to learn a new skill, for example, it is unlikely that you will be able to charge anything. However, if you are delivering a seminar, you would, of course, charge at your full billing rate. After all, you are working to your full capacity.

To keep a good relationship, make sure you do not nickel-and-dime your client to death. Throw in extra time for free sometimes (and let them know that). Perhaps call in with an idea on days when you are not there—gratis. Give a little to an important client just to keep a good relationship going.

What will your market bear?

After all of that, consider what is reasonable and customary in the market and for the company to which you are selling yourself. Would they pay someone like you $86 an hour? Or is that unlikely? If the market tends to pay only $50 an hour, that is what you are likely to get. If you get that amount, just be sure you understand that you are not making what you used to make— unless you manage to work 2,000 hours a year (or 1,600 hours, which allows for four weeks' vacation and 10 paid holidays).

Project-Based Pricing

Before you can possibly know what you want to charge a customer, you must figure out how much it will cost you to deliver the project. Go through the following steps:

Step 1.
List in detail the services you will provide, and who will provide them.

Step 2.
Price out these services using the billing rate for each person. This means you must be able to estimate accurately how much time you and/or every other person will spend on the project. Then you will apply your billing rate (perhaps two times cost).

Step 3.
Get it in writing.

Step 4.
Control your costs.

Now let's examine each step in detail.

*You have no idea what a poor opinion I have of myself
—and how little I deserve it.*
W.S. Gilbert

Step 1: List in detail the service you will provide.

List everything you will provide—both labor and out-of-pocket expenses. Be sure to include all planning and project-management time, as well as all clerical and other support time. It is not enough to include just the time you actually spend with your client. For out-of-pocket expenses, be sure to include items such as travel and printing costs.

Then estimate how much of each service will be provided. For example, how many hours do you think this project will take overall, for each component of it, and for each person working on it? How much travel will be involved (apart from routine travel to and from their office)?

Step 2: Figure out the price of each of those services.

Note the actual person or the level of the person who will be delivering each piece. Then use the billing rate for each person to determine the price of each service.

After you have priced each piece of the project, add up all the prices. This will tell you the total amount of revenue you will need on this project. It will also give you a feel for what goes into your project.

Step 3: Get it in writing.

Make sure the client understands what is included in the project and what is not. In Step 1, you detailed everything that would be included in the project. Make sure the client understands this. Put it in writing. As you get into the project, both you and the client will probably think of lots more you could do. Or the client will change the specifications. All of that is fine as long as the client understands what is included in the project fee, and what they must pay extra for (perhaps at your hourly billing rate) because it is outside the scope of what you originally agreed upon.

Step 4: Control your costs.

You must keep track of the number of hours you and everyone working for you spends on the

project—or you most likely will lose money, perhaps a lot of money.

Many consultants are so happy to get the projects that they overdeliver to the extent that they lose money. You must track the number of hours you spend on the project. In Step 1, you detailed all of the services you would deliver. Now you must see how you did against those projections of what you thought the project would include.

I have seen everyone from fine artists to senior executives bid on jobs expecting to spend a certain amount of time on them, and wind up spending twice or three times what they had originally projected. Then they are disappointed that they cannot make money.

Starting out

When you are starting out, it may be that you have to "give away the store" to get experience.

You have to figure out what the market will bear, perhaps take what you can get, build up your credentials, and market yourself to other companies. You may even decide to do a small assignment for free—perhaps for a not-for-profit or for a friend—just so you can say you are doing that kind of work.

On the other hand, you may think you are in a weak negotiating position when in fact you are not. I have worked with many an executive whose initial thought was to undercharge dramatically for his or her services.

Follow the rules for basic salary negotiation. If there are lots of people who can do what you do, and if you have no way to separate yourself from your competition, then you are in a weaker negotiating position. On the other hand, if you are offering a service that is somewhat unique and you cannot be easily replaced, you are in a solid negotiating position.

Life is to be lived. If you have to support yourself, you had bloody well better find some way that is going to be interesting. And you don't do that by sitting around wondering about yourself.
Katherine Hepburn

Salary Negotiation: Power and Positioning

Let's assume a company is about to make you an offer, and you want to prepare for the salary negotiation. What are your chances of getting the compensation you think you deserve? How can you tell whether you are in a strong negotiating position or a weak one?

Salary negotiation is about power. The more you are in demand, the better your chances of getting what you are worth. You need to know what you are worth in the market, but you also need to know how easily they could be satisfied with someone else. If it's easy for them to replace you, you have little room to negotiate. On the other hand, if you have convinced the hiring team that you and only you are the right person for the job, you are in a better position to get the offer and also to be paid fairly.

The earlier in the process that you differentiate yourself from your competition, the better. Establishing your worth takes time, and rarely happens during one interview. However, it can happen over a series of meetings where they get to know you better and appreciate you more.

Starting Out:
Little Room for Negotiation

A recent graduate may resemble the ten other people applying for the same job. Each has very little room for salary negotiation. Usually the best a person can hope for is to land the job by proving that he or she is superior to the other applicants, the same way experienced people do. Just landing the job may be a major accomplishment. When people are starting out, they usually have to pay their dues. They have little power.

After you gain some experience, you have more negotiating power—providing you can differentiate yourself from others.

Don't Accept or Reject a Job
Until It Is Offered to You

Sandy Bowers, Director of Career Services at Citibank, observed that job hunters often go into the interview thinking, "I want that job," or "I don't want that job." But the job hasn't even been

When God loves a creature he wants the creature to know the highest happiness and the deepest misery . . .
He wants him to know all that being alive can bring.
That is his best gift . . . There is no happiness save in understanding the whole.
Thornton Wilder, *The Eighth Day*

offered to them yet. It would be better if they had a more open mind, trying to assess the situation, and doing what they can to get an offer. As Sandy says, "*After* you have heard their best possible offer, *then* you decide to accept or reject it. Not before."

Position Yourself with Your Résumé

As you have seen in a previous chapter, "Four-Step Salary Negotiation Strategy," you are positioning yourself for the salary discussion in the first interview. But you are doing it even before that—when you are preparing your résumé. Examine the summary statement in your résumé—especially the first three lines. Make sure that people get the right impression of your level and what you have to offer them. If your description could work for someone who is lower level than you are, rewrite it.

Take a look at all the résumé samples in *Building a Great Résumé*. A lot of work went into the first three lines to make sure that people understand—within a few seconds—what each person has to offer and his or her level.

Position Yourself with Your Appearance and Demeanor

Do you look and act the level you say you are? You've heard people say, "Jane just looks like an executive." Be more conscious of how people look and act at the level at which you think you should be.

Position Yourself by Being in Demand

An important way to gain power is by having six to ten things in the works. Your increased self-esteem will cause you to come across differently, and you will be better positioned to play the game.

The Game: Unspoken Salary Negotiation While You Position Yourself

Much of the "salary negotiation" process is unspoken. Beginning with the very first meeting, you are thinking about the needs of the hiring team, and measuring yourself against your competition. You are assessing how well you are doing without overtly discussing salary. If you think that the job is too low level to warrant the salary you want, or that the hiring team likes your competition more than they like you, there is no sense in discussing salary. First redefine the job, if you can, to make it worth more. And then "kill off" your competitors.

Position Yourself versus Your Competition

You kill off your competitors by doing follow-up that is better than the hiring team could ever possibly get from anyone else. To do this well, you need to know where you stand regarding your competition.

After You Get the Offer, Is Your Competition Still Close Behind?

Even after you hear their best possible offer, you need to assess how far ahead of your competition you are.

There's a very big difference between "Let's offer it to John. If it doesn't work out, we can offer it to Jane" and "If John doesn't take it, we're dead. There's no one else who even comes close to what he has to offer." Certainly, you want to get the offer, but you also want to be a clear choice—far ahead of your other competitors. Be sure to ask:

- "Where are you in the hiring process?"
- "How many others are you considering?"
- "How do I compare with them?"

Remember, you need to uncover any objections they may have to hiring you. It is wise to ask, "Is there any reason why you might be reluctant about bringing me on board?"

When you get the offer, don't think you can necessarily start playing hardball. Is your competition waiting in the wings, or have you left your competition in the dust? As you become a more experienced job hunter, you will get better at finding out how you stand versus your competition.

Storybook happiness involves every form of pleasant thumb-twiddling;
true happiness involves the full use of one's powers and talents.
John W. Gardner, *Self-Renewal: The Individual and the Innovative Society*

Aim to Be Paid Fairly

Sometimes job hunters focus on getting a higher and higher salary, and lose perspective on what they are worth. Your goal is to get what you are worth. If you convince them to pay you more than that, they will expect more, and you may not be able to live up to their expectations. That's why it is so important to know what you are worth in the market, and then do your best to get it.

CASE STUDY: JUDY

In the Best Negotiations, You May Never Have to Say a Word

Judy, a retail manager earning $50,000, uncovered three job possibilities. One company in particular, Apex—a large retail chain—interested her. Apex had two openings—one higher level and one lower level.

Her first goal was to get the hiring team at Apex to see her as appropriate for the higher-level position. She spent some time doing library research about the company, and she talked to people she already knew who were Apex customers. She learned a lot about what the company could be doing better.

The next time she had a meeting with the prospective employer, she mentioned her findings and proposed changes that Apex could make to remedy these problems. The hiring team was very interested in her advice, and also admired her initiative. They knew she would be just as proactive on the job. Her future employer began to imagine her in the higher-level job, and told her that. They also told her that she had a number of competitors for that higher-level job.

Judy Positions Herself for the Higher-Level Salary

Judy did *more* work—to position herself against her competitors. She visited various store locations, and assessed what the store personnel seemed to be doing right or wrong. She asked more people what they thought of Apex, and came up with more ideas about what the company could do.

At her next meeting, she told them what she had done, and they were amazed. They wanted her for the higher-level job, and told her that. They also told her the salary range for that job, and it was very broad—anywhere from $50,000 to $75,000.

But remember, other companies were interested in Judy, and some spoke of offering her more money than Apex would pay her. She told the hiring manager that although she was talking to other companies, she wanted to work for Apex.

When they made her the offer, they did not want to risk losing her to *their* competitors—the other companies with whom Judy was talking. The hiring manager said, "We don't want to quibble, so we're going to offer you the very top salary to start, as well as a few other perks. We really want you here."

Judy never had to formally negotiate her salary. She positioned herself so well that their best offer came first.

Does this always work? No. But it is important for you to follow the same strategy that Judy did. You increase your chances of getting the best the company can offer when you:

- think about and outshine your competition;
- have other potential offers; and
- show the company what it would be like to have you in the job you want.

However, be sure you are qualified for that higher-level position, or your tenure in the job may be short lived.

CASE STUDY: RICK

Bargaining for What He Wants

This is an advanced technique that you may skip if you like. Sometimes a company may want you very much, but may be afraid to bring you in at the appropriate level. It may be too big a decision for them. You can help make that decision easier.

Rick, an architect, saw himself at the partnership level of a prestigious architectural firm. Although the company wanted to hire him, they

One can never consent to creep when one feels an impulse to soar.
Helen Keller

were afraid to bring him in as a partner. Job hunters think they are the only ones who are scared. But often companies are scared too—afraid of doing the wrong thing.

Rick said to them: "I believe this is the right place for me, and I believe that partnership is the right level for me. I'm so convinced of that, I'm willing to make an investment in this if you are. Bring me in at the level just below partner. But starting with my first day on the job, give me assignments at the partner level. At the end of three months, I'd like a salary and level review, and you decide."

The company felt very comfortable with this approach. If Rick could not perform at the level of partner, he would still be a good hire at the next-lower level.

At the *two*-month mark, Rick became a partner.

It's a Career-Management Issue

Job hunters say that they are often promised something in a new job, but it never materializes. And they are correct. Companies soon forget what they thought of you during the hiring process, and you are stereotyped by the new job. Everyone is soon back to business as usual.

The trick is to make sure they agree to do something *starting with your first day on the job* that reminds them of their promise to you. In Rick's case, for example, he asked for assignments at the partner level—starting with his very first day on the job. The following is another example.

CASE STUDY: CHARLIE
Negotiating a Career Change

Charlie is a great administrator. Department heads always succeed with him at their side. But he wanted to move into product management.

He interviewed for a product-management position, but the hiring manager realized what an asset Charlie would be as an administrative manager, and wanted him in that job instead.

Charlie said: "As your chief administrator, I would be able to help you greatly. But I want to move into product management. Perhaps we can negotiate something that will satisfy us both.

"Your department will take awhile to straighten out. I'm afraid that if I come in and kill myself working as your administrator, you will soon forget what I had really wanted.

"So let's make a deal. I'll come in as your administrator providing that, day one, you put me on a product-management task force or do something that gets me involved in product management. In the beginning, I'll spend 90 percent of my time on administration, and 10 percent on product management. At the end of the first year, I want to be spending 90 percent of my time on product management and 10 percent of my time on administration. I'll even find and train my successor."

The boss liked that idea. To prove his commitment, he allowed Charlie to spend the first week on the job working as part of a product-management team. That way, he got to know everyone in that group. When Charlie started working in the administrative area, he continued to go to the product-management staff meetings. It was clear to everyone what Charlie was promised, and he was able to make the transition.

It is unreasonable to expect people to remember the career promises they make to you during the interview. Even getting those promises in writing is not much help. With the press of everyday business—and because you are good at what you do—there is never a good time to make the transition, and you find yourself negotiating all over again while you are doing work you do not want to do. Over time, your resentment will build, and your only conclusion will be that people don't keep their promises.

Instead, your conclusion should be that you gave away too much. You should have negotiated something that reminded them on a daily basis what they had promised you. When a company wants what you have to offer, you are in a very strong position to negotiate a career change.

The
Five
O'Clock
Club®

Case Study: Stephen
"We like you, but . . ."

By Nancy Friedberg

Note: Look at http://www.FiveOClockClub.com for 150 Five O'Clock Club articles on job search and career development.

Question from Stephen:

Dear Five O'Clock Club Career Coach:

I interviewed with a company six weeks ago; I sent thank you letters to everyone; they asked for my references and I gave them to the hiring manager.

Today I spoke with the hiring manager who said: "We are through with the reference checking, everything is fine, we are still very favorable about you ... We've done some rethinking and have seen more people, ... we'll see a candidate on the 20th ... after that we'll be ready to make a decision ...I'll definitely call you that week (the 20th)." More info on the job: It will involve my relocating.

Please, what else can I do to sway things my way? Should I send another letter? What should I say in it?

I appreciate your help very much.

Ask: "Do you have any objections or concerns about hiring someone like me?"

Answer:

From: Nancy Friedberg, The Five O'Clock Club

That's an excellent strategy question, and the answer requires The Five O'Clock Club methodology for "turning job interviews into offers." The details of your meetings are not clear, so I'm reading between the lines about what the hiring manager said. The message seems to be "we're not 100 percent convinced you are the one we want to hire." Otherwise, they would have made you an offer. Having said that, you need to understand a few things about the interview process and the timing involved.

- We tell Five O'Clock Club members that when they're at the beginning of an organization's hiring process, time can work against them. In your situation, the hiring manager said, "we've done some rethinking." This may mean one of three things:
1. After the hiring manager met with you, he or she met with other candidates. The meetings with these candidates brought up new issues that made the hiring manager think differently about you or the position.
2. Some internal changes took place which caused them to re-evaluate their strategy.
3. There may be a potential concern about you that they haven't told you about.

- At The Five O'Clock Club we don't write thank you notes because job hunters really need to say more than "thank you." Instead, we analyze the needs of the company and compose an "influence" letter.

In your case, six weeks have gone by and you lack information about the current situation. You need to find out how their needs or views have changed. Call on contacts who can provide you with the best information. Do you have people in your network who can help you? Did you create a good rapport with the human resources manager, if there is one? Or perhaps you became friendly with a secretary there. One or all of these individuals can be an excellent source of information if they have a pulse on what's happening (the inside scoop).

Here's a recent example that's similar to your situation. One Five O'Clock Clubber was in discussions with a company for three months. Many of her decisions about how she should follow up with the various players came from the feedback she solicited from the HR manager—who definitely was backing her. She made sure to connect with the human resources manager every step along the way. She finally got an offer last week.

- Obviously, you can try to call the hiring manager to get information but your calls may not necessarily be as effective as trying to call someone else. Five O'Clock Club counselors want our members to figure out who has influence with the hiring manager—who can influence the hiring manager's thinking. So figure out who this might be, use your contacts to gather good information on the company's needs, and then work on "influencing the influencer."

- Finally, we recommend that our members ask a very important strategic question on every interview. If you haven't already done so, you should ask it at this point. The question is, "Do you have any objections or concerns about hiring someone like me?" If they do have a few objections (such as the fact that you will have to relocate), identify their concerns and address them as part of your follow-up strategy.

> **"Have six to ten things in the works at all times. Five will fall away through no fault of your own."**

Once you have addressed their concerns, you can apply another element of the Five O'Clock Club method:

- If you are actively speaking with only one employer, you will lose your edge. Of course, you know it's not smart to put all your eggs in one basket. That's why we recommend having "six to ten things in the works at all times." Five will fall away though no fault of your own.

So, if you are in discussion with other organizations, recontact all of them now and apply the strategies I mentioned above to try to turn those interviews into offers. That way, by the week of the 20th you can let the first organization know that you have other offers. Ask when they think they will be making their decision.

> **It may be more effective to call someone who can influence the hiring manager rather than calling the hiring manager directly.**

On the other hand, if you already have another offer right now, you can call them this week and gently apply some pressure saying something like, "I know you are seeing another candidate on the 20th and planning to come to a decision in the next couple of weeks. I am following up to let you know where I am in my process. I have an offer from another company and they are pressuring me for a decision. However, you are my number-one choice. I've been trying to put them off but it's getting difficult. Certainly I

can respect that you need to finish things up on your end. I was just wondering when you think you'll have an answer."

The bottom line: If they are truly interested in you, this will make them concerned about losing you and they might speed things up. If they are lukewarm about you—which is also good for you to know—they won't act concerned.

If this is the case and you've done everything you can think of, then you might want to back off and aggressively get on with your search so you don't sit around waiting for the phone to ring—which would only get you down and make you lose momentum. Good Luck.

Nancy Friedberg is a long-time career counselor with The Five O'Clock Club and also a member of The Five O'Clock Club's media team, appearing regularly on CNNfn.

This article originally appeared in *The Five O'Clock News.*

Want a Signing Bonus?

Everyone's getting them, right? But those who do are often giving up something—usually base salary. Most companies give signing bonuses to keep payroll costs down!

Louis Uchitelle reports in *The New York Times* that, "The hiring bonus is just the latest tool that companies have turned to in recent years to hold down wages. The others include profit sharing, flexible schedules, tuition subsidies, stock options, health club memberships and "performance" bonuses in lieu of raises for those already on the payroll. While wages are now rising a bit faster than they have in a decade, hiring bonuses are ballooning and spreading across the work force—absorbing some of the pressure for still-greater income." (Louis Uchitelle, "Signing Bonus Now a Fixture Farther Down the Job Ladder," *New York Times*, June 10, 1998)

The bottom line for you? You've made a deal when you get a signing bonus to make up for a lost bonus if you leave your present job. Otherwise, try to get money in your base rather than in a signing or other bonus.

Playing the End Game

This is the fun part—the part you've worked so hard to get to. You have had successful interviews, done thorough follow-ups. Now the offers are about to come in. Let's suppose you have a number of job possibilities. The game is to have them all come to closure within the same general time frame. It is not as effective to get an offer, turn it down, and a few months later, get another offer. Instead, try to have them happen at the same time. Then you'll seem more valuable in the marketplace, increase your chances of getting fair offers, and you'll be able to select the one that positions you best for the long run.

To do that, first get a lot of Stage 1 and Stage 2 contacts going all at once. When a company is interested in you, don't wait to see what they offer you. Instead, rush out and get more things going.

CASE STUDY: PAUL
No Longer Saw Himself As "Unemployed"

That's what Paul learned to do. He was unemployed, and felt that his situation was a major handicap. He had created a self-fulfilling prophesy.

When Paul got his first offer, from Englander, Inc., it was not a good one. The job was too low-level for him, and the pay was inadequate. He felt that the company was taking advantage of him because he was unemployed—and he was right.

They wanted him to drop everything and help out in an emergency by going on a sales call in another city—before putting him on payroll. They were acting as if "He's unemployed and desperate." Actually, Paul was feeling the same way about himself.

Despite his feelings of desperation, Paul declined to go on the trip. It would have made him feel worse. He told the company he was tied up with other things and simply could not make it.

Paul Decides to Play the Game

Instead of deciding whether to accept or reject the offer, Paul decided to play the game. Hiding his hurt and anger, he said, "I truly believe that yours is the company I want to work for. The problem is that I'm talking to a number of other companies right now, and I think it may take me a few weeks to wrap things up. I feel I owe it to myself to see these other possibilities through. Would it be okay if I got back to you in two weeks?" They agreed.

Paul then spent all of his energy making new contacts, getting new things in the works—and getting other offers.

The two weeks came and went as he continued to stay in touch with Englander, Inc., letting them know that he was still interested in them. He said that he would probably wind up working there, but that a few additional companies had expressed interest in him, and it would take a few weeks longer. Was that okay with them?

Paul wound up with 18 job possibilities and 8 job offers! He had written extensive follow-ups to every person in all 18 companies. That's how he turned his interviews into offers.

Many of the offers were excellent, and some were jobs he would consider taking only reluctantly. The other offers greatly enhanced his value in the eyes of every company with whom he was speaking—including Englander, Inc.

Paul continued to report back to them on the way he was being received in the marketplace. They started to see other roles for him in their company. His "unemployed" status was no longer relevant to them because it was no longer relevant to Paul. As he spoke to more and more hiring teams, he started feeling better about himself. The companies also sensed the difference. The issue was no longer Paul's status, but the fact that so many companies valued what he had to offer.

In the end, Paul's main decision had to do with the direction he wanted his career to take: He needed to decide which job would position him best for the long run. It was not easy.

As he continued his talks with all 18 companies, a number of them increased the responsibilities of the jobs they were talking to him about. Paul was having a lot of fun, and his self-esteem was greatly improved.

Increasing His Desirability

Paul ended up taking a position with Englander, Inc., after all—but not the position about which they were originally speaking to him. They offered him a job that was two levels higher than the original one, with greatly increased pay. What's more, they were proud to have him on board, and even issued a press release telling the world that he had joined their company.

By the way, you don't need eight offers to play the game. Three is a good number.

Slowing Down a Company
That Is Ahead of the Others

What can you do to slow down an offer while waiting for others to come through? If you are paying attention, you will most likely see an offer edging towards the finish line way ahead of the others. The time to slow it down is earlier on. When a company asks you back for another interview, and you feel it is getting too far ahead of the others, say, "I'm really eager to come back and meet with you again, but my schedule is pretty full next week. Could we schedule it for the week after that?" Use your judgment, of course. It may be that putting them off for a week would be inappropriate. If you feel you would just irritate them by postponing a meeting, then don't do it.

But what if Paul was not able to get so many other possibilities going? What if he had been made a terrible offer, and felt he was forced to accept or reject it with no assurance that others would come his way? This could well have been the case because, after all, offers are more likely to come your way when you have momentum—a lot of things going all at once. If Paul had really been in need of money, he might have decided to take that first offer and do well at it while he was

Charlie and Brad had no certain way to network into any companies besides the ones with which they had already met. And even if they could network in, that method would take too much time to uncover even one additional interested company.

They were willing to do a direct-mail campaign to sixty more companies. After all, they already knew how to express their idea in an appealing way.

Charlie and Brad quickly did research to find the names and addresses of the sixty companies, as well as the appropriate people to contact. They sent out a well-written one-page letter to each of them. In the letter, they asked the companies to call them if they were interested. (If they had decided to follow up each letter with a phone call, that would have been a targeted mailing rather than a direct-mail campaign.)

Within one day, an important company called. Within the next two weeks, three more called—including two highly prestigious companies they were very excited about. They met with those companies. Now they had a good reason to recontact the companies with which they had originally met. Within a short time, they received three offers. The numbers in their campaign were now as follows:

Companies Contacted	Companies Interested	Offers To Date
80	8	3

This was a lot of work, but it increased their chances of having something happen. Of the three offers they finally recieved, they accepted one that offered them the best of both worlds. They got 51 percent equity, a base pay higher than what either of them had been making in their previous jobs, plus full benefits.

> **The next time you want a company to make you an offer, instead of focusing on that, contact additional companies and try to get them interested in you. It actually shortens your search.**

You can get a job at any point in the process. You may not have to go to the lengths that Charlie and Brad and Paul went to. Luck can always be a factor. It is something you should allow for, but it is certainly not something you want to count on—and even if you're lucky once, it probably won't happen again in your next search.

The approach these job hunters used is the most dependable way to get a number of genuinely good offers in the shortest period of time.

In fact, I tried to conduct my whole career the way the big studios used to handle their actors. I did as many films a year as I could, to get the experience. If you sit around waiting for "the big one," when that opportunity finally comes along, you won't be ready for it. You won't have all that small time experience that adds up to big time ability. Success, it may surprise some to hear comes from doing, not negotiating, not counting lines, not weighing credits. Do it, do it, don't wait for it. Some very good actors sit out their entire lives while waiting for the right part. Make every part the one you've been waiting for. Learn the confidence you can only gain under fire. The confidence lends relaxation. Relaxation opens all your resources for the demands of your role. And when the big role does come along you'll need all 100 percent of what you've got to give. Don't be caught 25 percent short; don't be caught one percent short. Be completely available to whatever challenge comes your way, by being totally in charge of your craft, your material, yourself.

Michael Caine, *Acting in Film*

PART FIVE

KEEPING IT GOING

AFTER YOU'VE GOTTEN
THE JOB YOU WANT

Starting Out on the Right Foot in Your New Job

It is not the critic who counts;
not the man who points out how the strong man
stumbled or where the doer of deeds
could have done better.
The credit belongs to the man who is actually in the
arena, whose face is marred by dust and sweat and
blood; who strives valiently; who errs and comes
short again and again; who knows the
great enthusiasms, the great devotions;
who spends himself in a worthy cause;
who, at best, knows in the end
the triumph of achievement,
and who, at worst, if he fails,
at least fails while daring greatly,
so that his place shall never be with those timid souls
who knew neither victory nor defeat.
Theodore Roosevelt

Destiny is not a matter of chance,
it is a matter of choice;
it is not a thing to be waited for,
it is a thing to be achieved.
William Jennings Bryan

. . . be patient toward all that is unsolved in your
heart and try to love the questions themselves like
locked rooms and like books that are
written in a foreign tongue.
Rainer Maria Rilke

Starting out can be tricky: You are "on board" but "the jury is still out" on you. It is a time of trial. You are often being watched to see if you will work out. Here are some things you need to do to start out on the right foot and keep moving in the right direction.

Before You Start

• Say thank you. Contact all the people who helped you get the new position. Often people don't make this effort because they feel they'll be in the new job for a long time. But today, when the average American changes jobs every four years, the odds say you're going to change jobs again soon. You need to keep up those contacts.

Then think about ways to keep in touch with these contacts—if you read something that someone on your list would appreciate, clip it and send it.

Right Away

• Don't fix things or do anything "big" for the first three months. That is one of the biggest mistakes people make. Take time to learn the system, the people, and the culture.

You cannot possibly understand, in those first months, the implications of certain decisions you may make. You may be criticizing a project that was done by someone really important. Or you could be changing something that will affect someone on the staff in ways of which you aren't aware.

• Make yourself productive immediately. This does not contradict the point I just made. Do things that are safe. For example, install a new system where there has been none. This is "safe" because you aren't getting rid of some other system. What isn't safe? Firing half your staff the first week!

• Introduce yourself to everybody. Be visible—walk around and meet people as soon as possible, including those who work for you. Meet everybody. Too many managers meet only the "important" people while ignoring those who will actually do the day-to-day work.

• Don't make friends too fast. Someone who befriends you right away could also be on the way

Know how to ask. There is nothing more difficult for some people.
Nor for others, easier.
Baltasar Gracian, *The Art of Worldly Wisdom*

out. That doesn't mean you shouldn't be friendly, however. Go to lunch with several people rather than becoming known as someone who associates only with so-and-so. Get to know everybody, and then decide with whom to get closer.

- Take over compensation of your subordinates immediately. Look at review and raise dates, and make sure no one is overlooked. You can't afford to wait three months to get settled while one of your people is stewing about an overdue salary review.

- Get your budget—quickly. If it isn't good, build a better one. If you spend some time at the beginning trying to understand the budget, the things you hear over the next few weeks will mean more to you.

**Try not to do anything too daring for the first three months.
Take time to learn the system.**

In the First Three Months
- Learn the corporate culture. People new to jobs lose those jobs often because of personality conflicts rather than a lack of competence.

Keep your head low until you learn how the company operates. Some companies have certain writing styles. Some expect you to speak a certain way. In certain companies, it's the way they hold parties. Do people work with their doors open or their doors shut?

All those things are part of the culture, and they are unwritten. To learn them, you have to pay attention.

I had a client, for example, who lost his job because his management style rubbed everyone the wrong way. He is a "touchy feely" manager who, when he wants his employees to do things, schmoozes with them, saying things such as, "You know, I was kind of thinking about this and . . ." But the corporate culture was such that the employ-

ees liked and expected to be asked straight out. His style made them feel patronized and manipulated. And his own staff did him in.

Pay your dues before doing things at a variance with the corporate culture. After you build up some credits, you have more leeway. Let your personality emerge when you understand the company and after you have made some contribution.

- Learn the organizational structure—the real structure, not the one that is drawn on the charts. Ask your secretary to tell you who relates how with whom, who knows what, who thought of this project, who is important. You could be surprised.

- As far as subordinates are concerned, find out other people's opinions and then form your own. Consider that you may have a different perception because you have different values.

- Find out what is important in your job. For example, when I counsel people for a corporation, counseling is not the only important thing in my job. The people who come to me are sent by personnel, and I must manage my relationship with the personnel people. It doesn't matter how good a counselor I am if I don't maintain a good relationship with personnel.

- Pay attention to your peers. Your peers can prove as valuable to you as your boss and subordinates. Do not try to impress them with your brilliance. That would be the kiss of death because you'd cause envy and have a very large reputation to live up to. Instead, encourage them to talk to you. They know more than you do. They also know your boss. Look to them to teach you and, in some cases, protect you.

I know one executive who found out that her last three predecessors had been fired. She knew from talking to people that her boss was the type whose ego was bruised when someone had ideas. He had a talent for getting rid of these people.

**Pay attention to your peers.
Look to them to teach you
and, in some cases, protect you.**

To protect herself, she built relationships with her peers, the heads of offices around the country. After a year and a half, her boss's brother took her to breakfast and told her that, unlike her predecessors, she could not be fired: It would have been such an unpopular decision that it would have backfired on her boss.

• Don't set up competition. Everyone brings something to the party and should be respected for his or her talent, no matter what their level. Find ways to show your respect by asking for their input on projects that require their expertise.

• Set precedents you want to keep. If you start out working twelve-hour days, people come to expect it of you—even if no one else is doing it. When you stop, people wonder what's wrong.

• Set modest goals for your own personal achievement and high goals for your department. Make your people look good and you will too.

Three Months and Beyond . . .

• Continue to develop contacts outside the company. If you need information for your job, sometimes the worst people to ask are your boss and people around you. A network is also a tremendous resource to fall back on when your boss is busy—and you will seem resourceful, smart and connected.

You'll be busy in your new job, and may not keep up your outside contacts. In today's economy, that's a big mistake.

• Keep a hero file for yourself, a hanging file where you place written descriptions of all your successes. If you have to job hunt in a hurry, you'll be able to recall what you've done.

You will also use it if you stay. If you want anything, whether it be a raise or a promotion, or the responsibility for a particular project, you can use the file to build a case for yourself.

• Keep managing your career. Don't think, "I'll just take this job and do what they tell me," because you might get off on some tangent. Remember where you were heading and make sure your career keeps going that way.

Be proactive in moving towards your goal. Take on lots of assignments. If a project comes up that fits into your long-term plan, do it. If one doesn't fit into your plan, you can do it or you can say, "Oh, I'd love to do that, but I'm really busy." Make those kinds of choices all the time.

To act with confidence, one must be willing to look ahead and consider uncertainties: "What challenges could the world present me? How might others respond to my actions?" Rather than asking such questions, too many people react to uncertainty with denial.
Peter Schwartz, *The Art of the Long View*

The
Five
O'Clock
Club®

Thank You Note
After Getting a Job

Vivian Belen
400 First Avenue
Dayton, Ohio 22090

May 8, 20xx

Mr. Ellis Chase
3450 Garden Place
Des Moines, Iowa 44466

Dear Ellis:

The happy news is that I have accepted a position at Ohio State
Trust as Controller for their Ohio branches. I'll be responsible for
financial reporting and analysis, loans administration, budgeting
and planning. I think it's a great match and will make good use of
both my management skills and banking experience and the
environment is congenial and professional.

I really appreciated your interest in my job search. I very much
enjoyed speaking with people like you about your career and I
appreciated your advice and encouragement. The fact that you so
willingly gave of your time meant a great deal to me, and certainly
was beneficial.

If I can reciprocate in some way, please feel free to be in touch with
me. I will also probably be in contact with you in the months
ahead. My new office is at 75 Rockfast Corner, Dayton 22091.
You can reach me at 200-555-1212.

Sincerely,

Vivian Belen

. . . the country demands bold, persistent experimenta-
tion. It is common sense to take a method and try it.
If it fails, admit it frankly and try another.
But above all, try something.
Franklin Delano Roosevelt
Speech, Atlanta, 1932

There is no one way to job hunt; one neat solution to job hunting cannot answer it all. There are many ways.

The results of what you do in a job hunt are neither good nor bad; they are simply results to be observed and thought about. They are indicators of the correctness of the direction you are pursuing; they are not indictments. They are not personal; they are the world's feedback to what we are doing. These results can keep us on track, and if we look at them objectively, then they should not throw us off track.

Information is not good or bad, it is simply information. Things are changing so fast that we each need all the relevant information we can get. We may tend to block out information we find threatening—but that is precisely the information we need to get. Knowing the truth of what is happening around us may help us decide how to take care of ourselves. The information is not out to harm us—it is simply there.

To view your life as blessed does not require you to
deny your pain. It simply demands a more complicated
vision, one in which a condition or event is not either
good or bad but is, rather, both good and bad,
not sequentially but simultaneously.
Nancy Mairs (who has multiple sclerosis)
Carnal Acts

To be what we are, and to become what we are
capable of becoming is the only end of life.
Robert Louis Stevenson

There is a place for you, and you must look for it. Do not be stopped when others seem as though they are moving ahead. You, too, have a lot to offer if you would only think about yourself and not

them. You are on your own track. Put your energy into discovering what is special about you, and then hold on to it.

You will be knocked down enough during your job hunting. Don't knock yourself; push back. Push past the people who offer you discouragement. Find those nurturing souls who recognize your worth and encourage you.

. . . there are days when the result is so bad that no fewer
than five revisions are required. In contrast, when I'm
greatly inspired, only four revisions are needed.
John Kenneth Galbraith

Don't tell me the facts about yourself; tell me who you really are. When you are writing to someone, ask yourself, What am I really trying to say to this person? What would I say if this person were right here? You are writing to a real person, and when your personality comes through and you say what you mean to say, then your note is unique.

Read your work out loud. It will give you a sense of the timing, the flow. You will find out if it is readable. You will notice where it stumbles. Have someone else read it, too. Most people need an editor.

Take a few risks, but do it with some restraint. Don't be self-indulgent, but do let your personality seep through. You are not simply a "banker with twenty years' major banking experience." You are "mature, with worldwide contacts, and a sense of stability."

Pare down your writing. Get rid of the lines that have no energy. Think about getting rid of your first paragraph completely. Perhaps you wrote it just to warm up.

Write to make an impact, to influence the reader.

It is impossible to enjoy idling thoroughly
unless one has plenty of work to do.
Jerome K. Jerome

Continue to job hunt, but be easy on yourself. I worked on this book whenever I could, but some days I didn't feel like thinking, so I researched

Far better it is to dare mighty things, to win glorious triumphs, even though checkered by failure,
than to take rank with those poor spirits who neither enjoy much nor suffer much,
because they live in the gray twilight that knows not victory nor defeat.
Theodore Roosevelt

quotes, or made a chart, or organized my material. All of these things later made my writing easier—so I was always making progress.

The same can be applied to your job hunt. Some days you may research an industry or a number of companies, or you may write a proposal or a follow-up note. But you have to spend most of your time interviewing—just as I had to spend most of my time writing.

Job hunting takes practice, just as writing takes practice. I am not a professional writer, and you are not a professional job hunter. Neither of us, you or I, is perfect. But we are each trying to understand the process. This understanding will make us each less anxious, and more patient, about what we are doing.

Develop tricks to nudge yourself along. Find someone to report your progress to. If you cannot join a job-hunt group, then meet with a friend. Talking gives you perspective and gives you the energy to keep on going.

Set goals for yourself. For example, aim at all times to be in contact, either in person or in writing, with six people who are in a position to hire you or recommend that you be hired. Keep in touch with these six people. Strive to add more people to your list, because others will drop off. Plan to continue to network even after you find a job. Make networking a part of your life.

Keep pushing even when you get afraid—especially when you get afraid. On the other hand, if you have been pushing nonstop for a while, take a break completely, relax, and then push again.

Get together with a friend and talk about your dreams. In talking about them, they seem possible. And in hearing yourself say them out loud, you can test how you really feel about them. Then you can discover the central dream—the one that will drive you.

Where I was born and how I have lived is unimportant.
It is what I have done with where I have been
that should be of interest.
Georgia O'Keeffe

You will find endless resources inside yourself. Get inside yourself and find out what the dream is, and then do it. Stir yourself up. Go for it.

The fact is, if you don't try, no one will care anyway. The only reason to do it is for yourself—so you can take your rightful place in the universe. The only reason to do it is because we each have our place, and it seems a shame to be born and then to die without doing our part.

We are all controlled by the world in which we live . . .
The question is this: are we to be controlled
by accidents, by tyrants, or by ourselves?
B. F. Skinner

The world is big. There are many options; some job hunters try to investigate them all. Instead begin with yourself. Understand that part. Then look at some options and test them against what you are. You can hold on to that as a sure thing. You can depend on what you are for stability.

I am larger, better than I thought,
I did not know I held so much goodness.
Walt Whitman

A former client called me today. When I first met him, he had been out of work for a year. Now he was calling to say that he had been made vice president of his company. He has found his niche and has never been happier. Everyone notices it. And he keeps on networking—keeps on enjoying the process.

The world keeps changing. It won't stop. We must change, too. We are the dreamers of dreams.

We are the music-makers,
And we are the dreamers of dreams . . .
Yet we are the movers and shakers
of the world for ever, it seems.
Arthur O'Shaughnessy
"Music and Moonlight"

PART SIX

WHAT IS THE FIVE O'CLOCK CLUB?

"AMERICA'S PREMIER CAREER COUNSELING NETWORK"

The
Five
O'Clock
Club®

How to Join the Club

The Five O'Clock Club:

- **Job-Search Strategy Groups**
  - **Private Coaching**
- **Membership Information**

The Five O'Clock Club was founded
by Kate Wendleton in 1978 to provide
thoughtful career-development help
for busy people of all levels.
The programs and materials have helped
thousands take control of their careers
and find good jobs fast.

*The original Five O'Clock Club was formed in
Philadelphia in 1883. It was made up of the
leaders of the day, who shared their experiences
"in a spirit of fellowship and good humor."*

For a listing of local branches, or more
information on becoming a member,
please fill out the
Membership Application Form in this book,
sign up on the Web at:
http://www.FiveO'ClockClub.com
or call:
1-800-538-6645, ext. 600

*The median number of years men have been with their
current employer fell between 1983 and 1996 for most
ages, the Bureau of Labor Statistics reports: from 7.3
to 6.1 years for ages 35 to 44 and from 15.3 to 10.5
years for ages 55 to 64. But the overall median held at
about four years on the job, as the work force aged.
For women, the median tenure rose overall.*
Albert Karr, *The Wall Street Journal*,
February 11, 1997

The Five O'Clock Club Search Process

The Five O'Clock Club process, as outlined in
Kate Wendleton's books, is a targeted, strategic
approach to career development and job search.
Five O'Clock Club members become proficient at
skills which prove invaluable during their *entire
working lives*.

We train our members to *manage their careers*,
and always look ahead to their *next* job search.
Research shows that an average worker spends
only four years in a job—and will have 12 jobs,
in as many as 5 career fields—during his or her
working life.

Five O'Clock Club members find *better jobs,
faster*. The average job search for a managerial
position is now estimated at 8.1 months. The
average Five O'Clock Club member who regularly attends weekly sessions finds a job by his or
her tenth session. Even the discouraged, long-
term job searcher can find immediate help.

The keystone to The Five O'Clock Club process is in teaching our members an understanding of the entire hiring process. A first interview
is only a time for exchanging critical information.
The real work starts after the interview. We teach
our members *how to turn job interviews into offers*,
and to negotiate the best possible employment
package.

The Five O'Clock Club is *action-oriented*. **We'll
help you decide what you should do this very
next week to move your search along**. By their
third session, our members have set definite job
targets by industry or company size, position,
and geographic location, and are out in the field,
gathering information and making the contacts
which will lead to interviews with hiring managers.

Our approach evolves with the changing job
market. We're able to synthesize information
from hundreds of Five O'Clock Club members,
and come up with new approaches for our members. For example, we now discuss temporary
placement for executives, how to handle voice
mail, and how to network when doors are slam-
ming shut all over town.

Let us consider how we may spur one another on toward love and good deeds.
Let us not give up meeting together, as some are in the habit of doing, but let us encourage one another.

Hebrews 10:24-25

The Job-Search Strategy Group

The Five O'Clock Club meeting is a carefully planned *job-search strategy session*. We provide members with the tools and tricks necessary to get a good job fast—even in a tight market. Networking and emotional support are also included in the meeting.

The first part of the meeting is devoted to a forty-minute *main group presentation* on a particular aspect of job search; the second part, to *small group strategy sessions* led by trained career consultants.

The *main group presentations* are given on a rotating schedule, so a job searcher can join The Five O'Clock Club at any time. Members are encouraged to attend ten sessions in a row, after which they are free to stay with the main group or switch to the *advanced discussion group*, if one is offered.

Your *small group strategy session* is your chance to get feedback and advice on your own search, listen to and learn from others, and build your business network. All groups are led by trained career consultants, who bring years of experience to your search. The small group is generally no more than eight to ten people, so everyone gets the chance to speak up.

The first fifteen minutes of every meeting are given over to *informal networking*; the fifteen minutes between the main lecture and the small group strategy sessions are set aside for members to report on new jobs. The meetings are information-packed and action-oriented, move rapidly, and give you the tools and incentive to keep your search going.

Private Coaching

Visit us at http://www.FiveOClockClub.com or ask your local branch head for a list of career consultants available between group meetings for *private coaching*. Individual sessions help you answer specific questions, solve current job problems, prepare your résumé, or take an in-depth look at your career path. Please pay the consultant directly, as *private coaching is __not__ included in The Five O'Clock Club seminar or membership fee*.

From the Club history, written in the 1890s

At The Five O'Clock Club, [people] of all shades of political belief—as might be said of all trades and creeds—have met together. . . The variety continues almost to a monotony. . . [The Club's] good fellowship and geniality—not to say hospitality—has reached them all.

It has been remarked of clubs that they serve to level rank. If that were possible in this country, it would probably be true, if leveling rank means the appreciation of people of equal abilities as equals; but in The Five O'Clock Club it has been a most gratifying and noteworthy fact that no lines have ever been drawn save those which are essential to the honor and good name of any association. Strangers are invited by the club or by any members, [as gentlepeople], irrespective of aristocracy, plutocracy or occupation, and are so treated always. Nor does the thought of a [person's] social position ever enter into the meetings. People of wealth and people of moderate means sit side by side, finding in each other much to praise and admire and little to justify snarlishness or adverse criticism. People meet as people—not as the representatives of a set— and having so met, dwell not in worlds of envy or distrust, but in union and collegiality, forming kindly thoughts of each other in their heart of hearts.

In its methods, The Five O'Clock Club is plain, easy-going and unconventional. It has its "isms" and some peculiarities of procedure, but simplicity characterizes them all. The sense of propriety, rather than rules of order, governs its meetings, and that informality which carries with it sincerity of motive and spontaneity of effort, prevails within it. Its very name indicates informality, and, indeed, one of the reasons said to have induced its adoption was the fact that members or guests need not don their dress suits to attend the meetings, if they so desired. This informality, however, must be distinguished from the informality of Bohemianism. For The Five O'Clock Club, informality, above convenience, means sobriety, refinement of thought and speech, good breeding and good order. To this sort of informality much of its success is due.

Questions You May Have About the Weekly Job-Search Strategy Group

The Weekly Job-Search Strategy Group

is a Professional Career-Counseling Program
presented at branches of The Five O'Clock Club
"For busy, career-minded people"

Job hunters are not always the best judges of what they need during a search. For example, most are interested in lectures on answering ads or working with search firms. We will cover those topics, but, strategically, they are relatively unimportant in an effective job search.

At The Five O'Clock Club, you get the information you really need in your search—such as how to target more effectively, how to get more interviews, and how to turn job interviews into offers.

What's more, you will work in a small group with some of the best counselors around. In these strategy sessions, your group will help you decide what to do, this week and every week, to move your search along. And you will learn by coaching and being coached by others in your group.

Here are a few other points:
• For best results, attend on a regular basis. Your group gets to know you and will coach you to eliminate whatever you may be doing wrong—or refine what you are doing right.
• Those who think they need to come to a session only to ask a quick question are usually wrong. Often the problem started weeks before the job hunter realized it. Or the problem may be more complex than the job hunter realizes and require a few sessions to straighten out.
• You must be a member to attend the strategy group sessions. Some branches will allow you to pay for a single session, after which you must become a member before continuing in the group.
• Most branches charge for multiple sessions at a time to make administration easier. If you miss a session, you may make it up at any time. You may even transfer unused time to a friend.
• Although many people find jobs quickly (even people who have been unemployed a long

time), others have more difficult searches. Plan to be in it for the long haul and you'll do better.
• Carefully read all of the material in the Beginner's Kit that you get with your membership in The Five O'Clock Club. It will help you decide whether or not to attend.

The first week, pay attention to the strategies used by the others in your group. Soak up all the information you can.
• Read the books before you come in the second week. They will help you move your search along.

To register

1. Call 1-800-538-6645 ext. 600 or visit our Web site for the current list of branches.

2. After you become a member and get your Beginner's Kit, call your local branch head to reserve a space for the first time you attend. If there is a waiting list, preference is given to current members of The Five O'Clock Club.

3. Read the books ahead of time, or purchase them at your first meeting.

To assign you to a counselor, your branch head needs to know:
• your current (or last) field or industry,
• the kind of job you would like next (if you know),
• your desired salary range in general terms.

If you would rather see a private counselor before starting, call for suggested names.

What Happens at the Meetings?

Each week, job searchers from various industries and professions attend. Some branches specialize in professionals, managers and executives; others in recent college graduates, specific minority groups, or those over fifty years of age. Usually, half are employed; half unemployed.

The two-hour weekly program is in two parts. First, there is a lecture on a job-hunting topic appropriate to those in the audience. In the second hour, job hunters meet in small groups headed by senior full-time, professional counselors.

> *We find ourselves not independently of other people and institutions but through them. We never get to the bottom of our selves on our own. We discover who we are face to face and side by side with others in work, love, and learning.*
> Robert N. Bellah, et al, *Habits of the Heart*

The first week, you get the textbooks, hear the lecture, are assigned to your small group, and listen to the others in your group. You learn a lot by listening to how your peers are strategizing their searches.

By the second week, you will have read the materials. Now we can start to work on your search strategy and help you decide what to do next to move your search along. For example, we'll help you figure out how to get more interviews in your target area, or how to turn an interview into a job offer.

In the third week, you will see major progress in the other members of your group, and you may notice major progress in your own search as well.

By the third or fourth week, most members are conducting a full and effective search. Over the remaining weeks, you will tend to keep up a full search rather than go after only one possibility. You will regularly aim to have six to ten things in the works at all times. These will generally be in specific target areas that you have identified, will keep your search on target, and increase your chances of getting multiple job offers to choose from.

Those who stick with the process find that it works.

Some people prefer to just observe for a few weeks before they start their job search, and that's okay, too.

How Much Does it Cost?

The fees vary by location. Although each branch may charge what is appropriate for that location, a typical fee is 5 sessions for $225: 10 for $400. For administrative reasons, most branches charge for 5 sessions at a time. This avoids having a large number of people paying each week.

You must have the materials so you can look at them before the second session. That's why it is important for you to buy the books provided at the seminar. Otherwise, you will tend to waste the time of the others in the group by asking questions that are covered in the texts.

Is The Club right for me?

The Five O'Clock Club process is for you if:

- You are looking for a job or consulting work.
- You have some idea of the kind of work you want.
- You fit the salary profile of the branch.
- You want to participate in a group process on a regular basis.
- You realize that finding or changing jobs and careers is hard work . . . which you are absolutely willing and able to do.

If you have no idea about the kind of job you want next, you could see a counselor privately for one or two sessions, develop tentative job targets, and then join the group. On the other hand, some job hunters prefer to start the group program and see a counselor individually later if they still haven't come up with something. The choice is yours. Your branch head will be happy to provide you with the names of counselors you can see privately.

How long will it take me to get a job?

Although our members tend to be from difficult fields or industries, the average person who attends regularly finds a new position within ten sessions. Some take less time, and others take more. One thing we know for sure: *Those who get regular coaching during their searches get jobs faster and at higher rates of pay than those who search on their own or simply take a course.* This makes sense. If a person comes only when they think they have a problem, they are usually wrong. They probably had a problem a few weeks ago, but didn't realize it. Or the problem may be different from what they thought. Those who come regularly benefit from the observations others make about their searches. Problems are solved before they become severe, or are prevented altogether.

Those who attend regularly also learn a lot by paying attention and helping others in the group. This "vicarious" learning can cut weeks from your search. When you hear the problems of others who are ahead of you in the search, you can avoid those problems completely. People in your group will come to know you, and will point out subtleties you may not have noticed and interviewers will never tell you.

The Five O'Clock Club is plain, easy-going and unconventional. . . .
Members or guests need not don their dress suits to attend the meetings.
(From the Club History, written in the 1890s)

Will I be with others from my same field/industry?

Probably, but it's not that important. If you were a salesperson, for example, would you want to be with seven other salespeople?

Probably not. The search techniques are the same for the level handled by your branch. You will learn a lot and have a much more creative search if you are in a group with people who are in your general salary range but not exactly like you. Our clients are from virtually every field and industry. The process is what will help you.

We've been doing this since 1978, and understand your needs. That's why the mix we provide is the best you can get.

How can you charge such a small session fee?

1. We have no advertising costs because 90 percent of those who attend have been referred by other members.

We need a certain number of people to cover expenses. When lots of people get jobs quickly and leave us, we could go into the red. But so long as members refer others, we will continue to provide this service at a fair price.

2. We focus strictly on job search strategy, and encourage our clients to attend free support groups if they need emotional support. We focus on getting jobs, which reduces the time clients spend with us and the amount they pay.

3. We attract the best counselors, and our clients make more progress per session than they would elsewhere, which also reduces their costs.

4. We have expert administrators and a sophisticated computer system that reduces our overhead and increases our ability to track your progress.

May I change counselors at my local branch?

Yes. Some care is taken in assigning you to your initial counselor. However, if you want to change once for any reason, you may do it. We don't encourage group hopping: It is better for you to stick with a group so that everyone gets to know you. On the other hand, we want you to feel comfortable. So if you tell your branch head that you prefer a different group, you will be transferred immediately.

What if I have questions outside of the group?

Some people prefer to see their group counselor privately. Others prefer to meet with a different counselor to get another point of view. Whatever you decide, remember that the group fee does not cover counselor time outside of the group session. Therefore, if you want to be able to ask a counselor a "quick question" in between sessions, you would normally meet with the counselor first for a private session so he or she gets to know you better. "Easy, quick questions" are often more complicated than they appear on the surface. After your first private session, some counselors will allow you to establish an account by paying in advance for one hour of counseling time, which you can then use for quick questions (usually a 15-minute minimum is charged). Since each counselor has an individual way of operating, find out how the counselor arranges these things.

What if I want to start my own business?

The process of becoming a consultant is essentially the same as job hunting, and lots of consultants attend regular Five O'Clock Club meetings. However, if you want to buy a franchise or an existing business or start a growth business, you should see a private counselor, or attend the entrepreneurial program that is offered by a few of our branches.

What if I'm still not sure what to do.

Some branches allow you to pay for a single session before you become a member, for a modest fee. Then you can experience for yourself how we operate.

Whatever you decide, just remember that it has been proven that those who receive regular help during their searches get a job faster and at higher rates of pay than those who search on their own or simply attend a course. If you get a job just one or two weeks faster because of this program, it will more than have paid for itself. And you may transfer unused sessions to anyone you choose. However, the person that you choose must attend the branch from which you purchased your sessions.

The
Five
O'Clock
Club®

The Way We Are

The Five O'Clock Club means sobriety, refinement of thought and speech,
good breeding and good order. To this, much of its success is due.
The Five O'Clock Club is easy-going and unconventional.
A sense of propriety, rather than rules of order, governs its meetings.

J. Hampton Moore, *History of The Five O'Clock Club*
(written in the 1890s)

Just like the members of the original Five O'Clock Club, today's members want an ongoing relationship. George Vaillant, in his seminal work on successful people, found that "what makes or breaks our luck seems to be . . . our sustained relationships with other people." (George E. Vaillant, *Adaptation to Life*)

Five O'Clock Club members know that much of the program's benefit comes from simply showing up. Showing up will encourage you to do what you need to do when you are not here. And over the course of several weeks, certain things will become evident that are not evident now.

Five O'Clock Club members learn from each other: The group leader is not the only one with answers. The leader brings factual information to the meetings, and keeps the discussion in line. But the answers to some problems may lie within you, or with others in the group.

Five O'Clock Club members encourage each other. They listen, see similarities with their own situations, and learn from that. And they listen to see how they may help others. You may come across information or a contact that will help someone else in the group. Passing on that information is what we're all about.

If you are a new member here, listen to others to learn the process. And read the books so you will know the basics that others already know. When everyone understands the basics, this keeps the meetings on a high level, interesting, and helpful to everyone.

Five O'Clock Club members are in this together, but they know that ultimately they are each responsible for solving their own problems with God's help. Take the time to learn the process, and you will become better at analyzing your own situation, as well as the situations of others. You will be learning a method that will serve you the rest of your life, and in areas of your life apart from your career.

Five O'Clock Club members are kind to each other. They control their frustrations—because venting helps no one. Because many may be stressed, be kind and go the extra length to keep this place calm and happy. It is your respite from the world outside and a place for you to find comfort and FUN. Relax and enjoy yourself, learn what you can, and help where you can. And have a ball doing it.

There arises from the hearts of busy [people] a love of variety,
a yearning for relaxation of thought as well as of body,
and a craving for a generous and spontaneous fraternity.

J. Hampton Moore
History of The Five O'Clock Club

The original Five O'Clock Club was formed in Philadelphia in 1883. It was made up of the leaders
of the day, who shared their experiences "in a spirit of fellowship and good humor."

Use The Five O'Clock Club lexicon as a shorthand to express where you are in your job search. It will focus you and those in your group.

I. Overview and Assessment

How many hours a week are you spending on your search? Spend 35 hours on a full-time search; 15 hours on a part-time search.

What are your job targets?
   Tell the group. A target includes industry or company size, position, and geographic area.
   The group can help assess how good your targets are. Take a look at "Measuring Your Targets."

How does your résumé position you?
The summary and body should make you look appropriate to your target.

What are your back-up targets?
Decide at the beginning of the search before the first campaign. Then you won't get stuck.

Have you done the Assessment? If your targets are wrong, everything is wrong. (Do the Assessment in *Targeting the Job You Want.*) Or a counselor can help you privately to determine possible job targets.

II. Getting Interviews

How large is your target (e.g., thirty companies)? How many of them have you contacted? Contact them all.

How can you get (more) leads?
You will not get a job through search firms, ads, networking or direct contact. Those are techniques for getting interviews—job leads. Use the right terminology, especially after a person gets a job. Do not say, "How did you get the job?" if you really want to know, "Where did you get the lead for that job?"

Do you have six to ten things in the works?
You may want the group to help you land one job. After they help you with your strategy, they should ask, "How many other things do you have in the works?" If "none," the group can brainstorm how you can get more things going: through search firms, ads, networking, or direct contact. Then you are more likely to turn the job you want into an offer because you will seem more valuable. What's

more, five will fall away through no fault of your own. Don't go after only one job.

How's your Two-Minute Pitch?
Practice a *tailored* Two-Minute Pitch. Tell the group the job title and industry of the hiring manager they should pretend they are for a role-playing exercise.
   You will be surprised how good the group is at critiquing pitches. (Practice a few weeks in a row.) Use your pitch to separate you from your competition.

You seem to be in Stage One (or Stage Two or Stage Three) of your search. Know where you are. This is the key measure of your search.

Are you seen as insider or outsider?
See "How to Change Careers" for becoming an insider. If people are saying, "I wish I had an opening for someone like you," you are doing well in meetings. If the industry is strong, then it's only a matter of time before you get a job.

III. Turning Interviews into Offers

Do you want this job?
If you do not want the job, perhaps you want an offer, if only for practice. If you are not willing to go for it, the group's suggestions will not work.

Who are your likely competitors and how can you outshine and outlast them? You will not get a job simply because "they liked me." The issues are deeper. Ask the interviewer: "Where are you in the hiring process? What kind of person would be your ideal candidate? How do I stack up?"

What are your next steps? What are *you* planning to do if the hiring manager doesn't call by a certain date, or what are you planning to do to assure that the hiring manager *does* call you?

Can you prove you can do the job? Don't just take the "Trust me" approach. Consider your competition.

Which job positions you best for the long run? Which job is the best fit? Don't decide only on the basis of salary. You will most likely have another job after this. See which job looks best on your résumé, and will make you stronger for the next time.
   In addition, find a fit for your personality. If you don't "fit," it is unlikely you will do well there. The group can help you turn interviews into offers, and give you feedback on which job is best for you.

The Five O'Clock Club®

Dear Prospective Five O'Clock Clubber:

The Five O'Clock Club has helped thousands find jobs, change, or manage their careers!

At The Five O'Clock Club, we focus your search with real-world information that tells you exactly what you need to get more interviews . . . **and turn those interviews into offers.**

As a member, you also get—

❑ An attractive **membership card** and a **Beginner's Kit** containing information based on 12 years of research regarding who gets jobs and why, that will enable you to improve your job-search technqiues . . . immediately.

❑ A **subscription to** *The Five O'Clock News*, ten issues filled with information on career development and job-search techniques— information to help you thrive in your career.

❑ **Access to reasonably priced weekly seminars** featuring individualized attention to your specific needs in small groups supervised by our senior counselors.

❑ Access to **one-on-one counselor matching**.

❑ The opportunity to exchange ideas, experiences, and even role-play with other job searchers and career changers.

All that access, all that information, for the nominal membership fee of only $35.

The sooner you become a member, the sooner you can begin working on having a career that truly meets your financial, emotional, creative and intellectual needs.

Believe me, with self-examination and a lot of hard work with our counselors, you **can** find the job . . . you **can** have the career . . . you **can** live the life you always wanted!

The best of luck, whatever you may decide.

Sincerely,
Kate Wendleton, President

❑ Yes! I want access to the most effective methods for developing and managing my career, as well as for finding jobs.

. . . .

I enclose ❑ $35.00 for one year ❑ $60.00 for two years. I will receive a Beginner's Kit, a membership card, a subscription to *The Five O'Clock News*, a listing of current branches of The Five O'Clock Club, access to a network of career counselors and to reasonably priced seminars at branches of The Five O'Clock Club in the U.S. and Canada.

(If there is no branch near you, we will help you find a career consultant in your area, or you may choose to be counseled by phone.)

Name _____

Address _____

City _____ State/Prov. _____ Zip/Postal _____

Work Phone _____

Home Phone _____

Today's Date: _____

How I heard about you: _____

Interviewing and Salary Negotiation
. . . .

Method of payment:

❑ I enclose my check made out to The Five O'Clock Club, 300 E. 40th St., Suite 6L, NY, NY 10016.

❑ MasterCard, VISA or American Express:
(This form can be faxed to 212-286-9571)

Account Number: _____

Exp. Date: _____ Signature: _____
. . . .

The following information is for statistical purposes. Thanks for your help.

Salary range:

❑ under $30,000 ❑ $30-$49,999 ❑ $50-$74,999
❑ $75-$99,999 ❑ $100-$125,000 ❑ over $125,000

Age: ❑ 20-29 ❑ 30-39 ❑ 40-49 ❑ 50+

Gender: ❑ Male ❑ Female

Current or most recent position/title: _____

_____
. . . .

The original Five O'Clock Club® was formed in Philadelphia in 1883. It was made up of the leaders of the day, who shared their experiences "in a spirit of fellowship and good humor."

Once you fully apprehend the vacuity of a life without struggle,
you are equipped with the basic means of salvation.
Tennessee Williams

there, but continue to search for a job that was more appropriate for his experience.

Some people may consider it unethical to take a job knowing that they will continue to search for another one. But if you were a career counselor, you would see many cases in which a company hired someone—perhaps even moving his or her family—and then fired that person after a very short while for reasons having nothing to do with the employee. "Oh, I'm sorry we moved you here to Chicago. The project you were assigned to has been canceled. We'll give you some severance, but you are out of a job."

Companies are no longer dependable. Job hunters must fend for themselves and protect themselves. They didn't start this. Company executives did when they decided to cut people rather than retrain them or find another place for them inside the same company. In self-defense, employees must learn how to play the game—the new game of having a job in today's market.

You will give the company a full day's work for a full day's pay. What you are not giving them is your loyalty—until companies decide to be loyal back.

CASE STUDY: CHARLIE AND BRAD
The Numbers You Need

The company Charlie and Brad worked for decided they no longer wanted to be in the insurance business. They closed that business down.

Charlie and Brad had always wanted their own business and—with some severance pay in hand—they saw this as an opportunity to explore their dream. Perhaps they could sell their original business idea to a financial-services company—yet keep part of the equity. That way they could essentially have their own business but with the backing of a large organization.

The search Charlie and Brad conducted is exactly like a job search, and the numbers are the same. So see what you can learn from their experience.

Initial Contacts from Networking

At the time I met Charlie and Brad, they had already spoken to twenty large companies. They had actually known for some time that the business they were in would close, so as soon as they learned this, they had gotten to work. Four of the companies were somewhat interested in their idea. Charlie and Brad wanted me to help them make those four companies more interested.

Although they did not want to hear it, I told Brad that the problem was not with the four companies. Their numbers were too small, and they needed to drum up more interest in their idea. That would make their reluctant suitors more interested in doing a deal with them. When a company sees that others are pursuing you, they feel more secure about considering you for themselves. That's the way the game is played.

Here are the numbers that Charlie and Brad were working with:

Companies Contacted	Companies Interested	Offers To Date
20	4	0

After all Charlie and Brad had done, it would be difficult to get offers by working and reworkng their contacts with those same four companies. The number that first had to change is the number of companies contacted. Then the other numbers would also be likely to increase.

But human nature being what it is, Charlie and Brad did not feel like taking their eyes off the companies that were already interested. It took a number of weeks before they agreed to think about how to contact additional companies.

Networking, by Definition, is Serendipitous; Direct Mail Can Fill in the Gaps

Charlie and Brad had networked into those twenty companies. They both agreed that there were hundreds of companies that could possibly be excited about their idea, but most of those companies did not even know that there was an idea to be had.

Index

About the Author

Kate Wendleton is a nationally syndicated careers columnist and recognized authority on career development, having appeared on the *Today* Show, CNN, CNBC, Larry King, National Public Radio and CBS, and in *The New York Times, The Chicago Tribune, The Wall Street Journal, Fortune* magazine, *Business Week* and other national media.

She has been a career coach since 1978, when she founded The Five O'Clock Club® and developed its methodology to help job hunters and career changers of all levels in job-search-strategy groups. This methodology is now used by Affiliates of The Five O'Clock Club, which meet weekly in the United States and Canada.

Kate also founded Workforce America®, a not-for-profit Affiliate of The Five O'Clock Club, serving adults in Harlem who are not yet in the professional or managerial ranks. Workforce America helps each person move into better-paying, higher-level positions as each improves in educational level and work experience.

Kate founded, and directed for seven years, The Career Center at The New School for Social Research in New York. She also advises major corporations about employee career-development programs, and coaches senior executives.

A former CFO of two small companies, she has twenty years of business-management experience in both manufacturing and service businesses.

Kate attended Chestnut Hill College in Philadelphia and received her MBA from Drexel University. She is a popular speaker with groups that include the Wharton Business School Club, the Yale Club and the Columbia Business School Club.

While living in Philadelphia, Kate did long-term volunteer work for the Philadelphia Museum of Art, the Walnut Street Theatre Art Gallery, United Way, and the YMCA. Kate currently lives in Manhattan.

Kate Wendleton is the author of The Five O'Clock Club's four-part career-development and job-hunting series: *Targeting the Job You Want, Getting Interviews, Interviewing and Salary Negotiation* and *Building a Great Résumé.*

The original Five O'Clock Club was formed in Philadelphia in 1883.
It was made up of the leaders of the day, who shared their experiences
"in a spirit of fellowship and good humor."

Look to The Five O'Clock Club for the Best Job Search and Career Development Books on the Market

Building a Great Résumé
Second Edition

Includes scores of sample résumés and case studies as it takes you step by step through the entire process of creating a résumé that's just right for you. Covers more than 100 industries and professions.

1-56414-433-X, 208 pages, $12.99

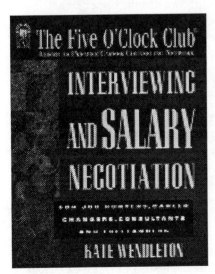

Interviewing and Salary Negotiation

The Five O'Clock Club has spent years helping job hunters land the best jobs at the best pay. Here are their latest ideas for getting what you want, including how to assess the interview and turn it into an offer.

1-56414-434-8, 192 pages, $12.99

Getting Interviews

Learn the secrets of the renowned career counseling and job-hunting organization that has helped thousands of people find their dream jobs.

1-56414-448-8, 192 pages, $12.99

Targeting the Job You Want
Second Edition

Finally, the best way to figure out what to do with your life in this tumultuous economy. Where are the jobs of the future? Where do you fit in? How can you stay marketable?

1-56414-449-6, 192 pages, $12.99

Available at Bookstores Everywhere, or call 1-800-CAREER-1

www.careerpress.com

About the Five O'Clock Club and the "Fruytagie" Canvas

Five O'Clock Club members are special. We attract upbeat, ambitious, dynamic, intelligent people—and that makes it fun for all of us. Most of our members are professionals, managers, executives, consultants and freelancers. We also include recent college grads and those aiming to get into the professional ranks, as well as people in their 40s, 50s and even 60s. Most members' salaries range from $25,000 to $400,000 (a third of our members earn in excess of $100,000 a year). For those who cannot attend a Club, *The Five O'Clock Club Book Series* contains all of our methodologies—and our spirit.

The Philosophy of The Five O'Clock Club

The Fruytagie Canvas by Patricia Kelly, depicted here, symbolizes our philosophy. The original, which is actually 52.5" by 69", hangs in the offices of The Five O'Clock Club in Manhattan. It is reminiscent of popular 16th century Dutch "fruytagie" or fruit tapestries which depicted abundance and prosperity.

I was attracted to this piece because it seemed to fit the spirit of our people at The Five O'Clock Club. This was confirmed when the artist, who was not aware of what I did for a living, added these words to the canvas: "The garden is abundant, prosperous and magical." Later, it took me only ten minutes to write the blank verse, "The Garden of Life," because it came from my heart. The verse reflects our philosophy and describes the kind of people who are members of the Club.

I'm always inspired by Five O'Clock Clubbers. They show others the way through their quiet behavior....their kindness....their generosity....their hard work....under God's care.

We share what we have with others. We are in this lush, exciting place together—with our brothers—and reach out for harmony. The garden is abundant. The job market is exciting. And Five O'Clock Clubbers believe that there is enough for everyone.

Part of Our Books

Because it so vividly represents our philosophy, we incorporated the Fruytagie Canvas into the covers of *The Five O'Clock Club Book Series*. The graphic element on each cover, designed by Steve Heiden, highlights a section of Kelly's canvas. *Targeting the Job You Want* contains the upper right-hand corner of the piece; *Job-Search Secrets* really is a secret—it has part of the grapes section of the tapestry, but upside-down. *Building a Great Résumé* shows part of the borders.

About the Artist's Method

To create her tapestry-like art, Kelly developed a unique style of stenciling. She hand-draws and hand-cuts each stencil, both in the negative and positive for each image. Her elaborate technique also includes a lengthy multi-layering process incorporating Dutch metal leaves and gilding, numerous transparent glazes, paints and wax pencils.

Kelly also paints the backside of the canvas using multiple washes of reds, violets and golds. She employs this technique to create a heavy vibration of color which in turn reflects the color onto the surface of the wall against which the canvas hangs.

The canvas is suspended by a heavy braided silk cord threaded into large brass grommets inserted along the top. Like a tapestry, the hemmed canvas is attached to a gold-gilded dowel with finials. The entire work is hung from a sculpted wall ornament.

Our staff is inspired every day by the tapestry and by the members of The Five O'Clock Club. We all work hard—and have FUN! The garden *is* abundant—with enough for everyone

We wish you lots of success in your career. We—and your fellow members of The Five O'Clock Club—will work with you on it.

—Kate Wendleton, President

The original Five O'Clock Club was formed in Philadelphia in 1883.
It was made up of the leaders of the day, who shared their experiences
"in a spirit of fellowship and good humor."

THE GARDEN OF LIFE IS abundant, prosperous and magical. ❦ In this garden, there is enough for everyone. ❦ Share the fruit and the knowledge ❦ Our brothers and we are in this lush, exciting place together. ❦ Let's show others the way. ❦ Kindness. Generosity. ❦ Hard work. ❦ God's care.